ENDORSEMENT

We live in an hour of great change and transition, not only in the Body of Christ but also in the nations of the world. G-d is strategically raising up reformers all over the earth who will be the tipping points for the greatest move of G-d in Church history. However, nations are not changed in a moment of time. In this devotional guide, Joe Pileggi offers daily insight and encouragement for those who are moving toward the prophetic, yet perhaps find themselves, like Joseph, "tested" by the word of the Lord. G-d desires us to enjoy the journey of "doing life" with Him. This devotional is a tool toward that end.

Abner Suarez
Founder and president
For Such a Time as This, Inc.
Dunn, North Carolina

OTHER BOOKS BY JOE PILEGGI

No Greater Love

FEARLESS

FEARLESS

90 Days to Eliminating Fear from Your Life

JOE PILEGGI

DESTINY IMAGE® PUBLISHERS, INC.
P.O. Box 310, Shippensburg, PA 17257-0310
"Promoting Inspired Lives."

This book and all other Destiny Image, Revival Press, MercyPlace, Fresh Bread, Destiny Image Fiction, and Treasure House books are available at Christian bookstores and distributors worldwide.

For a U.S. bookstore nearest you, call **1-800-722-6774.**

For more information on foreign distributors, call **717-532-3040.**

Reach us on the Internet: **www.destinyimage.com.**

ISBN 13 TP: 978-0-7684-0330-5

ISBN 13 Ebook: 978-0-7684-8570-7

For Worldwide Distribution, Printed in the U.S.A.

1 2 3 4 5 6 7 8 / 17 16 15 14 13

DEDICATION

There are precious few people in one's life who truly inspire to excellence and the pursuit of one's dream. For me, that one person is my bride and best friend, Lori. Relentless in pursuing her own God-given destiny, she has always been and continues to be my greatest encourager, inspiration, and cheerleader. This work would have died in the dust had she not believed in me and kept the vision alive.

If I could add a verse to the faith "hall of fame" chapter (see Heb. 11), her name would appear there. She is as ruthless as Deborah in battle with the enemy while possessing the grace and boldness of Esther in protecting her family. Yet she still makes time to sit at the feet of Jesus (next to Mary!) and exchange intimacies with the One who is her life.

Sweetheart, you are all He says you are: His princess and the beat of His heart. For Him to share you with me as my bride is the greatest of joys, the highest of privileges, and the most solemn of responsibilities. The level at which I have failed to fulfill all of this lays out before me the challenge for my life: "Greater love has no one than this, than to lay down one's life for his friends" (John 15:13).

This, by God's grace, I will do. You deserve no less!

ACKNOWLEDGMENTS

To my wife, Lori, who tirelessly typed the manuscript and kept the vision of the finished product alive and tangible—thank you. This work does not exist without your tenacity and encouragement.

Sometimes a life is transformed by someone without their ever being aware of it. For me, this person is Bill Johnson. Since he came to Mobile, Alabama in 2007, I have been "ruined" in pursuit of God encounters and a supernatural existence. Starting with his audio CDs, then his books, Bill has exploded an insatiable hunger in me for more of God, which has thrust me into offering the Bethel School of Supernatural Ministry curriculum on DVD to others with similar hunger here in the Mobile area.

D.L. Moody said, "The world has yet to see what God can do through one man who is totally sold out to Him." Bill, I believe the world is beginning to see the fulfillment of that statement through your life. Thank you.

Thanks to Destiny Image Publishers for believing in me and this work. You not only hold high literary standards for excellence, but seek an anointing from the Holy Spirit to rest on each work you publish. I am honored and humbled to have been considered to join your "hall of fame" of godly authors.

FEAR? NOT!

Men's hearts failing them from fear... (Luke 21:26).

It certainly seems like if ever we were living out these prophetic words of Jesus it is today:

- Banks and businesses either failing or being taken over (bailed out) by government

- Unemployment increasing by more than 370,000 per month

- Rogue nations developing and/or testing nuclear capabilities and threatening the U.S. and Israel with destruction

- Multiple murder/suicide incidents increase in scope and frequency as families and individuals buckle under immense stress of financial and personal failure

Wow! Is there any hope, anything that is *not* being shaken that we can cling to? Yes there is, but the question is, will we embrace it or will we continue to hold onto the false security of the world system?

God, speaking to His people (Israel), said, "...In returning and rest shall ye be saved; in quietness and in confidence shall be your strength: *and ye would not*" (Isa. 30:15 KJV). We have the same choice today as they did in Isaiah's day. Israel chose to find their security in Egypt (see Isa. 30:16) rather than in the rest, quietness, and confidence that their God was offering them if they would only "return."

In today's tumultuous world, we can find that same rest, quietness, and confidence in Father's often-repeated "Fear not." My prayer is that you will embrace each of them daily as you hear His heart for you.

When my children were in school, a popular phrase of sarcasm emerged that expressed the idea that a statement they had just made was not true. They would make the statement, and then, after a slight pause, would say loudly, "*Not!*" For example, my son might say, "Boy, I aced *that* test! *Not!* I guess that means we try again *next* week!"

In the same way, I want to express that even in these uncertain times we do not need to fear. David's words ring so true to us today: "God is our refuge and strength, always ready to help in times of trouble" (Ps. 46:1 NLT). The word *refuge* literally means "a shelter; hope, (place of) refuge, shelter, trust" (Strong's, H4268). One of the literal meanings of *strength* is "security." Is God our place of shelter and trust? Is our security in our relationship with Him? I believe that God is shaking everything that can be shaken so that only those things which cannot be shaken will remain (see Heb. 12:26-27; Hag. 2:6). Whaddaya think, gang (a little more youth lingo there)? Ya think we might be in the "times of trouble" David was referring to? The Hebrew word for *trouble* in this verse means, "tightness" (from a root meaning "narrow, a tight place; an opponent"), "rival, adversary, adversity, affliction, anguish, distress." Gee, I wonder—have you felt like some unseen adversary has you in a tight place lately? Sure describes me! But this is not a verse of trouble; it is a verse of praise! *He*, God, is my place of shelter and security in these times. So, shall I fear? *Not!*

THE FEAR OF CHANGE

After these things the word of the Lord came unto Abram in a vision, saying, Fear not, Abram: I am thy shield, and thy exceeding great reward (Genesis 15:1 KJV).

"**A**fter these things...." A whole bunch of things had happened to Abram: Terah, his father, had moved the family from their hometown and headed for Canaan. Before they left, Terah's other son, Haran, died. On their way to Canaan, they came to a city called Haran. What a coincidence! Trying to move on from a tragic loss, Terah comes to a city with the same name as his dead son. The Bible says that "they went as far as Haran, and settled there" (Gen. 11:31 NASB). It makes no further comment. We are only left to speculate as to why, with a goal of Canaan, they settled in Haran. Could it be that the city's name was too much of a reminder to Terah of his lost son? Overcome by grief, he could not go on and settled there to live out the remainder of his life there, in the city of grief, never reaching the goal of the promise God had put in his heart—a new land on which he could make a new start.

What about you? Has God given you a promise, a dream, a destiny toward which you were headed? But then, tragedy—the dreaded knock on the door from uniformed military officers with the news that a son, daughter, spouse, or grandchild would not be coming home from Iraq or Afghanistan. Or served with a notice—the marriage is over; the notice from the CEO—we're downsizing and cutting out your department; the phone call from the doctor's office—yes, the growth is malignant. You have bravely tried to move on only to come to the city "named" after the tragedy and you just couldn't go on. So you've settled there to grieve the rest of your life away. The real tragedy is stated in the next verse: "...and Terah died in Haran" (Gen. 11:32 NASB).

I'll never forget the Sunday after Mother's Day. I was dressing, getting ready for church, going over the message I was to preach in a couple of hours. The phone rang and a hysterical voice I could not at first identify was sobbing, "He's gone! He's gone, Joe. Dad is gone!"

It was my sister. Dad had passed in his sleep to join Mom who had moved in with Jesus four months (to the day) earlier. I don't remember preaching or doing much else that day; my wife had to make arrangements for us to fly home for Dad's "coronation" (life celebration) service. All the while, the nagging statement, "Why didn't you make it right between you while you had the chance?" screamed through my brain. I could have "settled in Haran" that day, but God graciously walked me through that "valley of the shadow of death" (Ps. 23:4).

You see, we all have that choice, because sooner or later, we all will lose a "Haran." The choice is, will we grieve and then refocus on "Canaan," the promise and destiny God has for us, or will we "settle in Haran" and lose the destiny of His blessing? May I encourage you? Chapter 12 of Genesis begins with the Almighty Creator having a conversation with Abram, Haran's brother. Abram now had lost his father *and* a brother. He had watched his dad waste away in grief, never to recover. God knew and understood Abram's loss, so He makes a house call! How cool is that? God's not too busy to come to your living room or bedroom today to be the Comforter to you that He promised to be. Paul calls Him:

> *...God of all comfort, who comforts us in all our affliction so that we may be able to comfort those who are in any affliction*

with the comfort with which we ourselves are comforted by God (2 Corinthians 1:3-4 NASB).

I had no intention to go in this direction when I began writing this, but I believe there are those who are terrified of the change they face—life without that loved one, life without that job or career, life without that marriage. The fear of change can paralyze us if we let it. But, we need not fear change of any kind if we remember and lay claim to God's promise of His presence and guidance: "The eternal God is a dwelling place, and underneath are the everlasting arms..." (Deut. 33:27 NASB). The journey's not over. You may just need to lean back and rest awhile in the "everlasting arms" of our Good Shepherd (see Matt. 11:28-30). So why don't you take today and do that? We'll continue our journey tomorrow.

THE FEAR OF UNFULFILLED PROMISES, PART 1

After these things the word of the Lord came to Abram in a vision, saying, "Do not fear, Abram, I am a shield to you; your reward shall be very great" (Genesis 15:1 NASB).

For a guy who just wanted to get married, stay at home, and raise a family, Abram's life sure was full of activity! After the Lord told him to complete the journey to Canaan, Abram received a promise from God: all the land he could see would be given to him and his descendants forever (see Gen. 12:7). There was just one little problem: Abram was 75 years old when the promise was made, a little old to be starting a family. Oh well. A minor detail.

Then came a famine in the land, necessitating another move—to Egypt. He was then deported from Egypt for lying to Egypt's president about his relationship with Sarai. Upon his return to Canaan, strife arose between his nephew Lot's employees and Abram's. So they split up.

It wasn't long until Lot got himself into trouble, captured by four kings in a war against his new hometown—Sodom. Abram heard that his nephew was a P.O.W. and took his 318 men and rescued Lot, his family, and his possessions. On the way home, Abram paid tithes of all he had to the high priest, Melchizedek (another study for another time, see Gen. 14:19). That's where

Genesis 15 picks up the story: "After these things…." These "things" happened over a span of years, and there was no further word from God after His initial promise to Abram in chapter 12.

How many years has it been since God made that promise to use you in ministry, bless you financially, restore that relationship, heal that condition, etc.? Since then, all "these things" have happened and the promise has gone unfulfilled. The encouraging word today is there is a time "after these things" when "the word of the Lord" will come again to reassure and reaffirm the promise. He will speak again. He has not forgotten!

The Hebrew for *word* in Genesis 15:1 means "a specific matter previously spoken of." The promise was given to Abram years earlier (see Gen. 12:1-3,7). In the meantime, "stuff" happened—necessary "stuff" but distracting "stuff." But after all the "stuff," God spoke to encourage Abram that He hadn't forgotten His promise and that it was still on time.

It was the Lord who spoke, *Yehovah*, "the Self-Existent or Eternal" One. As He spoke to Abram, so He speaks to us by His Spirit, just as directly and just as personally.

Do not fear the delay. Delay is not denial! Referring to this story, Paul says of Abraham:

> *With respect to the promise of God, he did not waver in unbelief but grew strong in faith, giving glory to God, and being fully assured that what God had promised, He was able also to perform* (Romans 4:20-21 NASB).

Should I fear the fulfillment of what He has promised for my life because it hasn't happened yet? Fear? *Not!*

THE FEAR OF
UNFULFILLED PROMISES, PART 2

*Some time later, the Lord spoke to Abram in a vision and
said to him, "Do not be afraid, Abram, for I will protect you,
and your reward will be great"* (Genesis 15:1 NLT).

God knows our heart. When He has made a promise and then time passes and nothing happens, time and His silence can bring discouragement. He is the God of encouragement.

Twice God showed Abram the land that God was going to give him and his descendants (see Gen. 12:7; 13:14-17). Wow! What a promise! Can you imagine looking at all that beautiful land and hearing God say, "I'm giving it all to you"? But there were a couple problems. The land was filled with hostile, violent, anti-God tribes who weren't about to just give up their land, and the second problem was Abram had no descendants, mainly because he had no children!

Well, years passed while all the "stuff" was going on and Abram probably began to wonder, "Is it ever going to happen? I'm not getting any younger, and neither is Sarai. Did I really hear from God, or was it just wishful thinking?"

Have you ever been there? You knew God spoke to you—at the time. Now you're not so sure. Nothing has happened; oh, yes, lots of "stuff" has happened that, if anything, has come *against* the promise being fulfilled. So fear begins to creep in: "Maybe I really didn't hear from God. What if it was just me? Maybe my spouse, child, or parent will never come to the Lord. What if God didn't say I was healed? What if I don't get that new job? What if…?" We're right there with Abram.

Then, just as with Abram, our faithful God shows up with a word of encouragement. First, He calls Abram by name. How personal is that? He says to us in Isaiah 43:1, "I have called you by name; you are Mine!" (NASB). Abram's name means "high father." So God calling Abram by name was both a personal, intimate address as well as a reminder of the promise.

God speaks to Abram in a vision; there was no Bible in those days. God spoke either audibly or inwardly, or He physically appeared in visions or dreams. The word *vision* here means, "to gaze at; mentally perceive, contemplate (with pleasure)." Abram was gazing at the Lord, hanging on every word the Lord was saying to him! Do we do that? Just come into and soak in His presence, hanging on every word He speaks to us through His word or in worship? That's where we'll get our answer.

Abram's answer? "Fear not." The word literally means "Do not be frightened." Hey, folks. That's God's word to all of us in these troubling times. Do not be frightened! Why? He tells Abram (and us), "I am your shield." The shield was the instrument the soldier used to protect himself from the enemy's arrows. The word literally means "to protect or defend, to hedge about." In other words, a protective hedge is built around us (His presence) through which the enemy's thought attacks cannot penetrate. It is the "shield of faith" of Ephesians 6:16. It is "taking every thought captive to the obedience of Christ" (2 Cor. 10:5 NASB). This word *shield* was used to describe the scaly hide of the crocodile that protects it from its potential enemies.

Is God our shield? He is if we allow Him to be. In these times of uncertainty and unfulfilled promises, His word to us is He is our protector. His invitation still holds: "Come to Me, all who are weary and heavy-laden, and I will give you rest" (Matt. 11:28 NASB).

Finally, God says to Abram, "...I am your shield, your exceedingly great reward". Sometimes, it's difficult to imagine God as being emotional. But imagine a parent running to the rescue of his or her child who is in trouble.

Having grown up on a dairy farm, I was always around machinery and the dangers that go with it. One day, we were out in the hayfield baling hay. My grandfather was driving the tractor and my dad and I were on the wagon stacking the bales. We were baling down a steep hill so Grandpa attempted to downshift the tractor into first gear. As he pushed in the clutch, the tractor began to careen down the hill as Grandpa struggled to get it into first. In the panic of the moment, my Dad turned to me and yelled, "Joey, come here!" He grabbed me and held me up against his chest to protect me from the impending impact.

The impact never came because Grandpa wisely turned the tractor to the right, and it harmlessly coasted to a stop. But the picture of my Dad vehemently running to me to protect me has stayed in my mind. That is the picture here with God. *Exceeding* means "to vehemently and speedily make something happen." It's the picture of a poker stoking the embers of a fire to rekindle what has been going out. Maybe the hope of God's promise was going out in Abram's life after all the years of delay, and he needed the fire rekindled.

Is the fire of your hope going out because what God has promised is yet unfulfilled? God knows the cry of your heart and He is *vehemently* running to stoke that fire again. And how is He stoking it? By telling you (and me) that He is our "great reward." That phrase literally means, "to increase payment of a contract, salary, or compensation." God has voluntarily placed Himself under contract, not only to fulfill His promise to us, but to *increase* the payment of that promise! Fulfilled, with interest! The apostle Paul refers to Abram's response to this statement: "(Abram) being fully convinced that what He had promised He was also able to perform" (Romans 4:21).

As the world seems to spiral out of control with skyrocketing unemployment, inflation, and ever-increasing government control, Father God wants us to remember—He has everything under His control and He is still our *Jehovah-jireh*, our provider, and He is vehemently running to our rescue to stoke the fires of our faith so we, too, along with Abram, can be fully persuaded that what He has promised He is able also to perform.

FEAR OF ABANDONMENT

*God heard the lad crying; and the angel of God called to
Hagar from heaven and said to her, "What is the matter with
you, Hagar? Do not fear, for God has heard the voice of the
lad where he is"* (Genesis 21:17 NASB).

Alone in the wilderness. A single mom and her son. No place to go. Out of provision. If it were just Hagar by herself, she could have endured it. But to see her son die with her and to be completely helpless to do anything—she couldn't handle it. So she sat him under a shade tree and went about 100 yards away so she wouldn't see him die. How is that for a hopeless situation?

Add to that, it was her mistress (Sarah) who demanded Abraham kick her out. The same Sarah who gave her to Abraham to produce a son for them in the first place! And it had happened. She bore them Ishmael. So what if she mocked Sarah after becoming pregnant with Ishmael? So what if she and her son made fun of Isaac years later? Oh, yeah, I guess sometimes our foolish moments can come back to haunt us. (They sure have in my life!) But I digress. The second incident so infuriated Sarah that she ordered Abraham to send them both away into the desert. To keep peace in the house, Abraham prepared bread and water for them and sadly sent them away.

It is here, in the depths of rejection and abandonment, that their cries were heard.

Okay. So your 15 minutes of stupidity have succeeded in getting you rejected by everyone, especially the ones you love the most. The one night stand (or discovered affair), the meltdown with the family member or boss, the gossip about your best friend gets back to them. And suddenly you're alone—all alone. Rejected and abandoned. Depression sets in. Motivation to go on…goes on without you. The house is now empty—after 20 years of marriage. You really *are* alone!

Notice it is in this setting that the lad cries out, and God hears—even though their circumstances were at least in part self-created. We need to remember this picture: God doesn't abandon those who cry out to Him, even if their own sin was what got them there in the first place. He hears us when we cry out to Him: "Call to Me and I will answer you, and I will tell you great and mighty things, which you do not know" (Jer. 33:3 NASB). David echoed, "Out of the depths I have cried to You, O Lord" (Ps. 130:1 NASB). Four times, God reminds His people, "I will never desert you, nor will I ever forsake you" (Heb. 13:5; see also Deut. 31:6,8; Josh. 1:5 NASB).

God heard the cry of Hagar and Ishmael. Look at the two different responses to the crisis. Hagar ran away (her name means "flight"). Ishmael cried out to God (his name means "God hears"). Could the boy have had a deeper insight into God's caring hand than his mother? I can remember the time, some 25 years ago, when I had to resign my church because of moral failure and everyone we loved abandoned us. I was without a job, in financial crisis, my marriage hanging by a thread. In the midst of the spiraling depression, self-hatred, and feelings of abandonment, my then five-year-old son came to me and said, "It's okay, Daddy. Jesus will take care of us."

David reminds us that, "The eyes of the Lord are toward the righteous, and His ears are open to their cry" (Ps. 34:15 NASB). Yes, the Lord heard the lad's cry. The word *heard* here means "to hear intelligently and pay attention to." The King James says, "And God heard the voice of the lad…" (Gen. 21:17).

The literal meaning of *voice* here is "to call out aloud." You see, our heavenly Father will hear us, but we have to give Him something to hear. We must pour out our desperation of loneliness, abandonment, and rejection. It's okay. He wants us to come to him. Say it: "Father, I feel so alone right now. My whole world is crashing down around me. Some of it is my fault, but it still hurts so much. I feel like I have nobody. I need Your presence; I need to know that You still love me, and You haven't abandoned me, too."

When we call out to Him aloud, He hears intelligently and pays attention to what we are saying. That means He cuts out all "background noise" and tells Heaven, "Shhh! Be still. My child is calling Me. I want to hear what he or she is saying." Yeah, that's right. It doesn't matter what the context of your cry is, He listens attentively. If it's important to you, it's important to Him. Why? Because you are His child. He doesn't need another reason.

As parents, our children's needs are important to us. Do you think it is any different with Abba (Daddy) Father? Again David says, "Just as a father has compassion on his children, so the Lord has compassion on those who fear Him" (Ps. 103:13 NASB).

In the fear of abandonment, Father wants us to call out to Him aloud and pour out our heart and hurts to Him. It's time. You've carried it around with you long enough. He is listening and paying attention, hanging on your every word.

Oooo! Did you hear that? I think He just called you:

> *Are you tired? Worn out? Burned out on religion? Come to me. Get away with me and you'll recover your life. I'll show you how to take a real rest. Walk with me and work with me—watch how I do it. Learn the unforced rhythms of grace. I won't lay anything heavy or ill-fitting on you. Keep company with me and you'll learn to live freely and lightly* (Matthew 11:28-30 MSG).

FEAR OF STOLEN BLESSINGS

And the Lord appeared to him the same night and said, "I am the God of your father Abraham; do not fear, for I am with you. I will bless you and multiply your descendants for My servant Abraham's sake" (Genesis 26:24).

Isaac grew up watching God bless his father, Abraham, because, "Abraham believed God, and it was counted unto him for righteousness" (Rom. 4:3 KJV). He saw "Dad" quietly and permanently trust (the meaning of "believe") whatever God promised, do whatever God asked, and reap tremendous blessings as a result. The word *counted* gives the idea of "being woven into," and included in the meaning for *righteousness* is "justice" and "prosperity." To paraphrase, we could say that because Abraham's relationship with God was one of a permanent, settled, quiet trust, God wove into Abraham's life justice (favor in all his personal and business dealings) and material prosperity beyond anyone's wildest dreams. In addition, Isaac knew he was to inherit those blessings. And that is exactly what happened: "After Abraham's death, God blessed his son Isaac..." (Gen. 25:11 NLT).

Those were the blessings promised to Isaac through God's promise to Abraham. But Isaac also followed in Dad's footsteps and "earned" his own blessings through his obedience. You see, God's blessings are generational, but He also requires obedience from us, too. Abraham had told his son that

God had promised to extend the blessings through Isaac and future generations. Now Isaac was experiencing them, a lesson in God's faithfulness and integrity.

In a time of famine similar to the one Abraham experienced, God told Isaac to stay in the promised land and *not* go to Egypt as He had instructed Abraham. Why? Because God wanted Isaac to learn to trust Him without any intervention from man (Egypt). So He told Isaac to plant his crops there, in the midst of the famine. And what happened? Listen:

> *When Isaac planted his crops that year, he harvested a hundred times more grain than he planted, for the Lord blessed him. He became a very rich man, and his wealth continued to grow. He acquired so many flocks of sheep and goats, herds of cattle, and servants that the Philistines became jealous of him* (Genesis 26:12-14 NLT).

But then something happened—opposition. There, at the height of enjoying God's blessing, Isaac was confronted by jealousy:

> *So the Philistines filled up all of Isaac's wells with dirt. These were the wells that had been dug by the servants of his father, Abraham* (Genesis 26:15 NLT).

Isn't it just like the enemy? You are seeing God's faithfulness in fulfilling His promise made to your parents or grandparents. Then, suddenly, the enemy comes and fills the wells of blessing with dirt. You dig another one, he fills that one, and on and on. What is going on?

Almost sounds like my life story. I had godly parents who prayed that God would use me in ministry. He did call me into pastoral ministry. And the cycle began. Enthusiastically embrace the pastorate. Pray and work hard (dig the well); see growth and God's presence. Then opposition—disagreement within leadership, families leave for almost any reason, etc. The enemy fills up the well with dirt, so we pull up stakes, move on, and "dig another well" only to have the same thing happen.

What about you? What wells of blessing has the enemy filled up with dirt in your life? Dream career? The perfect "godly" spouse? The call to ministry? You look back and every well you've dug and experienced God's blessing from is filled with the dirt of disappointment, disillusionment, and heartbreak. What went wrong? You begin to feel like Job when he lamented, "The thing which I greatly feared is come upon me..." (Job 3:25 KJV). The enemy has stolen your blessing. You examine yourself. Is it because of sin? (Isaac lied about Rebekah being his wife; like father like son!) You need a word from God. So did I.

It is there, at the lowest valley of disappointment with no apparent explanation, that God shows up. Isaac goes up to Beersheba, which means "the well of the oath." Ah, that's where God takes us. Back to the place where He first made the promise—the place of the oath. Where or when did God make His promise of blessing to you and your family? Did you write it down and date it? If not, think back and call to mind the promise and roughly when God spoke it. Find the verse, the prophetic word, and let God remind you of it. That's what He did with Isaac.

The same God (the Self-Existent One) who appeared to Abraham appeared to Isaac the same night he arrived at Beersheba. One of the meanings of the word *night* here is "adversity." Yeah, that's just like God. He takes us back to the place where He first called us and promised to bless us and shows up, not in the brightness of its fulfillment, but in the night of adversity. He reminded Isaac that his father's name was changed from Abram (*high father*—a title only) to Abraham (*father of a multitude*—a reality). Then God restated His promise in even more emphatic terms than He did with Abraham. He said that He *will* "multiply" (bring increase in abundance) to Isaac's descendants because of the promise He made to Abraham.

Remember, "God is not a man, that He should lie" (Num. 23:19 KJV). Let me encourage you with a few more of His promises to you:

Faithful is He that calleth you, who also will do it (1 Thess. 5:24 KJV).

And [Abraham] *being fully assured that what God had promised, He was able also to perform* (Rom. 4:21 NASB).

It is the same with my word. I send it out, and it always produces fruit. It will accomplish all I want it to, and it will prosper everywhere I send it (Isa. 55:11 NLT).

The Lord will work out His plans for my life—for Your faithful love, O Lord, endures forever (Ps. 138:8 NLT).

The thief's purpose is to steal and kill and destroy. My purpose is to give them a rich and satisfying life (John 10:10 NLT).

Has the enemy lied to you by filling your wells of promised blessing with the dirt of disappointment? Be encouraged and rest in His reminder to Isaac: Fear? Not!

FEAR OF A
STILLBORN DREAM, PART 1

*And it came to pass, when she was in hard labour, that the
midwife said unto her, Fear not; thou shalt have this son also*
(Genesis 35:17 KJV).

Rachel named her first son Joseph, which means "he shall add." After being barren her whole life, God finally heard her prayer and blessed her with a son. But Rachel was not satisfied with one. Her sister Leah had given Jacob six sons and a daughter. Rachel knew God had more for her. She had a dream—one more son.

Then she found out: she was pregnant again. Her dream would come true! She would have a second son. Nine months of planning and preparation. Rachel was willing to do whatever it would take; she couldn't wait to see what the fulfillment of her dream would look like.

For all the years she had been married to Jacob, she wanted to be fruitful and give him children. Watching her sister produce like a baby factory while she was barren broke her heart. Was God punishing her? If so, for what? She was the one Jacob fell in love with and worked 14 years to win her hand in marriage. Why could she not bless him with a son? Not only did she bless him with Joseph, now there would be a second son.

The time was at hand for her to deliver; but something was terribly wrong. The labor became intense. The word *hard* in the King James means "tough or severe." Rachel pushed with all the strength she had. This child must not be stillborn. Her dream must live, even if she must die to deliver it. And that is exactly what happened. The dream lived; Rachel died giving birth to it. The midwife, in the midst of the labor, spoke prophetically to Rachel: "Don't be afraid—you *will* have this son also! Your dream will *not* be stillborn. It will live."

The word *son* here means "builder of the family name." Your family name is "*Christ*-ian." You have been bought with a price; you are not your own (see 1 Cor. 6:20). The dream inside of you was conceived by the Holy Spirit. Your heart is for this dream to add (Joseph) to and be a "builder of the family name"—in other words, to glorify God. But it seems every obstacle in the universe has come against the birthing of this dream until you feel as though it will be stillborn or you will die giving birth to it. Why the heartbreak, struggle, disappointment, and pain in bringing forth what God Himself placed there?

The obvious answer is enemy opposition: "The thief's purpose is to steal and kill and destroy" (John 10:10 NLT). And it is true. We do not fight "against flesh and blood, but against principalities, against powers, against the rulers of the darkness of this world, against spiritual wickedness…" (Eph. 6:12 KJV).

But there is another reason for the struggle in birthing the dream. Rachel died giving birth to it. So must we! Our flesh must die! The desire for greatness in the eyes of others, the desire for recognition, credit, reward. Jesus taught His disciples that whoever wants to be greatest in His kingdom must become servant to all (see Matt. 20:26). Paul said:

> *I am crucified with Christ, nevertheless I live; yet not I, but Christ liveth in me: and the life which I now live in the flesh I live by the faith of the Son of God, who loved me, and gave Himself for me* (Galatians 2:20 KJV).

Ah, crucifixion, dying in childbirth. Isn't that something to look forward to? Yet that is the only way to experience the fulfillment of the dream of God's purpose for our life—dying to being recognized as the birthing agent and letting the dream live on its own merits, giving glory to the One who fathered it! As Jesus' cousin put it, "He must increase, but I must decrease" (John 3:30 KJV).

So what are you pregnant with? That book that's inside you? That home for troubled teenage girls? That Christian adoption agency? Starting that wild and crazy community youth center? Whatever it is, "Fear not," you *will* have that child that will add on and be a builder of the family name! But are you willing to die giving birth to it? The very birth of your dream depends on it!

FEAR OF A
STILLBORN DREAM, PART 2

And it came to pass, when she was in hard labour, that the midwife said unto her, Fear not; thou shalt have this son also (Genesis 35:17 KJV).

As most women will admit, the highlight of their life is to give birth to a child. With Rachel being barren for so many years, the joy of giving birth to a child was beyond belief. And, when she became pregnant with her second child, I think the joy was more than she could have ever imagined.

As a woman, I can identify with Rachel. I have gone through a long and painful 23-hour labor. During that long night and the following day, waiting and praying for the birth of the child, my fear was, "God, don't let my baby die." There is nothing more devastating than to see your newborn die, or give birth to a child who died in the womb. This was Rachel's fear. She was given a promise, "You shall have this son also." In other words, the dream (of having another child) would be fulfilled.

Just as in the natural birth, watching a dream die can be overwhelming. Are you afraid that you will never marry, or have children, or go to college or the mission field? What dream are you afraid of losing?

Rachel was told to *fear not*. She would give birth to the child—the dream. And she did. But she would give up her life so that the dream in her would live.

God asks us to give up our lives to Him. When we do that, God will see to it that our dream—*your dream*—will live.

Raise your hands to Heaven, surrender your life to God, and be amazed at what God will do with the dream that is in your heart.

Lori Pileggi

THE FEAR OF UNDESERVED BLESSING

And he [Joseph's servant] said, Peace be to you, fear not:
your God, and the God of your father, hath given you
treasure in your sacks... (Genesis 43:23 KJV).

It had been a tense journey. Joseph's brothers had to return to Egypt to ask to buy more grain. The first trip had not gone so well. They were ordered to leave one of them (Simeon) behind as hostage and to bring their youngest brother (Benjamin) back with them. But the worst part was when they had stopped for the night on their way home from the first trip, they discovered that the money they had paid for their grain had mysteriously reappeared in their sacks. Now, as they returned they were terrified that they, already having been accused of being spies, would now be accused of theft and *all* their lives might be in danger.

So when Joseph ordered them into his house upon their arrived, they thought, "Uh-oh. The jig is up. We're dead meat." (Well, maybe not those exact words, but you get the idea.) As Joseph's servant led them into the house, they offered a desperate explanation of what happened, assuring him that they had returned the money plus brought more for their current purchase. I can imagine the servant's sly, "I-know-what's-going-on-but-you-don't" smile as he answered them.

How about you? You've "paid the price," "denied self," "taken up your cross and followed Him," "crucified the flesh," and all the rest of the phrases we're taught we must do in order to "be worthy" of God's blessings and approval. Then, at some point early on in our journey, we look and realize what we offered up to God on the altar of sacrifice has been returned along with His blessings and provision!

Somehow, in our desire to please the Lord, we have come to believe we must sacrifice our dreams, talents, and desires of our heart. That leaves us to trudge through every day hoping that Heaven is better than life here as we're living it. Whatever happened to, "...the joy of the Lord is your strength," and, "Take delight in the Lord, and he will give you your heart's desires" (Neh. 8:10; Ps. 37:4 NLT)? Something's definitely missing. What is it?

I think the answer begins with identifying the "treasure." The word means "a secret storehouse; hence a secreted (buried), valuable; hidden riches." Every one of us has "a secret storehouse" of "hidden riches." They are our gifts, talents, ministries, and even material blessings. Why are we so afraid of developing them and using them for God's glory? Why do we feel we are undeserving of any blessings? I know that when I receive an unexpected financial gift, my immediate reaction is that I should give it all back to God because I don't deserve it, kind of like Joseph's brothers did. We are so afraid of being lifted up in pride (a legitimate concern) that we go to the other extreme and "bury the treasure." Where's the balance?

I believe it starts with realizing the Source of the "treasure." Joseph's servant said, "Your God...has given you treasure in your sacks" (Gen. 43:23 NASB). If it comes from Him: 1) it has to be good, and 2) He wants you to develop and use it for His glory. The *sack* represents your life. The word literally means, "to stretch out, something expandable." God pours His treasure into our lives and it stretches us; it sometimes is frightening to be stretched, but God does that to remind us that we are not the source of the treasure. The stretching also reminds us that we must be totally dependent on Him to develop and use the treasure so that He is the only one who receives glory from it.

Joseph's servant said, "Peace be to you, fear not...." Replace your fear of undeserved blessing with His peace (*shalom*). Remember, when the Jews say "shalom," they are conveying the thought of "being safe, complete, well, happy, healthy, and prosperous." That's God's desire for us—to be complete, happy, and prosperous; enjoying, developing, and using the treasure He has poured into us.

FEAR OF ENEMY TERRITORY

And He said, I am God, the God of thy father: fear not to go down into Egypt; for I will there make of thee a great nation (Genesis 46:3 KJV).

What a strange way to enjoy your "golden years." For those of you reading this who are under 40, that means retirement. Jacob, who had spent the first half of his life deceiving everyone in sight and the second half living for God, was probably looking forward to kicking back and enjoying the fruit of his labor while turning over the family business (shepherding the huge herds of livestock he had amassed) to his sons.

Think of it. Life was good for him now. He had found the son he thought was dead, was well taken care of in his old age, and so could die happy, without any more conflict. Yeah, right.

Just when he was getting comfortable in his comfort zone, he got an invitation in the mail, special two-humped camel delivery (the method after which we have patterned our current efficient mail delivery system) from none other than Pharaoh, Egypt's president, under whom his son Joseph served. Upon hearing the news that his son was still alive, Jacob wanted to make a trip to Egypt to see Joseph again before he died (see Gen. 45:28). Pharaoh did him one better. He told Joseph to tell his dad to bring everyone with him, his entire extended family and all of his livestock, and come live in Egypt. After all, the famine was still going on where they were and Pharaoh promised that he would give them the land of Goshen—the richest, most fertile section of land in Egypt.

So why not? Almost sounds like a no-brainer. So Jacob packed up everything and they began the massive move to Egypt. They stopped overnight at Beersheba, the southernmost border town in their land. They were about to cross over into Egypt.

Suddenly, Jacob was attacked by fear. "What am I doing?" he must have thought. "It's one thing to visit my son in Egypt, but move there and live? This is enemy territory. These people despise us" (see Gen. 43:32; 46:34). So Jacob did the only thing he knew to do—offer sacrifices to God (prayer and worship). It was there that God spoke to him and assured him he was doing the right thing.

Does that sound familiar? We're so comfortable in our middle-class homes and church. Even though there may be a spiritual famine there, we settle in and "make the best of it." Then we hear of good news from far away: a ministry we long thought was dead is instead thriving and suddenly we "get the urge" to visit—do a short-term missions trip or become involved in some other conscience-easing, comfortable ministry. But unexpectedly, we are invited to come live there. Settle there—in enemy territory. The name *Egypt* means "besieged places, to cramp, confine, hem something in, adversary, assault." Wow! Who in their right mind would want to live there? So we offer sacrifices. We pray and worship. We want a definite "word from God." Sure enough, He says, "Fear not; go down to Egypt."

What is your Egypt? A job in an ungodly atmosphere? Staying in a marriage to an ungodly spouse? A ministry to a people who are not hungry for God? Whatever it is, if God is in it, we must not fear to go down to Egypt. We must remember the same things he told Jacob:

1. "I am God, the God of your father…" (Gen. 46:3).

   We must not forget who He is—Elohim, the Creator of the universe. "…If God be for us, who can be against us?" (Rom. 8:31 KJV). When Jesus commissioned the disciples to "go into all the world and preach the gospel," He added, "…I am with you always, even to the end of the age" (Mark 16:15; Matt. 28:20 NASB). The promise of the I AM's presence should be enough to dispel all fear and move us to immediate obedience.

2. "Do not be afraid to go down to Egypt…" (Gen. 46:3 NIV).

   How can we win the lost and make disciples if we don't go to where they are? As a chaplain at our city's rescue mission, I am among addicts of all kinds. I have no clue how to minister to them; I must totally rely on God to minister through me. Did He not say He would set a table for us in the presence of our enemies (see Ps. 23:5)? Jesus told His disciples that He was sending them out as "sheep among wolves" (see Matt. 10:16 NIV). That sounds like Egypt to me. There is no more gray area in the world anymore. The world has become so anti-God that the mere mention of His name brings persecution, lawsuits, and in some cases, arrests. We are in Egypt. Get used to it. The world used to tolerate us. Then they mocked us. Now they want to obliterate us. All-out war has been declared. But God still says, "Do not be afraid to go down to Egypt." Why?

3. "…for I will make you a great nation there" (Gen. 46:3 NASB).

   That's end-time harvest! The scene in Heaven describes the "new song" being sung around God's throne, saying, "…your blood has ransomed people for God from every tribe and language and people and nation" (Rev. 5:9 NLT). That's why He's commanded us to go down and live in Egypt; not to participate in their sin, but we are to "turn many to righteousness" (Dan. 12:3).

Do not fear living in the enemy's territory. When you are there by the providence of your God, His word says, "When a man's ways please the Lord, he maketh even his enemies to be at peace with him" (Prov. 16:7 KJV).

FEAR OF DETHRONING GOD

And Joseph said unto them, Fear not: for am I in the place of God? (Genesis 50:19 KJV)

Finally. A legitimate fear. The fear of dethroning God in some area of our life and usurping the authority that is rightfully His. Thank goodness none of us have ever done that! R-r-r-right!

Joseph had finally been reunited with his brothers. He was thrilled; they were scared to death. They had all just returned from burying their father, Jacob. As long as "Dad" was alive, they knew he would act as a "buffer" between them and Joseph. Once he was gone, what would stop Joseph from getting even with them for what they had done to him? Listen to their fear as they contemplated what Joseph might do:

> But now that their father was dead, Joseph's brothers became fearful. "Now Joseph will show his anger and pay us back for all the wrong we did to him," they said (Genesis 50:15 NLT).

It was the old philosophy, "What goes around comes around." They went into "survival mode." Just as they had concocted a story to tell Jacob after they sold Joseph into slavery, they came up with a plan to tell Joseph to spare their lives:

So they sent this message to Joseph: "Before your (notice they didn't say "our") father died, he instructed us to say to you: 'Please forgive your brothers for the great wrong they did to you—for their sin in treating you so cruelly.' So we, the servants of the God of your father, beg you to forgive our sin" (Genesis 50:16-17a NLT).

Looking back through the text, I find nowhere that Jacob said those words. I guess we'll say anything when it comes to saving our own neck!

But Joseph did not question the accuracy of their statement. In fact, it says, "…When Joseph received the message, he broke down and wept" (Gen. 50:17 NLT). Why would he cry over their request? What an opportunity to make 'em squirm! Instead, he weeps over the fact that they would even think he would want revenge. This is what prompts his response: "…Don't be afraid of me. Am I God, that I can punish you?" (Gen. 50:19 NLT).

Umm, yeah—people have wronged me. Even my own (Christian) brothers, even those in the ministry have sold me out. What about you? Ever been gossiped about by those "closest" to you—those you told personal, confidential stuff to, only to hear about it through the church or work grapevine? Ever been passed up for a promotion you know you qualified for in favor of the boss's relative? How about being falsely accused of something that gets you demoted or fired at work or passed over or run out of the ministry? Welcome to Joseph's world—sold into slavery for 13 years and then thrown into prison on a false rape accusation. How did that not embitter him to seek revenge against his brothers?

Somehow, he had come to grips with the New Testament principle of forgiveness taught by Jesus, Paul, Peter, etc. Joseph realized that God was in charge of judging and punishing, and for him to do it would be dethroning God, usurping His authority, and placing himself in the place of God. We must do the same.

Paul quotes Deuteronomy 32:35 when he reminds the Roman Christians, "Dear friends, never take revenge. Leave that to the righteous anger of

God. For the Scriptures say, 'I will take revenge; I will pay them back,' says the Lord" (Rom. 12:19 NLT).

Yes, it hurts when those closest to you sell you out, walk away from the relationship, and leave you open and bleeding. Somehow we think the only way we can heal is for them to "get theirs." And we want to be the administrator of it. I know. I've been there—and still am. I recently had a car mechanic tell me he had replaced the blown engine in my car only to find out after I had paid him 800 dollars that he had not touched it! I couldn't find him, couldn't get my money back, and filed with a small claims court—all to no avail. Talk about wanting revenge! I have also had major disappointments in ministry—everything from contrary church boards to pastors who marginalized, ignored, or gossiped about God's call on my life. I have gone through years of bitterness until I allowed God to enroll me in Joseph's "school of forgiveness."

When Jesus taught the Sermon on the Mount, He said, "You have heard that the law of Moses says, 'Love your neighbor' and hate your enemy. But I say, love your enemies! Pray for those who persecute you!" (Matt. 5:43-44 NLT). Later, in chapter 6, after Jesus gave us the Lord's prayer, the only part of the prayer He taught on was "forgive us our sins, as we have forgiven those who sin against us" (Matt. 6:12 NLT). Then He editorialized, "If you forgive those who sin against you, your heavenly Father will forgive you. But if you refuse to forgive others, your Father will not forgive your sins" (Matt. 6:14-15 NLT). Wow! Our being forgiven by God is not only dependent on our repentance, but also on the degree to which we forgive those who have wronged us. That's a sobering thought!

Jesus illustrated this truth with the story of the slave, though just forgiven a huge debt by his master, had thrown into prison a fellow slave who owed him a very small debt (see Matt. 18:21-35). The result was the master retracted his forgiveness of the original slave's debt and had him thrown into debtor's prison "...until he had paid his entire debt" (Matt. 18:34 NLT). Jesus ended the story by saying, "That's what my heavenly Father will do to you if you refuse to forgive your brothers and sisters from your heart" (Matt. 18:35 NLT).

Forgiveness is not optional for us. We cannot afford to harbor unforgiveness in our heart. To seek revenge is to set ourselves up in God's place, and that is truly a fearful place to be. To forgive and go on allows us to focus on the pursuit of God's presence and purpose for our life. That's what enabled Joseph to go from slave and prisoner to vice-president of Egypt! He said it himself: "You intended to harm me, but God intended it all for good. He brought me to this position so I could save the lives of many people" (Gen. 50:20 NLT).

David, another man who went from fugitive to king, wrote, "For promotion cometh neither from the east, nor from the west, nor from the south. But God is the judge: he putteth down one, and setteth up another" (Ps. 75:6-7 KJV).

Today, let's determine to give those who have hurt and wronged us a "Fear? Not!" Let's adopt Joseph's perspective that although they may have meant it for evil, God meant it for good so that we could save the lives of many people.

FEAR OF REVENGE

Now therefore fear ye not: I will nourish you, and your little ones. And he comforted them, and spake kindly unto them (Genesis 50:21 KJV).

There are actually two fears we can address here because we can find ourselves on either side of the "revenge" word. We can be like Joseph; we are the one who was wronged and, given the opportunity, are tempted to exact our "pound of flesh," balance the scales of justice, and get even with the person who wronged us. We covered that yesterday, but today's Scripture takes it one step further.

What about being on the receiving end of revenge, like Joseph's brothers were? They knew they had wronged him, knew he would be justified in whatever he desired to do to them. He now had the power; they were powerless, at his mercy. Yet instead of seeking revenge, Joseph told his brothers:

> "No, don't be afraid. I will continue to take care of you and your children." So he reassured them by speaking kindly to them (Genesis 50:21 NLT).

How would you feel if you were in the brothers' position, fearing retribution from someone you had wronged, fearing public humiliation, a lawsuit, loss of job, or your very safety? Would you plead for mercy like they did, knowing that you are indeed at their mercy? Would you not want to hear the words of Genesis 50:21 spoken to you? I know I would.

Notice that Joseph did not stop with the act of forgiving his brothers. He took it one step further. He promised them that he would *nourish* them. That literally means to "maintain," including to "feed" and "make provision; sustain, provide sustenance for."

Forgiveness is not passive; it is not merely a mental assent to let go of an offense. It is active. Joseph promised his brothers he would take care of them and their families, providing them with food and shelter. Here Joseph, living some 2,000 years before Jesus' ministry, displayed Christ's teaching:

> *But I say unto you, Love your enemies, bless them that curse you, do good to them that hate you, and pray for them which despitefully use you, and persecute you* (Matthew 5:44 KJV).

Paul continues the thought, quoting Proverbs 25:21-22, in his letter to the Romans:

> *If your enemies are hungry, feed them. If they are thirsty, give them something to drink. In doing this, you will heap burning coals of shame on their heads* (Romans 12:20 NLT).

That is what Joseph did with his brothers. The Bible says he also *comforted* them, which means "to sigh, breathe strongly, to pity or console." Joseph's promise to provide for them caused the tension between them to dissipate and they "breathed a sigh of relief." It brought healing to the relationship which had been severed for 17 years.

Then Joseph "spoke kindly" to them, which gives the idea that he verbally communicated specifically how he would take care of them so as to leave no doubt to his sincerity. Forgiveness in action!

How about that for a challenge for us today?

1. Do something to help "take care of" the one who hurt you.

2. Speak kindly to them.

3. Reassure them of God's love and your forgiveness.

Do those three things on a consistent basis and nothing will be able to withhold God's full blessing and purpose from being fulfilled in your life!

FEAR OF THE ENEMY, PART 1

And Moses said unto the people, Fear ye not, stand still, and see the salvation of the Lord, which he will shew to you to day: for the Egyptians whom ye have seen to day, ye shall see them again no more for ever (Exodus 14:13 KJV).

From delightful to desperate. Ever have a day go like that? Israel had started their journey in triumph. Suddenly, a look over their shoulder revealed a cloud of dust, the noise of horses, and the roar of chariots. The enemy was closing in on them and they were trapped—no way of escape.

How did they get to that place? From Joseph's family being welcomed by the Pharaoh under whom Joseph served, to utter slavery 430 years later under a ruthless pharaoh. Because God's favor was upon them, the Hebrews multiplied in number enough to threaten to outnumber the very Egyptian population they served. So Pharaoh reasoned that the only way to control them was to enslave them.

Hmmm. Doesn't that sound like our enemy (satan, in case you were wondering)? We begin our life in Christ living amongst a people who do not know or serve Him, but they welcome us and our experience with Christ—at first. But as God blesses us and they see us increase spiritually (in joy and purpose) and materially, jealousy sets in and they begin to feel threatened.

Their only solution to "control" us is to enslave us. The resulting isolation tempts us to compromise our standards, and the enemy's trap is set. The desire for acceptance, affirmation, and relationship tempts us to trade our inheritance for a "bowl of lentils" (see Gen. 25:34).

Esau was not the only one to fall in that way. It is my story as well. Going through school as the class "Urkel" (*nerd* to those of you unfamiliar with the TV series *Family Matters*) and suffering from an acute case of acne, I was not very popular with the ladies. Longing for that acceptance mixed with teen-age hormones can be a deadly combination. So although I was a Christian called into ministry, my outlet became pornography. Its icy tentacles soon became a vice grip around my mind, and like an insatiable monster it was never satisfied. Pictures soon became movies, and soon watching others "do it" was no longer enough. I was an Egyptian slave, totally at the mercy (of which there was none) of my taskmaster. While on the one hand I played the part of caring pastor and youth pastor, on the other I was mercilessly in bondage to pornography and multiple affairs.

Like Israel, I was a child of God but in bondage to Egypt (sin). Would there be a day of deliverance for me as there was for Israel? Yes, but not until I cried out to Him in repentance and asked Him to deliver me from this addiction (see Exod. 2:23). When I did, like Israel, deliverance came, which prompted spiritual warfare as I had never experienced before. That is the fear of which I speak here. The fear of the enemy; the fear of recapture and return to slavery.

When you have been in slavery for 430 years (20 in my case), that's the only lifestyle you know. Israel thought they were rid of Egypt. The 10 plagues, the miraculous exodus, carrying the riches of Egypt with them, and headed for the Promised Land. What could be more exciting for them—and for you and me? Delivered from our addictions and sin and set on a course for our Jeremiah 29:11 purpose, our Promised Land.

Let's pause here for a word. The word is, "Duh!" Did we really think satan would let us go unopposed when Christ "...has rescued us from the kingdom of darkness and transferred us into the Kingdom of his dear Son" (Col. 1:13 NLT)? We've been divinely and miraculously delivered from bondage, standing on the shores of our Red Sea, ready to cross over on our journey to our Promised Land (His plan and purpose for our life), when suddenly we hear the rumble of enemy horses and chariots coming after us to re-enslave us. The fear of the enemy can be terrorizing, until we hear the declaration from our "Moses" (Christ):

> But Moses told the people, "Don't be afraid. Just stand still and watch the Lord rescue you today. The Egyptians you see today will never be seen again. The Lord himself will fight for you. Just stay calm" (Exodus 14:13-14 NLT).

Tomorrow, we'll take apart that victory statement and shout the shout of victory, even while the enemy is charging toward us and we seemingly have no place to run. Victory belongs to the Lord!

FEAR OF THE ENEMY, PART 2

*But Moses said to the people, "Do not fear! Stand by and see the salvation of the Lord which He will accomplish for you today; for the Egyptians whom you have seen today, you will **never** see them again **forever**"* (Exodus 14:13 NASB).

I used the New American Standard translation here for emphasis. There are three things that God wants us to know and embrace here. Let's look at each one.

First—the need for supernatural intervention. Moses' command was to stand still and see the salvation of the Lord. The situation was such that only the God of the universe could turn back the enemy's attack and bring victory. Moses knew it; the people knew it. Do you? Facing foreclosure on the house? Divorce? Children in rebellion? Terminal illness? Financial shipwreck? Trying to do what God called you to do?

You know the enemy is coming in like a flood (see Isa. 59:19) and you desperately need the Spirit of the Lord to lift up a standard against him—now! In crisis, the natural man will either panic or attempt to figure out a solution himself.

Lori and I are senior leaders of Mobile School of Supernatural Ministry, a school based on Bill Johnson's curriculum from Bethel School of

Supernatural Ministry, to train the body of Christ to move in supernatural signs, wonders, and miracles of healing as they discover and pursue the passion that God has placed within them. Teaching has always been my passion; the school has been *our* passion for at least three years. We have experienced tremendous spiritual opposition as well as little interest from other pastors. The personal attacks in our thought life and fear of failure have at times been overwhelming. Our anchor has been in Scriptures such as today's.

The word *salvation* in Hebrew is "Yeshua." (Jesus!) It means, "something saved; deliverance, aid, victory, prosperity." How can we fear the enemy when we have the promise of *Yeshua* standing beside us?

The children of Israel were moving in obedience to God—leaving Egypt, heading to the Promised Land, taking the route God ordered them to take. Yet here they are, seemingly trapped, with no route of escape, annihilation imminent. Is this the reward for obedience? God's deliverance from the enemy's bondage one day, replaced by an even more ferocious attack the next? Perhaps you are saying, "I thought God delivered me from the bondage of addiction, promiscuity, depression, etc. If I belong to God now, why this onslaught of temptation, financial crisis, or sickness (or insert your own personal attack here)? The more I try to live in obedience to God, the greater I'm assaulted by the enemy." Ever hear the saying, "New level, new devil"? The enemy's tactics have not changed. We are the "children of Israel" today. Anyone who sells out to God and determines to follow Him and fulfill their destiny and passion He has given them, meets with tremendous opposition from the enemy. Jesus warned us, "In the world you will have tribulation…." But He doesn't stop there! He adds the great promise: "…but be of good cheer, I have overcome the world" (John 16:33).

This is what the children of Israel couldn't seem to grasp. If God told them to do it, He would see to it that no enemy would be able to stop them from accomplishing it. When Jesus told the disciples, "Let us cross over to the other side" (Mark 4:35), a demonically-inspired storm threatened to destroy them en route. After their panic-stricken plea to Jesus for help, Jesus simply calms the storm, then says to them, "Why are you so fearful?"

(Mark 4:40). That's the question He asks us today. We look around us at the crumbling global economy, our precious God-given freedoms being taken away, the threat of terrorist attack at home and a nuclear-armed Iran abroad, and the tendency in the natural is to panic and cry out with the disciples, "Lord, don't You care that we are perishing?" Yet His answer to us is the same: "Why are you so fearful?" Has He ever failed us? Has He not promised that He would never leave us nor forsake us (see Heb. 13:5)? If we are in the place of obedience, we and God are a majority: "...greater is he that is in you, than he that is in the world" (1 John 4:4 KJV). Elisha said to his servant, "Do not fear, for those who are with us are more than those who are with them" (2 Kings 6:16).

Second—we must remember that it is He (God) who will accomplish the victory. Moses told the people to see what the Lord would accomplish for them. Paul said, "Now thanks be to *God* who always leads us in triumph in Christ..." (2 Cor. 2:14). Jesus warned His disciples, "Without Me you can do nothing," while Paul stated the logical conclusion of that statement, "I can do *all* things through Christ who strengthens me" (John 15:5; Phil. 4:13). Christ secured our victory at the cross and the empty tomb. We are seated with Him in heavenly places (see Eph. 2:6) and so are "more than conquerors through Him who loved us" (Rom. 8:37). Your crisis, my crisis, must bow its knee to the One who said:

> *"No weapon formed against you shall prosper, and every tongue which rises against you in judgment you shall condemn. This is the heritage of the servants of the Lord (you and me), and their righteousness is from Me," says the Lord* (Isaiah 54:17).

Finally, Moses promised the people that they would never again see the enemy who was pursuing them that day. We must remember that the bondage and control of the enemy has been broken over us forever. The cross and empty tomb were not meant as a temporary fix, but as a daily lifestyle of victory that we don't have to strive for, but rather to rest in. Consider Matthew 11:28-30 to be your invitation, because, "There remains therefore a rest for the people of God. For he who has entered His rest has himself also ceased from his works..." (Heb. 4:9-10).

FEAR OF THE ENEMY, PART 3

*Only do not rebel against the Lord, nor fear the people of the
land, for they are our bread; their protection has departed
from them, and the Lord is with us. Do not fear them*
(Numbers 14:9).

The choice was simple—the promise or the wilderness. That's what Israel faced. A simple choice. Walk into and claim His promise that He had prepared for them—or stay in their own wilderness. The problem with going in and claiming what was rightfully theirs was that it would mean warfare. There were enemies in the land who wouldn't give up without a fight. There would be a price to pay. And from the reports, the enemy was bigger than they were and outnumbered them. What would they choose to do? What would you choose? God has prepared a supernatural lifestyle in His presence, bringing "as it is in Heaven" to earth. All the prophetic promises spoken over you stand ready to be fulfilled. You stand at the edge of your promised land. But there is an enemy in your land of promise and you know there will be warfare to lay hold of it.

Let's get specific. God has spoken to you about a supernatural financial breakthrough, ministry, or healing. You fill in the blank. Now He has prompted you to take the first step of faith, to go in and begin to lay claim to what you know is rightfully yours through declaration. But... The enemy.

To lay claim to it means you have to face unexpected bills and expenses, thoughts and feelings of inadequacy, bad medical reports, etc. Doing what God has called you to do may involve some or all of these and more. There are giants in your promised land. "...And we were like grasshoppers in our own sight, and so we were in their sight" (Numbers 13:33).

That perspective will breed fear every time. In fact, it is the perspective of fear. And it paralyzes us into inactivity and leaves us in the wilderness of unfulfilled destiny. But check out the different perspective of Joshua and Caleb (Num. 14:9). They did not deny reality.

1. It was a land "flowing with milk and honey."

2. There were giants in the land.

But, as with Joshua and Caleb, people of faith are given a different perspective of the outcome: they see into the spiritual realm and see that the principalities and powers have been "disarmed" (see Col. 2:15). Listen to Joshua and Caleb: "their protection has departed from them." The word for *protection* in the Hebrew means "shade" or "hovering over; to shade or shadow." The evil spiritual principalities and powers that "hovered" over the "giant" opposition, giving them their muscle, had been removed. The word *departed* there means, "to turn off, call back, depart, pluck or take away, remove, withdraw, be without."

The angelic hosts that were with Israel had already disarmed their enemies. The enemies only looked formidable. They didn't even realize the enemy's demonic power had been taken away. Joshua and Caleb had seen into the spirit realm and had seen that the battle had already taken place there and God had Israel set up for victory. All they had to do was march in and lay claim to it. That's why these two godly men were so excited.

We are living in a fearful time. Our nation, founded on godly, moral standards seems to be crumbling around us. Corruption runs rampant in public office. The economy is being "set up" for collapse. Most of all, those who love God and righteousness are now viewed as a threat and labeled "domestic terrorists." There are indeed "giants" in the land. And in the natural, we might see ourselves as "grasshoppers," unless we purpose to see as Joshua and Caleb saw—into the spirit realm and begin to declare it with our words: "Greater is He that is in me than he that is in the world" (see 1 John 4:4). "I (Jesus) give you the authority to trample on serpents and scorpions, and over all the power of the enemy, and *nothing shall by any means hurt you*" (Luke 10:19). Best of all, let's adopt God's perspective:

> *Why do the nations rage, and the people plot a vain thing? The kings of the earth set themselves, and the rulers take counsel together, against the Lord and against His Anointed, saying, "Let us break Their bonds in pieces and cast away Their cords from us!"* **He who sits in the heavens shall laugh; the Lord shall hold them in derision** (Psalm 2:1-4).

Daddy God doesn't seem to be concerned over the chaos being brought on by world leaders. *Fear not* is still God's message to His children. Be like Joseph of the Old Testament: prepare for hard times as God directs you while trusting Him for supernatural provision for you and your family. Every crisis is an opportunity for Daddy God to show up and show off!

FEAR OF HIS PRESENCE

And Moses said to the people, "Do not fear; for God has come to test you, and that His fear may be before you, so that you may not sin" (Exodus 20:20).

The word *fear* is used twice in this verse, but they are not the same. The first refers to that cowering fear that makes you run and hide. The other speaks of a healthy respect, honor, and reverence.

Which is your response to His presence? Moses was telling Israel not to be terrified of God because He wanted to be with them. His holy presence, Moses said, would generate a healthy, reverent respect for Him.

God's heart has always been for fellowship and relationship. We see that from the Garden of Eden. Yet since the time of Moses to today, we have meshed these two words together and we think respecting and honoring God is cowering in fear, afraid of His punishment!

That's the way I was raised. I honored and respected my earthly father in fear of the strap or belt. On the other hand, my mother, as godly a woman as she was, was afraid she wouldn't be "good enough" to make it to Heaven. So as a result, my life has been one of performance, always trying to work my way into Father's favor (and always feeling I wasn't doing enough to please Him).

But, in recent years, through being introduced to teachings by Bill Johnson, Heidi Baker, and others, I have come to understand how unconditionally I am loved by Father; how much *He* desires *my* presence.

And so, I am "on a quest," to use a Bill Johnson phrase. A quest for living intimately in His presence. Instead of running away from the mountain of His presence, I'm running toward it. Because *He* wants me to! And He wants you to as well. And it's not about our worthiness. If we have asked Christ into our life and asked for His blood to cleanse us from our sin, then that blood makes us worthy to pursue His presence. You do not have to be afraid of someone who loves you!

I highly recommend Bill Johnson's book, *Face to Face with God: The Ultimate Quest to Experience His Presence.* In that book, Bill Johnson addresses this very issue. He says, "The Israelites were afraid they would die if they heard His voice, not realizing that the death they feared was in the absence of His voice."[1] In contrast, Bill continues, "...[Moses'] perception of all the fireworks God set off on the mountain was completely different."[2]

He then explains, "The word 'fear' occurs twice in this statement. Moses was pointing out that there was a wrong fear of God and a right fear. The wrong kind leads us to hide from God, while the right kind leads us to draw near to Him in purity and reverence."[3]

Which "fear" will you embrace?

NOTES

1. Bill Johnson, *Face to Face with God* (Lake Mary, FL: Charisma House, 2007), 62-63.

2. Ibid., 64.

3. Ibid.

INTIMIDATING FEAR

Then the Lord said to Moses: "Do not fear him, for I have delivered him into your hand..." (Numbers 21:34).

"**I**f I have to go through one more battle..."

We've all been there. Maybe you're there now. It seems one crisis barely ends before another is staring us in the face. Financial ruin seems imminent as bills go up and income goes down. Tests from a nagging physical condition produce a bad medical report. Upheaval and dissatisfaction in the church leaves an unquenchable thirst for a God encounter that is real. A promising godly relationship suddenly disintegrates, leaving a crushed and shattered heart. Yet words prophetically spoken over you and confirmed in the Word have promised financial blessing, divine health, "Song of Solomon-like" intimacy with God, and a soul mate to partner with in pursuing your God-given destiny. God has faithfully navigated you through each land mine—as you walked to Him and with Him on the water of your storm—speaking "Peace, be still" to each one as He provides financial miracles, divine healing, spiritual refreshing, etc.

Now, here you are, facing yet another battle. And you are just plain battle weary. "God, can we please have a couple of weeks with smooth sailing?" That is God's *fear not* message to us today.

This is where Israel was in Numbers 21. The Canaanites had taken some of the Israelites captive. Israel made a "deal" (vow) with the Lord that if He would give them victory over the Canaanites, they would destroy the cities of the enemy, which He did. As was often the case after a great victory, Israel moved further into the wilderness, became discouraged, and responded wrongly by murmuring against God and Moses.

I sense the Lord wants me to pause here to encourage you. The Canaanites were the descendants of the cursed son of Noah, Ham, who saw his father's nakedness and mockingly told his brothers. The curse was that Ham's descendants, the Canaanites, would be servants to his two brothers' descendents, which included, eventually, the Israelites (from Shem). So here, the Canaanites attacked Israel in a bitter battle and took prisoners.

For some of you, Canaan (representing the kingdom of darkness) has attacked you and taken some prisoners (your children?). You vowed to the Lord to destroy their cities (the habitation of evil—Internet pornography, movies, etc.) from your environment if God would deliver the enemy into your hand. He has—the "prisoners" have been freed and you have experienced a great victory. But beware! As mentioned above, often on the heels of a great victory comes a time of wilderness experience (spiritual dryness) that can bring discouragement (see Num. 21:4).

Compare Elijah's experience after his victory against the prophets of Baal and Jesus' after the words of His Father at His baptism. It is essential that our response during this time be like Jesus', declaring the Word, rather than like Elijah and Israel—discouraged and complaining. This latter response opens the door to further attack (fiery serpents, see Num. 21:6).

The key was that Jesus kept His focus on the reason why He was here. Elijah and Israel did not. All three faced enemy attacks after great victories. Two lost their focus and settled in the wilderness of discouragement and hopelessness. One did not. He is our model.

Moses' message was clear: "Do not fear him (the next battle), for I have delivered him into your hand" (literally, "given you victory over him"). It is a message of courage and confidence—courage to face our next battle without fear because our Commander in Chief has already declared the outcome before we've even engaged the enemy. Victory!

FEAR OF POSSESSING HIS PROMISES

Look, the Lord your God has set the land before you; go up and possess it, as the Lord God of your fathers has spoken to you, do not fear or be discouraged (Deuteronomy 1:21).

Moses had begun recounting the 40-year history of Israel's journey to the new generation that was now poised and being readied to go in and possess the land.

The quote here is from the first promise made to the previous generation as they stood at the border of God's promise! One generation later and they were still there—one river away from God's fullness and blessing. Fear had kept them in the wilderness of lack and discouragement, when just across the river was the fullness of God's promise. They had experienced a taste of that promise when the spies returned carrying *one* cluster of grapes that had to be tied to a pole and carried by two men! That was God saying, "See what awaits you? See the blessing I have prepared for you?" But then, an evil report—giants and walled cities—brought fear that outweighed and negated what they had seen and heard.

Fear does several sinister things when we choose to embrace it rather than God's promise:

1. It causes us to forget God's past protection.

   Ten plagues came upon the Egyptians—not one touched Israel. What plague has God protected you from? Cancer? Crime? Accidental death?

   A thousand may fall at your side, and ten thousand at your right hand, but it shall not come near you. ...No evil shall befall you, nor shall any plague come near your dwelling (Psalm 91:7,10).

2. It causes us to forget God's provision.

   The Egyptians *gave* Israel their gold, silver, jewelry, and live-stock! Then God provided food, water, shelter from the desert sun (the pillar of cloud), and light (fire at night). Not to mention their clothes and shoes didn't wear out. Have you forgotten all of God's past provisions and are now fearful of what may lie ahead in your financial future? You see the economy spiraling out of control, the threat of terrorism, natural disasters; all that has brought security is being shaken to its very foundation. "I have been young, and now am old; yet I have not seen the righteous forsaken, nor His descendants begging bread" (Ps. 37:25). Evil report or God's promises? Which will we believe? That is our choice.

3. It causes us to lose focus on God's ultimate purpose—to bless us so we can be a blessing (see Gen. 12:2).

   God's purpose was originally stated to Moses: "...to bring them up...to a good and large land, to a land flowing with milk and honey" (Exod. 3:8). God always brings us out so He can bring us in. He never brings change to leave us in the wilderness but to bring us to a higher and greater provisional destiny. He never closes one door without opening another. There may be a time of testing and preparation, but a land of "milk and honey" awaits.

An 11-day journey (see Deut. 1:2) turned into a 40-year, generation-passing nightmare for one reason only—*fear*, which led to unbelief, which led to murmuring and complaining, which led to open rebellion and desire to return to Egypt. They desired the security of slavery over the adventure of freedom.

Destiny involves risk, trust, and adventure into the unknown. The joy is not so much in the destiny as it is in the journey: "If Your Presence does not go with us, do not bring us up from here" (Exod. 33:15).

OVERWHELMING FEAR

Then I said to you, "Do not be terrified, or afraid of them"
(Deuteronomy 1:29).

Moses now reminded Israel of the ugly incident of the fear-filled report of the ten spies and their subsequent decision not to go up and take the land, which resulted in the 40-year "road to nowhere" experience. It is noteworthy that Moses added a word to the "fear" word we've seen so far. The Hebrew word means, "to awe, to harass, to be terrified, oppress, shake terribly." It's a step up from fear—it's terror. I guess looking into the face of an army of nine-foot giants would qualify as terror!

"Terror" and "terrorism" have become common vocabulary words since 9/11, so much so that the government no longer uses the term but prefers to define terrorist attacks as "man-made disasters." As we approached the 10-year anniversary of the attack, we realized that we were living in a different world. Today, the Middle East is "on fire," nation after nation rising in revolution as their people seek freedom, only to have their government clamp down or be replaced with an even more ruthless regime. All of these nations have aligned themselves against Israel, promising, along with Iran, to "wipe Israel off the map."

At home, our economy (and the dollar) is collapsing around us; prices are skyrocketing while unemployment remains at depression-like levels. "Big Brother" government now controls once free-market industries, such as healthcare, automotive industries, housing, student loans, banking, and more. Some economists predict that within a year a loaf of bread may cost 60 dollars. Corn has already doubled in price in the last six months as we use more and more of it as fuel instead of food.

Enough giants for ya? Makes you want to turn back into the wilderness and build a cabin in the woods, grow your own food, and forget the rest of the world is out there—kind of like the Amish do, bless their hearts. Sometimes I envy their simplicity.

Yet we have this mandate from our Commander in Chief to "Go therefore and make disciples of all the nations..." (Matt. 28:19). In this mess we call a world? Where's the Rapture when you need it? As I sit and write this, it is a day after a cult got nationwide attention by predicting that Jesus would return on May 21, 2011, judge and destroy the world (and the Church), and take the "true believers" back to Heaven with Him. I just went outside to get my morning paper and as far as I could tell, the world around me was still there and so am I. Guess I missed the Rapture. *Darn!* I was so looking forward to it!

Israel was a new generation here; the generation that God brought out of Egypt had died in the wilderness—by their own words. Be careful what you speak in your crisis: you are prophesying your future. They said, "...if only we had died in this wilderness" (Num. 14:2). God's response was, "...as you have spoken in My hearing, so I will do to you" (Num. 14:28). And they did, except for Joshua and Caleb. Now, this new generation was facing the same challenge—the same giants. Moses was charging them to have a different response.

You and I are facing the "perfect storm" of giants as mentioned above. What will our response be? Why did Moses admonish the people to not be terrified or afraid? His next statement answered that question and it became their battle cry. I pray, as we advance Papa God's kingdom in the face of our giants, it will be ours as well: "The Lord your God, who goes before you, He will fight for you…" (Deut. 1:30).

In so doing, "terror" can be used to describe the enemy rather than us. Bill Johnson, in his daily devotional book, *A Life of Miracles*, which is a compilation of quotes from his other books, cites several principles of spiritual warfare in "Day 107: Biblical Secrets of War." His third principle applies perfectly here:

> *In no way alarmed by your opponents—which is a sign of destruction for them, but of salvation for you, and that too, from God* (Philippians 1:28 NASB).

> When we refuse fear, the enemy becomes terrified. A confident heart is a sure sign of his ultimate destruction and our present victory! Do not fear—ever. Return to the promises of God, spend time with people of faith, and encourage one another with the testimonies of the Lord. Praise God for who He is until fear no longer knocks at the door.[1]

Amen, Bill!

NOTE

1. Bill Johnson, *A Life of Miracles* (Shippensburg, PA: Destiny Image Publishers, 2009), 113.

DISPELLING FEAR: REMEMBERING HIS FAITHFULNESS

And the Lord said to me, "Do not fear him, for I have delivered him and all his people and his land into your hand..." (Deuteronomy 3:2).

When facing a challenge, it is always good to pause and meditate on His past faithfulness. Moses here reminded Israel of God's faithfulness in delivering a formidable king and his army into their hands. It must have been a great victory, perhaps unexpected, for it to be cited as a motivation to move ahead into the challenge before them.

We face great challenges today in our society. Ever-expanding government power and control, economic crises worldwide, and rampant sin and crime in our own nation, can cause a fear for our own and our family's survival. What lies ahead? Fear of the future can be paralyzing.

How do we overcome it? How do we maintain and even grow our faith in the face of today's challenges? One way, as Moses did here, is to recall God's supernatural intervention and provision in the past. Can you recall a past crisis in your life where the enemy seemingly overwhelmed you and God intervened, showed up, and showed off?

Jeremiah said, "Through the Lord's mercies we are not consumed, because His compassions fail not. They are new every morning; great is Your faithfulness" (Lam. 3:22-23). Has God been there for you in the past? Healed you? Supernaturally provided for you? Restored a relationship that you thought was lost forever? All of the above?

When Israel crossed the Jordan into the Promised Land, God instructed Joshua to tell the head of each of the 12 tribes to pick up a stone from the dry riverbed as they crossed over and to, "…leave them in the lodging place where you lodge tonight" (Josh. 4:3). Why? Joshua said, "…that this may be a sign among you when your children ask in time to come, saying, 'What do these stones mean to you?'" (Josh. 4:6). This would give them opportunity to explain to their children God's faithfulness in bringing them into their inheritance. It would be "…a memorial to the children of Israel forever" (Josh. 4:7).

Where is your pile of "stones of remembrance"—your memorial to God's faithfulness? Have you made one lately? In these days of uncertainty, are you confident that the God who has never left you nor forsaken you is still with you and will continue to provide "all your need according to His (not the economy's) riches in glory" (Phil. 4:19)?

I remember as a child singing an old favorite from our church hymnbook: "Count your blessings; name them one by one. Count your blessings, see what God has done." How about it? Sit down, ask the Lord to bring to your mind all the times He has already proven Himself faithful to you in the past and begin to write them down. Make a list. Space is provided below for you to start. Refer to the list and add to it every day as the Lord reminds you. As the song says, "…and it will surprise you what the Lord has done."

_____

_____

_____

_____

_____

COURAGE: FEAR'S REPLACEMENT

*...Your eyes have seen all that the Lord your God has done...
so will the Lord do.... You must not fear them, for the Lord
your God Himself fights for you* (Deuteronomy 3:21-22).

Joshua's assignment: lead Israel into the Promised Land—a land filled with giants. That prospect had already frightened one generation away to wander and die in the wilderness. Now, here they were again—new generation, new leader, same challenge.

Why does the Lord do that? He brings us to the edge of our destiny; then we realize there are "giants" of opposition we must conquer in order to move into that destiny (past hurts, unforgiveness, feelings of inadequacy, unworthiness, etc.). So, despite His promise to be with us, assuring victory, we turn tail and retreat back into our spiritual wilderness, where He teaches us how to fight (rather than run from) giants. Then He brings us back to the same river-crossing we ran from a generation ago—wise, battle-ready, and confident in our new Leader (Jesus).

One of the weapons God teaches us to use in the current challenge is memory of His faithfulness in past battles. Moses has just reminded the people of their greatest wilderness victory: King Og of Bashan (see Deut. 3:1-3). How "big" was that victory? Verse 11 describes King Og's bed as being nine cubits long by four cubits wide. That's thirteen and a half feet long by six feet wide! The frame was made of iron in order to hold him up! That's one big boy! Gives a whole new meaning to "king-size bed"! Yet, Moses reminds them of the complete victory God gave them, "...until he had no survivors remaining" (Deut. 3:3).

Pause here, dear one. Let the Lord remind *you* of the "King Og" that He gave you *complete* victory over in your life. Got it? Okay. Now, fast forward to today. You're once again on the shores of your destiny, facing the same giants as last time. But this time you have the weapon of memory: "Your eyes have seen all that the Lord your God has done." Confidence for today's battle begins in memory—remembering His faithfulness. "Great is Thy faithfulness, morning by morning new mercies I see" (song based on Lam. 3:23-24).

The second weapon we have is the basis for God's command of "You must not fear them," and that is, "...the Lord your God Himself fights for you." What a revelation! He is not just the Coach on the sidelines, cheering us on. He is not only *in* the game, He's taken charge of the game! From the cross, He "...disarmed principalities and powers" and "made a public spectacle of them, triumphing over them..." (Col. 2:15). Yes, He is the One who fights for us. Now, all we have to do is put on the full armor of God (see Eph. 6:10-18), take and use the authority He has given us (see Luke 10:19), and declare His promise that "...no man (opposition to your destiny) shall be able to stand before you all the days of your life..." (Josh. 1:5).

I recommend you watch the DVD, *Indescribable,* hosted by Louie Giglio, as he takes you on an unbelievable journey into the vast universe through the Hubble Telescope and shows you the handiwork of our God. It is He who fights for us, indeed, and has already secured the victory. We need to go on offense, declaring His promises aloud and possessing all that He has paid such a great price for.

FEAR OF RISK (LOSS)

And he [the priest] *shall say to them, "Hear O Israel: Today you are on the verge of battle with your enemies. Do not let your heart faint, do not be afraid, and do not tremble or be terrified because of them; for the Lord your God is He who goes with you, to fight for you against your enemies, to save you"*
(Deuteronomy 20:3-4).

This message seems to be the same as the last (see Deut. 3), and to an extent it is. Moses was again reminding the people not to panic when they were on the verge of battle with their enemies because it would be God who would go with them and fight for them. I don't mind if God reminds me of that every day. Do you? We don't know what "enemy" we will face on any given day. All we need to do is to strap on the "full armor of God" and let Him do the rest (see Eph. 6:10).

But this reminder focuses on specific groups of people among the Israelites who had a specific reason to fear going to battle. These were the exemptions from serving in the military. But we must remember one thing: we are not exempt from the enemy's attack. When we embraced Christ's love, we "switched sides" and joined the army of the righteous and thus became a target of the enemy, whose aim is to get us back or destroy us. Satan doesn't exempt us from attack, so I'd say Moses' statement applies here.

The first exemption Moses cited was that of a man "...who has built a new house and has not dedicated it" (Deut. 20:5). This, to me, gives a picture of a young man starting a family, which may include purchasing a home. A new marriage, a new baby, a new career—all that is included in establishing a home. A comfort zone is formed that says, "I can't go to war; I have a new family, career, etc." What we need to understand is that new whatever-it-is becomes a target of the enemy who comes to steal, kill, and destroy (see John 10:10). Yes, it does need to be dedicated to God. The very act of dedication is an act of war. It is building a hedge or wall of protection around our home and family by declaring Psalms 91 and 121 protection over them and making Jesus owner of them. That's the act of war that allows God to fight for us.

The second exemption is seen in verse 6: "Also what man is there who has planted a vineyard and has not eaten of it?" It seems shepherds and vine-dressers were the two main careers in ancient Israel. Having been raised on a farm, I know the labor (and risk) involved in raising crops. There is a help-less dependency on weather (drought, flood, hail, etc.), danger of insect or disease damage, and so much more that could destroy months of labor in one day.

What about your vineyard? Vineyards produce grapes, which are har-vested and made into wine. In the New Testament, new wine is used to depict the Holy Spirit (see Matt. 9:17; Eph. 5:18). The message I believe the Lord is giving here is—before going to war for others (intercession), guard your own "vineyard" (your spirit life) so that you may "eat of it," i.e., live a Spirit-empowered supernatural lifestyle, seeing and experiencing miracles, signs, and wonders on a daily basis. Why should you (and I) be a casualty of ministry and let someone else partake of the fruit of our labor?

Tragically, I learned this lesson the hard way. Pouring myself into pas-toral ministry, I neglected my own vineyard, eventually falling into moral failure and fulfilling the last part of verse 6: "...lest he die in the battle and another man eat of it." It took 20 years in the spiritual wilderness to bring healing and restoration to my marriage first and then ministry.

Moses' third exemption was for those who had been "...betrothed to a woman and [had] not married her" (Deut. 20:7). There are two messages here, I believe. One continues the thought from above—family and marriage come before career or ministry. Mr. Businessman, your first ministry is to your wife, not your career! Mr. Pastor/Minister, your primary responsibility is to meet the needs of your wife, not your church or ministry. Spousal neglect is the number one cause for ministerial failure and divorce among Christian couples. Violate that principle and fulfill the end of verse 7: "...lest he die in the battle and another man marry her."

The other principle is "double loyalty." Joshua challenged Israel, "...choose for yourselves this day whom you will serve..." (Josh. 24:15). Jesus taught the reason why a choice is necessary:

> *No one can serve two masters; for either he will hate the one and love the other, or else he will be loyal to the one and despise the other* (Matthew 6:24).

Both of these refer to placing things (*mammon,* or riches) on an equal plane with God. To whom are you betrothed? Maybe the gal or guy you're engaged to has no desire to participate in your God-ordained destiny. Time to choose! Can't serve 'em both! One will ascend to the throne of your life, the other will be rejected.

The fourth and last exemption Moses gave was for those who were "fearful and fainthearted" (Deut. 20:8). Afraid and feeling "closed in" is what those words mean. Ever been there? Circumstances, finances, losses, and medical reports bring fear and the feeling of being closed or hemmed in, trapped in a circumstance you can do nothing about. The greatest encouragement I can give you is Papa God's words we began with:

> *Do not let your heart faint, do not be afraid, and do not tremble or be terrified...for the Lord your God is He who goes with you, to fight for you against your enemies, to save you* (Deuteronomy 20:3-4).

FACTS THAT MELT FEAR

Be strong and of good courage, do not fear nor be afraid of them; for the Lord your God, He is the One who goes with you. He will not leave you nor forsake you (Deuteronomy 31:6).

When I was growing up in upstate New York, I loved the early spring season. After months of the frozen tundra of a New York winter, the warmth of the spring sun began melting the snow and thawing the ground. The smell of spring was in the air; new life was emerging as the crocuses, daffodils, and lilies pushed through the soil reaching for the warmth of God's resurrection of nature.

As we walk through these dark days that have fallen on our nation and the world, we may feel we are entering a moral ice age as all references to God are methodically being legislated out of our lives. Like Israel, we face a ruthless enemy—giants in the land who dare us to oppose them. It seems they have all the power.

- The fear of man is very strongly associated with unbelief.[1]

This was the fear of the new generation whose assignment was to go in and conquer the land, the land of promise, the land "flowing with milk and honey"—a land filled with giants. So, what was the Lord's word of encouragement to His people with this seemingly-impossible assignment? To be of good courage and to not be afraid of them. Easier said than done, except for the *reason* why they are not to fear. God promises to do three things as they lay claim to the land of promise:

1. God will be with them.

   Bill Johnson's experience of walking in the supernatural lifestyle began with his quest for God's Presence. In His Presence, the impossible not only becomes possible, it becomes easy. Bill advises, "Rather than going after miracles, go after His Presence." In His Presence is contained all the supernatural power needed to defeat any giant.

2. God will not leave them.

   The King James uses the word *fail*, which means "to slacken." God promises He will not slacken or lag behind in His partnership with His people.

3. God will not forsake them.

   The word means to loosen, relinquish, or permit. God is saying He will not abandon them in the heat of battle. A covenant gets stronger in hard times; abandonment is not possible in true covenant.

So what impossibility are you facing today? What promises has God spoken to you? And what giants are striking fear into your heart and keeping you from going in and taking possession of your destiny? Unemployment? Finances? Health issues? Marriage crisis? Who are your giants? I believe God's message to ancient Israel is our message today:

- "Be strong and courageous. There is no need to fear, My child. With the assignment—moving into your destiny—goes the promise that I am with you and no opposition can stand before Me. Stay in My presence and I will make a way where there is no way. I will open doors no man can shut."

Do you trust Him, the One has called you and who will be faithful to do it (see 1 Thess. 5:24)? How big are your giants and how big is your God? How you answer that question will determine the degree of your "promised land" (destiny) you will claim!

NOTE

1. Bill Johnson, *When Heaven Invades Earth* (Shippensburg, PA: Treasure House, 2003), 46.

THE CALL TO FEARLESS LEADERSHIP

*And the Lord, He is the One who goes before you. He will be
with you, He will not leave you nor forsake you; do not fear
nor be dismayed* (Deuteronomy 31:8).

As the leader goes, so go the people. Moses had just challenged the people to be strong and courageous and to not fear. But what good would that do if their leader was fearful in facing the challenge that lay ahead? Moses now turned his attention to Joshua, his successor, and virtually repeated the challenge he just gave the people, adding, "He is the One who goes before you." The word *before* there can be translated "in the face of." God would be in the face of the enemy, going ahead of Joshua, disarming each foe, making them ripe for defeat. Joshua had to be confident and convinced of this before he could transfer that confidence to the people.

This message, I believe, is to the leaders of today, both church and political. It is time for apostolic leadership to rise with renewed boldness as in the book of Acts (see Acts 4). Facing the "deep darkness" on world governments and economies today, it is time to "Arise, shine; for your light has come! And the glory of the Lord is risen upon you" (Isa. 60:1). Leaders, God has promised in this age of spiritual and moral corruption, "...But the Lord will arise over you, and His glory will be seen upon you" (Isa. 60:2). No more compromise! No more spineless social gospel. It is time to declare the Kingdom "on earth as it (already) is in heaven" (Matt. 6:10). The supernatural must become the normal Christian life. The book of Acts chronicles the explosion of the early church amidst the antagonistic Jewish and Roman cultures. Once again, in this final generation, the cry of the early apostles must be heard among our leaders:

> *...grant to Your servants that with all boldness they may speak Your word, by stretching out Your hand to heal, and that signs and wonders may be done through the name of Your holy Servant Jesus* (Acts 4:29-30).

Where are you, leaders of today? Your people have been challenged to rise up and take back the land the enemy has stolen! They need modern-day Joshuas who will unashamedly and uncompromisingly stand up to the deep darkness covering the earth today and proclaim, "Choose you *this day* (now) whom ye will serve...but as for me and my house, we will serve the Lord" (Josh. 24:15 KJV).

FEAR OF OBEDIENT RISK-TAKING

Have I not commanded you? Be strong and of good courage;
do not be afraid, nor be dismayed, for the Lord your God is
with you wherever you go (Joshua 1:9).

It is one thing dealing with fear in the midst of an enemy attack. But what about when God gives us a clear assignment to step out with Him in defiance of all logic? John Wimber said, "Faith is spelled R-I-S-K." Is there something in your spirit that you know God has called you to—a destiny that is so big, so overwhelming, you know it is "impossible" to accomplish in the natural? If you were to sit down and write the dream God has placed in your heart, if there were no limitations (including money) in accomplishing it, what would it be? Does it frighten you? That's what Joshua faced in today's text.

"Moses my servant is dead. Now therefore, arise..." (Josh. 1:2). Is God doing a "new thing" in your life (see Isa. 43:19)? New job, promotion, ministry? Retirement (like me), relocation? Change always seems to bring a certain level of anxiety with it (fear of failure or the unknown). God reassures Joshua in a couple of ways:

1. He commands him to "be strong and of good courage" or "very

courageous" three times (Josh. 1:6,7,9).

The words God uses are very emphatic. *Strong* means "to be manly, established, firm, fortified, obstinate, and mighty." To be *of good courage* means "to be alert, physically on foot or mentally in courage." Being alert and standing firm, obstinate, and mighty in the face of opposition to our God-given dream is a command God gives us. He would not command (give a charge to) us to do something if it were not possible to achieve: "Have I not commanded you?" In other words, "Haven't I appointed you to accomplish this assignment?" We call that a rhetorical question. If you have said to Him, "This is impossible. I can't do this, especially in this economy," His answer will be the same: "I've commanded you to do this, so why do you think it's impossible?" Paul encouraged the Thessalonians, "He who calls you is faithful, who will also do it" (1 Thess. 5:24).

2.   Twice, God tells Joshua that He will be with him (Josh. 1:5,9).

"...As I was with Moses, so I will be with you. I will not leave you nor forsake you" (Josh. 1:5). And, "...the Lord your God is with you wherever you go" (Josh. 1:9). Gee, no mention of the economy, the government, or any other source of opposition. Just His promise that, "Every place that the sole of your foot will tread upon *I have given you*..." (Josh. 1:3). Wow! John says of Jesus, "...knowing that the Father had given *all things* into His hands..." (John 13:3). Then Paul makes the ridiculous (but true) statement, "For all things are yours" (1 Cor. 3:21). Okay. So the Father gave "all things" to Jesus. Jesus gave "all things" to us (see Matt. 28:18-19), and now "all things" are ours. What is included in "all things"? Paul lists some of them in First Corinthians: "... the world or life or death, or things present or things to come— all are yours" (1 Cor. 3:22). That's our inheritance!

The greatest reason not to fear, though, is the promise of His presence (see Josh. 1:5,9; Matt. 28:20). We never step out of the boat alone. What we accomplish will always be in and with His presence. The "risk" is always the first step—out of the boat, into the Jordan, etc. Start that business, give to that ministry, reconcile that relationship. His presence will go before you, giving you favor, walking beside you, comforting, exhorting, and encouraging you on and following behind you, protecting you from sneak attacks, confirming His word with signs, wonders, and miracles (provision).

FEAR *AFTER* FAILURE

Now the Lord said to Joshua, "Do not be afraid, nor be dismayed; take all the people of war with you, and arise, go up to Ai. See, I have given into your hand the king of Ai, his people, his city, and his land" (Joshua 8:1).

It was supposed to be easy. God promised to be with him. That was proven by Jericho—an impenetrable fortress fell, just as God said it would. Then Ai, a city a fraction of the size of Jericho, defeated Israel, setting them to flight. What happened?

Sin, in the form of greed, had infiltrated and breached the covenant with God, and as a result His presence had lifted and subjected the whole nation to defeat. Joshua cried out to God for revelation and the sin was exposed and dealt with. Then, God gave Joshua instructions to go back to Ai, the place of defeat, and engage the enemy again. What was different? It's simple but profound: "See, I (God) have given into your hand...Ai." The "I will be with you" covenant was back in force.

What about you? Have you gone through your own "Ai" experience? Moral failure? Failed marriage, ministry, or business? I have. Called into ministry at 17, I went off to Bible college the next year to prepare. But underneath were unresolved issues—rejection, need for acceptance, not to mention teenage hormones! That was a lethal combination.

Wherever I pastored, I seemed to have Jerichos—attendance doubling or tripling, salvations, baptisms, Holy Spirit moves. Wow! Walls came tumbling down! But underneath, I was secretly planting the seed of my Ai—moral failure—cheating on my wife, in plain English. God mercifully gave me 10 opportunity-filled years to repent, but as long as I could keep it hidden (Achan buried the evidence in his tent), I felt like I was "getting away with it." In September of 1982, I experienced my "Ai" and my house of cards came tumbling down around me.

So, how do I (and you) recover from our Ai? The same way Joshua did:

1. The sin must be exposed (see Josh. 7).

    When sin is exposed it loses its power or hold over us. But it is the thing we fear most because of shame and humiliation. Yet light *is* the only thing that dispels darkness. David said:

    When I kept silent [about my sin], my bones grew old through my groaning all the day long, for day and night Your hand was heavy upon me; my vitality was turned into the drought of summer. I acknowledged my sin to You, and my iniquity I have not hidden. I said, "I will confess my transgressions to the Lord," and You forgave the iniquity of my sin (Psalm 32:3-5).

2. The sin must be dealt with (see Josh. 7:20-26).

    Achan was pre-Calvary. Our "death penalty" was taken there. Instead, with confession comes forgiveness and cleansing (see 1 John 1:9).

3. Return to the place of failure (see Josh. 8:1).

    That's our subject today—the fear of returning to the place of failure, getting back on the horse after he's thrown you. I was "on the shelf" for 20 years after my "Ai," partly because of the work and healing the Holy Spirit was doing in me (because He knew, though I didn't, that He wasn't through with me), and partly because of this fear. "If I stay out of ministry, then if I fall again, at least I won't be publically humiliated," I reasoned. This is what the Lord had to get out of me—*me*. It was all about me. The focus had to change and become all about Him, His presence, His love (yes, He still loved me).

To do this, in part, He took me to Hebrews 12:5-11 to remind me a Father disciplines His son, and if He doesn't, then he is not a son. Then He reminded me that He would restore the years the locusts had eaten (see Joel 2:25). And He has!

The reason Joshua did not have to fear returning to Ai was God's statement, "I have given into your hand…Ai." God was back in charge.

Friend, repentance and submitting to Father's discipline and restoration will bring His promise that He will give into your hand the very enemy that caused you to fail, resulting in a great victory for which He will get all the glory!

FEAR OF UNGODLY ALLIANCES

And the Lord said to Joshua, "Do not fear them, for I have delivered them into your hand; not a man of them shall stand before you" (Joshua 10:8).

A similar message was given by God to Joshua here as in Joshua 8:1—"Do not fear them, for I have delivered them into your hand." The message was similar but the circumstances were different. Here, the Gibeonites had deceived Joshua into making a treaty with them, a decision Joshua made without inquiring of the Lord. Now the Gibeonites were being threatened by five city-kings, and they quickly appealed to Joshua for help on the basis of their agreement. There are two things that stand out to me in this story that I believe can encourage and challenge us.

1. What do we do when we have errantly made a decision without going to Papa God first to get His wisdom?

    "…But they (Israel) did not ask counsel of (inquire at the mouth of) the Lord" (Josh. 9:14). The result was, "Joshua made peace with them, and made a covenant with them…" (Josh. 9:15).

Have you ever signed a contract, indebted yourself with a purchase, started a business, or even married an unbeliever, something that sounded reasonable, so much so that you felt that it *had* to be God and so you didn't feel you needed to pray specifically about it? I have. I've started many home-based businesses and locked myself into contracts, only to strain the budget and realize little or no profit. It sounded good, perhaps Christian-owned, etc., so it *must* be God. Only after Joshua "sealed the deal" did he realize who they really were. Now what?

> *Then all the rulers said to all the congregation, "We have sworn to them by the Lord God of Israel; now therefore, we may not touch them"* (Joshua 9:19).

The answer is, we honor our word unless it would be illegal or immoral to do so (see Matt. 5:37). Yes, there are consequences when we move presumptuously without getting God's direction (see Prov. 3:6). But that leads to the second point of this passage.

2. When we live up to the covenant we've made, God promises to rally to our support and overcome obstacles that arise as a result of that decision.

    Whether it's potential bankruptcy, stress on the budget, or crisis in the marriage, do not fear or "go on a guilt trip." God promises He, too, will honor the covenant you made and "deliver the enemy into your hands." He will make a way where there seems to be no way. Just go to Him, ask Him how to honor your commitment, and trust Him to provide "exceedingly abundantly above all that we ask or think, according to the power that works in us" (Eph. 3:20).

COMMUNICATING THE "FEAR NOT" MESSAGE

Then Joshua said to them, "Do not be afraid, nor be dismayed;
be strong and of good courage, for thus the Lord will do to all
your enemies against whom you fight" (Joshua 10:25).

Joshua had heard from God. So many times God had encouraged him to "Fear not" and admonished him to "be of good courage." And that's okay. God knows our tendency to look at overwhelming opposition and become anxious or fearful. He is an encourager and will consistently reassure us that we have nothing to worry about because He is still in control (see Matt. 6:25-34).

But at some point, especially if we are a leader or head of a household, we must become convinced of Papa God's message and begin to communicate that message to those whom God has placed under us to steward. If we, as leaders, have a tendency toward being fearful in a crisis, how much more will those we lead be fearful—especially if, when they look to us for courage, they see fear instead? It has been accurately stated that as the leader goes so go the people. God knows that, so He speaks to the leader who then is responsible to communicate that message to those he or she leads. We lead by example. For Israel to continue to face future enemies courageously and know that no enemy could stand before them (and God), they had to hear it from their leader and see the fire in his eyes.

Today, America and the world are in crisis, facing everything from global terrorism to nuclear war threats to economic collapse, not to mention the continuing loss of our freedoms here in America. It would be very easy to look at this perfect storm and live in fear, if not panic. So how do we avoid doing so?

Father's message has not changed. Joshua had five kings imprisoned in a cave. So God said, "See what I did with your (overwhelming) enemies so far? So what are you worried about?" Then He made the most victorious prophetic promise in the Old Testament: "...for thus the Lord will do to *all* your enemies against whom you fight" (Josh. 10:25). That's pretty all-inclusive.

I am not belittling the seriousness of the times in which we live, nor am I saying not to stand for righteousness in our culture or at the ballot box. It is our responsibility to do so. But we must remember and rest in the fact that, "The king's heart is in the hand of the Lord, like the rivers of water; He turns it wherever He wishes" (Prov. 21:1).

So the message of this "leader" is: "Fear? *Not!*"

TURNING THE TABLES

*And Jael went out to meet Sisera, and said to him, "Turn
aside, my lord, turn aside to me; do not fear"* (Judges 4:18).

Sin, oppression, war, victory. Israel had entered this cycle after Joshua's generation died, a cycle that persisted throughout their history. Here, once again,
Israel "...did evil in the sight of the Lord" (Judg. 4:1). And God allowed another
enemy to oppress them (see Judg. 4:2). As was their pattern, under oppression,
"...Israel cried out to the Lord..." (Judg. 4:3), both in repentance and a plea for
deliverance. God, in His mercy and compassion, heard and responded by raising
up Deborah as judge, to whom He gave a strategy for victory.

So complete and overwhelming was their victory that the enemy general,
Sisera, ended up abandoning his iron chariot and fleeing on foot. He met his
demise by accepting an invitation from a woman to come into her tent—a
woman whom he supposed to be his ally, and who tells him to "Fear not"!
Talk about turning the tables.

Now, I am *not* telling you to pound a tent stake through the temple of
your enemy. That's Old Testament. Jesus taught the opposite (see Matt. 5:44).
But what lesson does this hold for us today?

Names in the Bible have meanings. Sisera was the general of the Canaanite
army. *Sisera* means "battle array." He was a genius in battle and commanded

an army of 900 chariots made of iron, which made them indestructible. Spears and arrows would bounce off of them like toothpicks. Opposing armies (including Israel) were terrified. But God spoke to Deborah (whose name means "honeybee") to tell Barak (whose name means "lightning") to amass 10,000 troops and go to battle and God would rout the enemy.

So the "honeybee" went with "lightning" to battle the brilliant "battle array" general, and they sent him fleeing in terror into the tent of Jael. *Jael* means "wild goat," which means she probably wasn't afraid of anything.

First of all—ladies, you are equally anointed to hear from God in receiving His wisdom and strategy for your family's battle. He can use a little sweet "honeybee" or an aggressive, fearless "wild goat" to accomplish His purposes. Both Deborah and Jael fulfilled the roles of wife and warrior. They are not contradictory. The centurion told Jesus, "I also am a man under authority, having soldiers under me" (Matt. 8:9). Paul said that in Christ there is "...neither male nor female..." (Gal. 3:28). Godly spiritual leadership is not gender-specific.

Second, what the enemy intended for evil, God meant for good (see Gen. 50:20). God turned the tables of fear and terror from Israel onto the enemy:

> And the Lord routed Sisera and all his chariots and all his army...and Sisera...fled away on foot...and all the army of Sisera fell by the edge of the sword [which is the Word of God, see Ephesians 6:17]; not a man was left (Judges 4:15-16).

Jesus "...disarmed principalities and powers, He made a public spectacle of them, triumphing over them" (Col. 2:15). "Now thanks be to God who always leads us in triumph in Christ..." (2 Cor. 2:14), because "...greater is he that is in you, than he that is in the world" (1 John 4:4 KJV).

Turn the tables on the enemy! Use the weapons Christ has made available to you (see Eph. 6:10-18; 2 Cor. 10:4-5) and experience the victory His blood intended for us—one will chase a thousand, and two will put ten thousand to flight! (See Deuteronomy 32:30.)

FEAR OF SPIRITUAL DARKNESS

Also I said to you, "I am the Lord your God; do not fear the gods of the Amorites, in whose land you dwell." But you have not obeyed My voice (Judges 6:10).

I never cease to be amazed at the extent to which Papa God will go to respond to His children. Here, once again, through their own disobedience, the Israelites find themselves "impoverished" and oppressed by the enemy (see Judg. 6:6). Yet, "…when the children of Israel cried out to the Lord…the Lord sent a prophet…" (Judg. 6:7-8) to speak to them, reminding them of what He had done for them (past deliverance) and why He allowed the current discipline of enemy oppression (disobedience). His next step was to prepare and send a deliverer—Gideon (see Judg. 6:11).

Father gives us His recipe that, if we will live in awareness of each ingredient, will enable us to live in His presence, "far above all principality and power" (Eph. 1:21).

1. "I said to you."

    God's first reminder to us is: a) who the speaker is, and b) who the final authority is. Growing up in an old-fashioned Italian home, when Dad spoke, he left no doubt. And if I asked Dad "Why?" his answer was, "Because I said so!"

Jesus said, "My sheep *know* My voice," (see John 10:4). God has a word for you today: He does not want you to question, "Was that God or was that me?" You know His voice because you are one of His sheep.

2. "I am the Lord your God."

    Papa then reminds us of His identity. Jehovah—the Self-Existent One. Elohim—the Almighty, Supreme God. Moses asked, "When...they say to me, 'What is His name?' what shall I say to them?" (Exod. 3:13). God's answer was, "...I AM WHO I AM...I AM has sent me to you" (Exod. 3:14).

    We have derived the English title *Jehovah* from the Hebrew, which literally means "the Self-Existent One." And, as if that weren't enough, He further identifies Himself as *God*—Elohim—the "Almighty Supreme God." Put them together, and it is "the Self-Existent One" who is "the Almighty Supreme God"! *Wow!* Good enough for you? No? Then how about this? In between these two descriptions is a little pronoun—*your*. Yes, He (not me) identifies Himself as *your* God! Stop here, and spend some quiet time meditating on this. He voluntarily offers Himself to you, to become your possession. He is saying, "I am *yours*. I belong to *you*. You are possessed...by *Me!*" You have not earned that level of intimacy. He offers it.

    We casually identify our spouse as "my wife" or "my husband." In the same level of intimacy, He says, "I am my beloved's and He is mine" (see Song of Sol. 6; John 17). He, the Creator of the universe, is the One who is speaking to you today. That's how important you are to Him! And what does He have to say to you?

3. "Do not fear the gods of the Amorities, in whose land you dwell."

    The main god of the Amorites was called *Marduk*, a Babylonian god. Marduk was said to have conquered all the others gods and thus became their chief god. According to Wikipedia, he was known by several names: "Lord, lord of lords, leader of the gods, the wise lord of oracles, and reviver of the dead."[1] Do you see the parallels in these descriptions and those in Scripture? Satan, as the angel of light, still seeks to be worshiped as God. Further, Wikipedia describes man's purpose under Marduk's rule: "Under his reign, humans were created to bear the burdens of life so the gods could be at leisure."[2] In other words, slavery. Bondage is always the result of serving satan.

But God says do not be afraid of them, even though you dwell in their land. There is much darkness in our land today. Our freedoms are quickly being eroded and expression of our faith is now not without judicial limitations. Personally, many face unemployment or great stress on the job, economic crisis or disaster, terminal illness or addiction. In the midst of this, God is declaring over you, "*Do not* be afraid!" He sums up this age by saying:

…darkness shall cover the earth, and deep darkness the people; **but** *the Lord will arise over you, and His glory [the weightiness of His presence] will be seen upon you* (Isaiah 60:2).

Gee! The darkness of this age doesn't seem to move God at all. In fact, He wants to pierce the darkness with His light…through you! Your call, your destiny has not been derailed by the economy or any other circumstance. When Jesus told the disciples they were going to the other side, no storm was going to prevent it from happening. That's why Jesus was able to sleep in the boat. Bill Johnson says, "The only storm you have victory over is the storm you can sleep through." In other words, you can live in perfect peace, speaking peace to the storm because your trust is in Him who has given you the authority over every opposition (see Isa. 26:3; John 14:27; Phil. 4:6-7; Luke 10:19).

One last cautionary note: God's promises are always conditional, and that condition is obedience. Israel was in bondage because of disobedience;

the last statement of Judges 6:10 negated the entire previous promise of God's victory. Our victory is also contingent upon our personal obedience to Him. We must follow the instructions Mary gave the wedding attendants at Cana: "Whatever He says to you, do it" (John 2:5).

NOTES

1. "Marduk," Wikipedia, Late Bronze Age, accessed March 27, 2013, http://en.wikipedia.org/wiki/Marduk.

2. Ibid.

FROM FEAR TO PEACE

Then the Lord said to him [Gideon], *"Peace be with you; do
not fear, you shall not die"* (Judges 6:23).

I identify with Gideon; do you? Son of a farmer, doing his chores, timid
and fearful. Gideon was living in such an oppressive environment that he
would do his daily chores looking over his shoulder, ready to run and hide at
the appearance of the enemy. That's what makes the sudden angelic greeting
so bizarre: "...The Lord is with you, you mighty man of valor!" (Judg. 6:12).

Later, when Gideon prepared a meal for Him and brought it to Him, the
angel lit an instant barbeque with the end of His staff, then disappeared (see
Judg. 6:19-21)! The incredibly perceptive Gideon then "perceived that He
was the Angel of the Lord..." (Judg. 6:22). Gideon's response? "I'm going to
end up like the goat I just prepared—dead meat!" He knew that no one could
look on the face of God (pre-incarnate Jesus) and live (see Exod. 33:20). That
was why Gideon needed the assurance of verse 23. Why was he so fearful to
realize he was in the presence of the King? Why are we? I submit to you one
simple but profound reason—unworthiness.

We have been taught for so long that we are "sinners saved by grace"
that we grovel into His presence, being so sin-conscious that we never enjoy
Him when He shows up. I believe that's why so many avoid prayer; in fact,

I frequently hear Christians preface their prayer time with: "Lord, we are so unworthy to come into Your presence." *What?* Unworthy? Then what was His blood shed for? We need to put this one to rest once and for all!

Paul tells us that when we come into Christ we are a new creation—a partaker of the divine nature (see 2 Pet. 1:4). "Old things have passed away," the sin nature has passed away, and "all things have become new" (see 2 Cor. 5:17; also Gal. 2:20; Rom. 6).

Additionally, Paul tells the Colossians that, through Christ's finished work on the cross, He has "forgiven you *all* trespasses," having *canceled* the debt we owed, and "…having nailed it to the cross" (Col. 2:13-14). So, instead of being saddled with our sin, He "…made us sit together in the heavenly places in Christ Jesus" (Eph. 2:6).

We have been adopted into a royal family, making us a son or daughter of the King (see Rom. 8:15). That makes us a prince or princess, able to call God "Abba, Father" (Daddy)! It makes us "heirs of God and joint heirs with Christ" (see Rom. 8:17). As a result of this family status, we are told to "…come boldly (with confidence) to the throne of grace (His presence)" (Heb. 4:16). Even when we are disciplined by Him, it is because we are "sons"—family members (see Heb. 12:5).

Besides, how can you be a sinner and still be saved? If you were a sinner before you were saved, and you're still a sinner after you're saved, then the blood of Jesus is worthless! It did nothing to change your character.

Bottom line is this: I am "accepted in the Beloved"—Christ (Eph. 1:6). So, when I bring my offering of praise and worship to Him as Gideon did, I do not have to fear His presence as Gideon did because of who I am in Him—an adopted member of His family. The Lord said to Gideon, "Peace (*shalom*) be with you." That encounter so overwhelmed Gideon that he named the altar *Jehovah-shalom*—"the God of peace was here."

The blood of Jesus has made you worthy to come into (and live in) His presence. I speak His *shalom* upon you as you are refreshed in Daddy God's presence daily!

FEAR OF INSECURITY

And now, my daughter, do not fear. I will do for you all that
you request, for all the people of my town know that you are a
virtuous women (Ruth 3:11).

The devastation of the premature death of an immediate family member brings a hollowness to the soul that it seems no one can fill. Naomi, already a widow, lost both of her sons. Ruth lost her husband. She was young, in the prime of life, so to speak, but her dream of the security of a husband to take care of her and children to bless her was gone. Except for an also grieving mother-in-law, Ruth was now alone in a famine-plagued foreign land. All security and hope was suddenly gone.

Are you Ruth? Have you lost your spouse, your life soul mate? Are you Naomi? Do you find yourself alone with no companionship, provision, or security for your future? Is this where a life filled with promise and purpose writes its final chapter?

Naomi, whose name means "pleasant, delightful, lovely," married Elimelech, which means, "My God is King"! How could you be anything but a "Naomi" when you are married to an "Elimelech"? But, suddenly, all that their names meant—the joy of being in intimate relationship with the King—evaporated in unexplained tragedy. In the ash heap of destroyed hope and vision, can there still be "a future and a hope" (Jer. 29:11)? When your world comes crashing down around you without warning, is Jeremiah 29:11 still true?

From Papa God, hear His gentle answer, "Yes, My child." Feel His embrace as He takes you up in His arms and puts your tears into His bottle (see Ps. 56:8). His answer speaks to you from today's text:

1. "And now."

   God is the God of the present. He is a "now" God. David said, "My times are in Your hand…" (Ps. 31:15). Are yours? You may have no understanding as to the why of what happened (neither did Job or Joseph), but Papa God wants you to know He has a "now" for you—a continuation of His perfect plan; it hasn't changed or been derailed. It's still there and on course! Today is your "now." As you embrace Him, He will reveal your "now" to you.

2. "My daughter."

   Your "now" begins with Papa God reminding you who you are—His daughter, a princess to the King! If you identify yourself in any other way, you are believing a lie, and believing a lie empowers the liar. *Daughter* here literally means "apple of my eye"! As a protective Father, He says, "…he who touches you touches the apple of His eye" (Zech. 2:8).

It is perfectly legitimate for you to go to Him and say, "Daddy, I know what You say is true, but I sure don't feel like the apple of Your eye right now. I feel abandoned and all alone. I feel like everything has been taken away from me. I really need to feel Your tangible embrace right now." Then put on some gentle worship music and soak in His presence. Weep, sob, and rest in Him. Words need not be spoken; there is an intimacy that doesn't require words, only Presence.

3. "Do not fear."

   This one is easier said than done, isn't it? The thoughts race through your mind, "What now? What do I do now? What's going to happen to me now? I don't think I can make it without _____."

   Psalm 46 has been my answer in these times. Read this Psalm through, several times a day, if necessary. Make it personal:

   "God is *my* refuge and strength, a very present help in trouble. Therefore, *I* will not fear, even though the earth be removed, and though the mountains be carried into the midst of the sea (circumstantial upheaval). ...The Lord of hosts is with *me*; The God of Jacob is *my* refuge. ...*I will* be still, and know that *You are God*" (see Psalms 46:1-2,7,10).

4. "I will do for you all that you request."

   No interruption will derail Father's pursuit of fulfilling His daughter's requests. He knows your heart has been after Him and as you "delight yourself" in Him, which means to remain soft and pliable in His hands. He commits to "...give you the desires of your heart" (Ps. 37:4). As you "Commit your way to the Lord," literally roll off onto Him everything—your emotions, plans, hopes, and dreams—and "Trust also in Him...He shall bring it to pass" (Ps. 37:5).

5. "For all...know that you are a virtuous woman."

   Virtuous here means having an inner strength and determination to persevere through to victory. It is a military term depicting an army persevering through the battle until victory is secured. You may not feel that way right now, but God knows that is who you are. You are a fighter. You may be a "wounded warrior" right now. That's why He calls you to rest in Him right now, letting

Him be your strength, as He said to Paul: "…My strength is made perfect in [your] weakness" (2 Cor. 12:9).

He is so proud of you! Let Him heal your heart in these difficult days. He has wept with you but promises, "…weeping may endure for a night, but joy comes in the morning" (Ps. 30:5), and you will declare: "You have turned for me my mourning into dancing; you have to put off my sackcloth and clothed me with gladness" (Ps. 30:11).

A REASON TO FEAR

And about the time of her death, the woman who stood by her said to her, "Do not fear, for you have borne a son." But she did not answer, nor did she regard it (1 Samuel 4:20).

Having a child, especially a son, in biblical times was always a cause for celebration. Except here. Why would Eli's daughter-in-law not rejoice in giving birth to a son? Well, the obvious reason would be that she knew she was dying in childbirth. But the real reason goes much deeper than that and can be seen in the name she gave her son as she died—Ichabod, meaning "the glory has departed." There was something more important in this woman's life than the maternal instinct of bearing a son. It was experiencing the *shekinah* glory of Father God's presence!

Her husband, Phinehas, and his brother, Hophni, were sons of Eli, the priest. Both sons corrupted the house of God by taking for themselves the meat offerings people brought that were supposed to be given to God as burnt offerings (see 1 Sam. 2:12-17) and also by sleeping with the women "...who assembled at the door of the tabernacle" (1 Sam. 2:22).

The names of these men reveal how evil they were. *Hophni* means "pugilist" (boxer, fighter). He evidently was a bully, probably physically threatening worshipers to give to him what they had brought as an offering to the Lord. His brother's name, *Phinehas*, means "mouth of a serpent." (As an aside, what mother would give birth to a cute little boy and say, "Aw, look, sweetheart. Isn't he cute? Let's name him "mouth of a serpent." I don't know; I'm just sayin'!)

Phinehas was probably a blasphemer, false teacher, and gossiper, dropping the names of the women he slept with, ruining marriages and reputations. It was under this oppressive and corrupt environment that the call came for the ark of His Presence to be carried into battle against the Philistines.

I doubt very much that anyone, including Eli, bothered to consult God as to His direction. As a result, the ark was captured, Hophni and Phinehas were killed, and Israel was defeated. Just a note here—God is not obligated to bring victory to His people when they live in compromise. It opens up a door for the enemy to torment and harass.

Phinehas's wife heard the news of the outcome of the battle and the death of her husband. The sorrow and grief sent her into labor, possibly prematurely, which resulted in complications and death. But what strikes me about her is that the name she gave the baby, Ichabod, reflected the reason for her sorrow—"the glory has departed." She grieved unto death, not over the loss of her husband, but over the loss of the glory of God's Presence.

Her midwives tried to encourage her that she should take joy in the birth of her son, thinking she was grieving over her husband's death. But it says, "...she did not answer, nor did she regard (pay any attention to) it" (1 Sam. 4:20). The loss of God's Presence overshadowed the loss of her husband and the joy of a newborn son. Nothing else mattered!

When Nathan the prophet exposed the sin of David with Bathsheba, David wrote out of the anguish of his soul, "Do not cast me away from Your presence, and do not take Your Holy Spirit from me" (Ps. 51:11).

What about us? How important to us is the habitation of His Presence? Do we fear losing intimacy with Papa God more than anything else? We should. If there ever was a legitimate fear, this is it! Listen to the cry of David's heart:

As the deer pants for the water brooks, so pants my soul for You, O God. My soul thirsts for God, for the living God. When shall I come and appear before God? My tears have been my food day and night... (Psalm 42:1-3).

O God, You are my God; early will I seek You; my soul thirsts for You; my flesh longs for You in a dry and thirsty land where there is no water (Psalm 63:1).

Like David, in the wake of immorality in my life, I lost the ministry and was on the verge of losing my marriage and children. All friends abandoned me. In the fear of losing everything, my greatest fear was David's cry in Psalms 51:11, for I believed that verse had already happened to me and I feared it might never be restored. I struggled with the guilt, shame, and sense of unworthiness to come to Him for 25 years!

It was through the teachings of Bill Johnson and the Bethel School of Supernatural Ministry that Papa God showed me how precious I am to Him, and that I was truly forgiven and accepted in Him and that my destiny had not been derailed. He spoke Joel 2:25 to me: "So I will restore to you the years that the swarming locust has eaten...." In addition, He said, "The glory of this latter temple shall be greater than the former" (Hag. 2:9), and that "...my [strength] You have exalted like a wild ox; I have been anointed with fresh oil...[I] shall still bear fruit in old age; [I] shall be fresh and flourishing" (Ps. 92:10,14).

What about you? Has something in your life—a past (or present) sin—kept you from His Presence and you feel that the separation can never be reconciled? Liar, liar! (That's addressed to the devil—*not you!*) Come to think of it, this chapter actually *is* a "Fear not"! As David did, cry out to Him, repent, and know that you are *immediately* restored to fellowship in His Presence (see 1 John 1:9). David was restored under the old covenant; we are told we have a "better covenant" (Heb. 8:6). Paul said that *nothing* can separate us from the love of God (see Rom. 8:35-39). How will you know you've been restored into His Presence? Joy! (See Psalms 16:11.) So, confess, repent (change the way you think), then go into the bathroom, look at yourself in the mirror and *laugh!*

Laugh…and be renewed in His love (see Zeph. 3:17).

Laugh…and be renewed in His strength (see Neh. 8:10; Isa. 40:31).

He's so smack in love with you, He can't help Himself. So go ahead, sit back, relax in His presence, and have an old-fashioned, belly-bouncing, silly giggle session with Papa God! That's what Jesus was describing in John 10:10: "…I have come that you might have life and have it more abundantly" (to the full, overflowing).

FEAR OF MAKING A WRONG CHOICE

Then Samuel said to the people, "Do not fear. You have done all this wickedness; yet do not turn aside from following the Lord, but serve the Lord with all your heart" (1 Samuel 12:20).

Israel's "king" had always been God. Though following leaders such as Joseph, Moses, Joshua, and the judges, they had always acknowledged God, who had delivered them from Egyptian bondage, as their ultimate leader.

But here, Samuel, current judge over Israel, was turning that office over to his two sons, Joel and Abijah. Unlike Eli's sons, Samuel's sons were named after God. *Joel* is a form of "Jehovah" and *Abijah* literally means "Father God." However, like Eli, Samuel failed to raise his sons to serve the God after whom they were named. Most times, names given to individuals in the Bible described their character. Perhaps Samuel hoped or even fully believed that naming his sons after God would cause that character to develop in them. But godly character doesn't happen to our children just by calling them godly names. Godly principles must be taught (see Deut. 6:6-7; 2 Tim. 1:5,13; 2:2). And that is our responsibility as parents, not the church's! The church should reinforce what we are teaching our children at home. Not doing this is what produced the corruption in Eli's and Samuel's sons.

Israel had suffered through this corruption a generation ago with Eli's sons and now they were about to be subjected to it again with Samuel's sons: "But his [Samuel's] sons did not walk in his ways; they turned aside after dishonest gain, took bribes, and perverted justice" (1 Sam. 8:3). Not this time! Israel had had enough, so they came to Samuel and said, "Look, you are old, and your sons do not walk in your ways. Now make us a king to judge us..." (1 Sam. 8:5).

The point here is—to whom do we turn in reacting to injustice? God or government? This is an especially critical question for America today. Our recent history has shown we have made the wrong choice. Looking to government as our "Jehovah-jireh" (provider) is progressively moving us toward a welfare-state status, totally dependent on and equally controlled by a strong, centralized government. That's what happened to Israel: Saul became a king-dictator, paranoid about losing power.

Samuel proclaimed God's answer: God would honor their demand, but told Samuel, "...they have not rejected you, but they have rejected Me, that I should not reign over them" (1 Sam. 8:7).

From the Garden of Eden to today, God honors the choices we make, even if they are wrong. Yet even when they are wrong, He does not forsake us. When the people realized what they had done, they begged Samuel to ask God for mercy (see 1 Sam. 12:19). Samuel's answer lays out a good plan for us to follow when we realize we have made a wrong decision (see 1 Sam. 12:20):

1. "Do not fear."

   God is a gracious God, quick to forgive and will never leave us or forsake us (see Exod. 34:6-7; 1 John 1:9; Heb. 13:5). We are never abandoned; our adoptive Father looks for our return and runs to meet and restore us (see Rom. 8:15; Luke 15:20).

Banning Leibsher, youth pastor at Bethel Church in Redding, California, tells the story of a time when he was faced with a potentially life-changing decision. He hesitated in making it, praying, "God, if I make the wrong decision here, it may derail Your whole plan for my life." Immediately, he sensed the Lord respond, "You give yourself too much credit. Do you think that one wrong decision can derail the destiny I have ordained for you? You're not big enough to do that!"

Sometimes we analyze until we're paralyzed. When we've made a wrong choice, sure, there may be consequences (divorce, single parenthood, financial lack, etc.), but if we will go through Psalms 32:5, we can then return to Proverbs 3:6. As we acknowledge Him in *all* our ways from that point on, He promises to direct our paths. The word *direct* there literally means to "make straight and right." In other words, as we go to Him now, He will literally "straighten out" what we have messed up. Your destiny is still intact! Start walking toward it again without fear of falling in the ditch!

2. "Do not turn aside from following the Lord."

    Following in the Hebrew means "the hind part." If you are following directly behind someone, what part of him or her do you see? The "hind part." That means they are out front—*leading*. Is He leading and are you following? Or have you "turned aside"—turned off onto another path that you think is better? Choices, choices.

3. "Serve the Lord with all your heart."

    This speaks of a lifestyle of complete, sold-out devotion birthed from an intimate love encounter that has settled all priorities, "...that in all things He may have the preeminence" (Col. 1:18). Wrong choices are not fatal to God's plan. I am living proof of that. God always moves from the present forward; His Kingdom is always moving forward, never in retreat. So why should we be? Wrong choices repented of are nothing more than speed bumps used by Father as learning tools in fulfilling our destiny in Him!

So, forward...*march!*

FEAR OF PHYSICAL HARM

Stay with me; do not fear. For he who seeks my life seeks your life, but with me you shall be safe (1 Samuel 22:23).

A soap opera, thriller, and suspense drama all rolled into one—this best describes this story of David and Saul. Saul had become obsessed with destroying David because he knew David had been anointed by God to replace him as king. David was hiding out in the cave of Adullam (see 1 Sam. 22:1) after stopping at the house of the priest, Ahimelech, to ask for food and a weapon. Doeg, a servant of Saul, happened to be there, and reported the event to Saul. Ahimelech and all his sons were brought before Saul and interrogated. Saul determined them to be traitors and had them all executed. One, Abiathar, escaped and fled to report to David what happened. David was devastated, stating, "I have caused the death of all the persons of your father's house" (1 Sam. 22:22). David then invites Abiathar to stay with him, offering him protection and refuge, and from that context comes his consolation, "Do not fear" (1 Sam. 22:23).

To feel responsible for another's death is horrific enough. How much more an entire family, and that family was in the ministry! No wonder David passionately vowed to Abiathar "…with me you shall be safe."

Fear of death or physical harm is probably the ultimate fear in life. It seems the first fifteen minutes of every newscast covers personal assaults and/or murders that happened in the last 24 hours. The next news segments will cover national and world atrocities. How can we feel safe in such a world? One word—trust.

Trust in God and build trusting relationships with one another. The Scripture is replete with promises of God's presence and protection over us. My favorite is Psalm 91. In fact, I have done a word study on this Psalm and it is breathtaking in the range and detail of the fatherly, protective promises He speaks over His children. I often declare Psalm 91 over myself and every member of my family. On more than one occasion, my wife or I have been awakened in the night to pray for our children who were traveling at the time. They later related to us that they narrowly avoided a car wreck at the precise time we felt the urgent need to intercede for them.

On one occasion, our son was driving home from college with some friends. One of the wheels of the car began making a loud noise, so they pulled over to check it out. When they removed the hubcap, all of the lug nuts were off, lying in the hubcap! They had had the car checked out before leaving and evidently the lug nuts weren't tightened sufficiently. Had the wheel come off at interstate speeds, the results could have been tragic. On another occasion, he related that the right front tire *did* come off while he was driving home from work on the Tampa, Florida bypass interstate, in the third lane of six lanes of traffic. He said, "Dad, all of a sudden I see my tire running out ahead of me through three lanes of traffic, then bouncing over the guard rail. Then sparks flew everywhere as the axle hit the pavement. I knew my only hope was to get to the shoulder of the road. Somehow, I was able to maneuver through two lanes of traffic to the shoulder without causing a wreck or flipping over!" Psalm 91 protection!

What about believers who *have* suffered loss? There are many theories we could advance to explain the "why does God allow...?" question.

In the midst of declaring a "no-cancer zone" at Bethel Church in Redding, California and seeing incredible miracles in that area, Pastor Bill Johnson relates the story of how he lost his own father and executive secretary to cancer. How do you reconcile that? Pastor Bill addresses this issue of disappointment and loss in his book, *The Essential Guide to Healing*.

- Disappointment is inevitable for everyone pursuing this miracle lifestyle. ...Learning to live with the unexplainable is one of the most necessary ingredients of the Christian life. ...If we do not give up our right to understand, we will seldom experience the peace that passes understanding that Philippians 4:7 talks about.[1]

Trying to understand why God *didn't* do something can start us on a dangerous downward spiral toward the sin of unbelief. Bill cautions that "One of the most spiritually vulnerable moments in a Christian's life is when loss or disappointment comes."[2] So how do we deal with disappointment when Psalm 91 or prayer for a sick loved one doesn't "work"? Bill presents a very tender and balanced answer:

- It is normal for questions to arise during loss. ...The danger comes when these questions lead us away from God and His Word into human reasoning in conflict with God's Word.[3]

These questions can lead us to actually question God's goodness. Bill cautions, "To question the goodness of God is one of the most dangerous spiritual diseases. It comes on the heels of disappointment." It is okay to be honest with God, but "don't accuse Him."[4] On many occasions Bill has stated his conclusion on the matter (with which I completely agree): "I choose to not focus on what God has *not* done, but to glorify Him for what He *has* done." To me, that is the answer. We live in a fallen world and we will not have explanations for everything. We must follow Solomon's advice: "Trust in the Lord with all your heart, and lean not on your own understanding" (Prov. 3:5).

David could not explain to Abiathar why God "allowed" his entire family to be murdered by an insane king trying to get at David. David could do only two things—grieve with Abiathar and encourage him by walking through the tragedy with him, assuring him "with me you shall be safe" (to grieve *and* recover). Sometimes coming alongside the grieving and assuring them we are there for them is the assignment God gives us to minister. No words are necessary; just reassurance that they are in a safe place: "Pure and undefiled religion before God and the Father is this: to visit orphans and widows in their trouble..." (James 1:27).

NOTES

1. Bill Johnson and Randy Clark, *The Essential Guide to Healing* (Grand Rapids, MI: Chosen Books, 2011), 153-155.

2. Ibid., 155.

3. Ibid., 155-156.

4. Ibid., 156-157.

THE COVENANT OF A FRIEND

And [Jonathan] *said to* [David], *"Do not fear, for the hand of Saul my father shall not find you. You shall be king over Israel, and I shall be next to you"* (1 Samuel 23:17).

Can you imagine having a friend like Jonathan? He was the legitimate heir to the throne—son of Saul the king. Yet he says to David his friend, "*You* shall be king over Israel." Jonathan could have killed David—legally. David was his competition for the throne. According to lineage, Jonathan was rightfully the successor to Saul to rule Israel. As friend to friend, he could have said, "Hey, Dave, dude. I love ya, man. But look. I know the old man's a jerk, but he is my dad. So that puts *me* next in line. So don't try to muscle in on my turf, or I might have to hurt ya." (Did they talk like that back then? I don't know.)

Let's bring the scenario into today's world. You are working for a corporation. You become best friends and work side by side with the CEO's son. The CEO is retiring and wants his son to succeed him. However, the board of directors appoints you instead. This enrages the CEO and he embarks on a campaign to get you fired. His son comes to you and says, "Don't worry, dude. My dad can't fire you. You will be the next CEO, and you will have my full support." What level of character would one have to have in order to genuinely display that attitude?

Jonathan had developed a godly character that understood what God was doing and why. That character elevated him above the human tendency to strive after power and position that, through heredity, he could have rightfully claimed. He had a higher understanding of God's ways than his own father had.

What a blessing to have a friend of character! Every David needs a Jonathan. They are few and far between. Evidently David taught this value to *his* successor Solomon: "A friend loves at all times, and a brother is born for adversity" (Prov. 17:17). *Friend* here can also mean "companion, neighbor, fellowman, a familiar person" (Strong's, H7453). A friend loves (is loyal) at all times—even when he or she gets the promotion I felt I should have gotten. Mature, godly character understands, "For promotion cometh neither from the east, nor from the west, nor from the south. But God is the judge: he putteth down one, and setteth up another" (Ps. 75:6-7 KJV).

This is true on both sides of the coin—whether we get the promotion or our friend gets it instead. On the one, we need a friend of character who will assure us to *fear not*, there will be no competition when we are promoted. The relationship is more important, and they will rejoice with us. I can honestly say I have about three friends who I know are of that character.

On the other, I must be that friend of character who will likewise say to my friend, "Fear not," when they get the promotion I thought I deserved. This is the key issue: "A man who has friends must himself be friendly, but there is a friend who sticks closer than a brother" (Prov. 18:24). How do you get to *have* a friend who sticks closer than a brother?

Be one!

FEAR OF PERSECUTION

So David said to him, "Do not fear, for I will surely show you kindness for Jonathan your father's sake, and will restore to you all the land of Saul your grandfather; and you shall eat bread at my table continually" (2 Samuel 9:7).

As I write this, I am listening to reports of global economic collapse. It is now being predicted that within three to six months the Euro will collapse, which will create a domino effect across the globe. We are being advised to have at least 30 days' worth of cash on hand (because banks will close due to the collapse) as well as three to six months' worth of food stored up. In such a situation, governments will likely seize control of everything, from money to food distribution. Personal freedoms will vanish. Scary, isn't it?

So what do you do when a government feels it has a legitimate right to silence or even destroy you?

Mephibosheth was in such a situation. The grandson of Saul—who had tried to kill the current king, David—feared for his life and was in hiding in Lo-Debar, which means "no pasture"—in other words, the wilderness. Here he was—royalty hiding in the wilderness. Do you feel that way? At one time, you knew who you were, with a divine destiny. But because of generational sin, others have been promoted in your place and now you fear retribution; they now have the power to destroy you if they so choose. So you languish in spiritual and emotional, if not physical, hiding. But Mephibosheth's name means "dispeller of shame." God ordained his destiny to be the one who ended the shame of Saul's legacy. Dropped and crippled as a child by his caretaker as she fled the palace when David was crowned king, it hardly seemed to Mephibosheth that his life could ever represent the *end* of shame for him and his family. Yet that was God's plan. What is His plan for you?

1. "I will surely show you kindness."

   You thought God was disappointed in you, possibly even angry with you, whether over your own past sin or that of your heritage. "How could He ever be proud of me?" you might ask. Because you are royalty, regardless of what your forefathers (or you) have done! As a believer, you have been adopted into the royal family, making you a prince or princess of the King (your Father)! Even if you *have* failed Him, He still is determined to show you kindness. Why? Because it is the kindness of God that leads to repentance (see Rom. 2:4 NASB). He sees the "gold" in you, even in your disappointing "Lo-Debar" (wilderness) residence.

2. "I will restore" (literally, "return back to the starting point").

   The enemy has stolen some things from you—ministry, relationships, finances, promotion, health, etc. God is saying to you today: "I will restore to you the years that the swarming locust has eaten..." (Joel 2:25). The thief is required to "restore sevenfold" what he has stolen (see Prov. 6:30-31). Jesus identifies the thief and his purpose in John 10:10 but counters it with His purpose—to give you life and give it more abundantly, to fill you to the full and overflowing. That is His promise—you are entering restoration of all you have lost!

3. "You shall eat bread at my table continually."

   In fact, God's in-your-face attitude toward satan is to "prepare a table before [you] in the presence of [your] enemies" (Ps. 23:5). He forces your enemy, the one who tried to saddle you with shame instead of your destiny, to sit there and watch you eat at God's table, enjoying fully His presence (see Ps. 16:11).

God leaves no doubt. You have His favor; you are restored, and you have full intimate fellowship with Him *continually*.

So fear not the threats of the enemy! God has your back and will turn it around for your benefit and His glory (see Gen. 50:20; John 9:3).

FEAR OF LACK

And Elijah said to her, "Do not fear; go and do as you have said, but make me a small cake from it first, and bring it to me; and afterward make some for yourself and your son"
(1 Kings 17:13).

As I mentioned yesterday, economists are predicting an imminent global economic collapse. I asked the Lord that if this "doomsday" prediction is true, what should the body of Christ be doing, if anything, to prepare? I believe His answer to me was, "It is for this reason I have named you Joseph." So, as Joseph in Genesis prepared for famine, I am preparing for what may be coming and advocating others to do so as well.

In this prophetic light, it is easier to understand the context of Elijah's and the widow's situation, although theirs is the end-game result of what we may soon face—extreme famine. Whether the widow had stored food or not, she was now at the point of having only enough left to prepare *one more meal* for her son and herself, and she had resolved they would then starve to death. There were no government subsidies like food stamps or food pantries. Famine affects everyone, so her neighbors couldn't help her—they were in the same situation or perhaps had already died. She couldn't raise her own food or livestock—famine is drought, no rain; everything dies!

It is in this setting that Elijah appeared, at whose word the heavens were shut up in the first place. To add insult to injury, Elijah made a seeming death-sentence request of the widow—take of what she had and make *him* a cake *first*, then prepare for her and her son from what she had left. Dismal prospect at best.

Have you ever been or are you now in a tight financial situation such that you feel that you have enough for "one more meal" or round of paying bills for your household before your bank balance shows a zero? Then God comes along and strongly impresses on your heart to sow a sacrificial amount into His Kingdom. Immediate thought: "This is *nuts!* How can I give (or tithe) when I can't even pay my bills?" Yet the "knowing" is there. It's in your spirit; you recognize it; it's happened before. It still doesn't make it easy.

But it's not a fatalistic choice: "If I give to God, I won't have enough to pay…" whatever. After the widow responded to Elijah's request, she was given an assurance of provision: "The bin of flour shall not be used up, nor shall the jar of oil run dry, until the day the Lord sends rain on the earth" (1 Kings 17:14). Supernatural provision until the natural order of things resumes. That's God's promise: obedience to His faith-stretching request brings unending provision and abundance. This is what gives God the opportunity to prove His faithfulness to us. "Playing it safe" requires no faith. Giving the minimum will bring provision but not abundance. As a young pastor, I remember figuring my tithe to the penny. If our income for the week was $523.42, my tithe check was $52.34! There, that's a tithe—10 percent, exactly. I don't think God was angry with me; I think He was amused, if anything. We got by—barely. I never had the faith to give as this widow did, and so I never gave God the opportunity to fulfill His promise of supernatural abundance.

Rather than admonishing you to give out of your need, I just feel I should leave you with scriptural examples and promises and let God comfort and speak to your heart. I know that there are a lot of single women (like this widow) struggling to provide for their families. Be encouraged! The Lord says He is your husband and will provide for you—His princess bride!

King David sinned by "numbering the people"—an arrogant act of measuring his power without acknowledging God as the Source. He knew it and wanted to offer a sacrifice to God as an act of repentance (see 2 Sam. 24). To do this, he wanted to purchase a threshing floor and oxen from a local farmer. The farmer, knowing this was the king, offered to give it to him (see 2 Sam. 24:22). But David refused, saying, "No, but I will surely buy it from you for a price; nor will I offer burnt offerings to the Lord my God with that which costs me nothing" (2 Sam. 24:24).

Yes, discipleship will cost us something. But this same king, in the twilight of his life, wrote, "I have been young, and now am old; yet I have not seen the righteous forsaken, nor His descendants begging bread" (Ps. 37:25). David's son, Solomon, spoke of how God's economy works:

> *There is one who scatters, yet increases more, and there is one who withholds more than is right, but it leads to poverty. The generous soul will be made rich, and he who waters will also be watered himself* (Proverbs 11:24-25).

Somehow in God's economy, the more we "scatter" and "water" (give into God's Kingdom), the more He increases blessing back to us, echoing Jesus' words:

> *Give, and it will be given to you: good measure, pressed down, shaken together, and running over will be put into your bosom. For with the same measure that you use, it will be measured back to you* (Luke 6:38).

The apostle Paul phrases the same idea in the farming terms of sowing and reaping, the principle being: "He who sows sparingly will also reap sparingly, and he who sows bountifully will also reap bountifully" (2 Cor. 9:6). Jesus praised the widow for giving her two mites, which were all she had (see Mark 12:42). Paul spoke of the Macedonians who gave out of their "poverty" (see 2 Cor. 8:1-4), but assured all of us that God is "...able to do exceedingly abundantly above all that we ask or think, according to the power that works in us" (Eph. 3:20) and that He will "…supply all your need according to His riches in glory" (Phil. 4:19).

All of these promises and more should encourage us not to fear lack in this or any economy! He is our Abba (Daddy) Father, and He said He would honor His Word above His name. We just need to trust in Him with all our heart (see Prov. 3:5), "casting *all* your care upon Him, for He cares for you" (1 Pet. 5:7).

FEAR OF
OVERWHELMING OPPOSITION

*So he answered, "Do not fear, for those who are with us are
more than those who are with them" (2 Kings 6:16).*

Since the Garden of Eden, the battle between light and darkness has
raged. In fact, that is the story of Scripture—the redemption of humankind from the bondage of darkness (sin). We know that. We also know that
victory was won at Calvary and sealed at the empty tomb. So why does it
seem that world events are spiraling out of control along with our personal
circumstances as well? I thought we were winning! This was probably what
Elisha's servant thought when he woke up and went outside to see them surrounded by the enemy (see 2 Kings 6:15).

Syria hated Israel and tried to eradicate them at every opportunity. But
God revealed the evil king's strategy to Elisha every time and Elisha reported
the plan to Israel's king (Jehoram) every time, thus avoiding ambush. This is
God's first and most crucial step in establishing us in His victory lifestyle—
prophetic revelation of the enemy's intention. Paul said, "...we are not igno-
rant of his devices [purpose, strategies]" (2 Cor. 2:11). How is that possible?
Most of us are blindsided by an enemy attack and are immediately put on

the defensive, running to God, yelling, *"Help!"* How can we know what the enemy is going to do before he does it? God desires to give us:

> *"...the spirit of wisdom and revelation in the knowledge of Him, the eyes of [our] understanding being enlightened"* (Eph. 1:17-18).

There are prophets in the land today who have been warning of difficult times ahead. I believe we are entering those times now. Christianity has been demonized in America, its public expression becoming illegal in many venues. It is now illegal for a U.S. Air Force chaplain to refer to God in any context! We seem to be surrounded by the enemy trying to silence the witness of Father's love. From a nation founded on the principle that government "shall make no law respecting an establishment of religion, or prohibiting the free exercise thereof" (Amendment I to the Constitution of the United States of America) to today's suppression of *any* expression of faith, we could probably more easily identify with the apostle Paul's statement:

> *We are hard-pressed on every side, yet not crushed; we are perplexed, but not in despair; persecuted, but not forsaken; struck down, but not destroyed* (2 Corinthians 4:8-9).

But a study of Paul's life shows supernatural intervention protected him from certain death. God revealed the plans of the enemy—just as in Elisha's case. The same is true today. Many (including me) are sensing the urgency to prepare by storing food and water; others report supernatural multiplication of food, miracles of healing, and even resurrections from the dead. God will reveal to you the enemy's strategies before he attacks, whether to warn the body of Christ or you personally—if you seek and live in intimacy with Him.

How do we live in peace when we seem to be surrounded by so much darkness? We can when we ask what Elisha prayed for his servant: "...open his eyes that he may see" (2 Kings 6:17). That spiritual insight will show that "those who are with us are more than those who are with them" (2 Kings 6:16). We are not outnumbered—they are!

It is easy to experience peace when the water is still. But Jesus called for peace in the midst of the storm. Isaiah called out, "Arise, shine; for your light has come! And the glory of the Lord is risen upon you" (Isa. 60:1). But look at the context in which that light is called forth: "For behold, the darkness shall cover the earth, and deep darkness the people; but the Lord will arise over you, and His glory will be seen upon you" (Isa. 60:2). Contrast! The light shines brightest in the blackest of darkness. We are the "light of the world" (Matt. 5:14). Paul assures us that we are "...more than conquerors through Him who loved us" (Rom. 8:37), and John reminds us that "...He who is in you is greater than he who is in the world" (1 John 4:4). Remember that these statements made by these biblical authors were made under governmental regimes far more oppressive than ours. When Paul commanded us to "Rejoice in the Lord always. Again I will say, rejoice!" (Phil. 4:4), he was sitting in a Roman prison not knowing whether he would be released or executed.

This is the greatest day to live! Multitudes are living in fear over world events and are looking for answers, direction, and peace. We must arise and shine, declaring:

> God is our refuge and strength, a very present help in trouble. Therefore **we will not fear**, even though the earth be removed, and though the mountains be carried into the midst of the sea (Psalm 46:1-2).

Indeed, those who are with us *are* more than those who are with them!

Fear not!

CONSEQUENCES OF DEFIANCE

And it was so, at the beginning of their dwelling there, that they did not fear the Lord; therefore the Lord sent lions among them, which killed some of them (2 Kings 17:25).

This is one of the most tragic and sad narratives in the Bible. It is the account of the death of a nation—Israel. After Rehoboam, Solomon's son, foolishly listened to his contemporary (peer) advisors rather than the elders who had been Solomon's advisors, Israel revolted, appointed their own king, and created a separate nation (see 1 Kings 12).

Rehoboam remained king over those remaining loyal to David's lineage, and his land became Judah, the southern kingdom. Our text here deals with the northern kingdom—Israel. It is incredible to note that in the 200-plus years of their separate existence, Israel did not have one godly king! The fruit of rebellion never ends well.

Hoshea (which means "deliverer") was Israel's last king. His name reflected what God intended for him to be—Israel's deliverer. God has a destiny for each of us—whether or not we fulfill it largely depends on our choices and their consequences. *Hoshea* is a form of *Joshus*, from which is derived *Jeshua*—Jesus! This king was the last chance for Israel to repent as a nation. If Hoshea had lived up to his name, Israel's judgment might have been averted, or at least delayed. When a nation embarks on a highway to destruction, God gives ample exit ramps for her to get off and get on the entrance ramp in the opposite direction—repentance leading to godliness. I believe America is approaching her final exit ramp, and if we don't appoint (elect) a true "Hoshea" who will turn us back to God, we may face the same godless demise Israel faced as narrated here. As I read this text, I was chilled by the parallels between Israel then and America now. Here are some of the most obvious, just from Second Kings 17:

1. "And he (Hoshea) did evil in the sight of the Lord..." (2 Kings 17:2).

   Like Israel, America was established on a godly covenant by our founders, but we have strayed far from those godly principles. To a large degree, many of our leaders are walking as Hoshea did.

2. "...and Hoshea became his vassal (servant) and paid him tribute money" (2 Kings 17:3).

   America has gone from a lender to a debtor nation, and a very wise "president" (Solomon) wrote, "...the borrower is servant to the lender" (Prov. 22:7). America's unbridled spending on entitlement programs has plunged us into insurmountable debt (now over $16 trillion at this writing!), $2 trillion to China alone. Like Hoshea, we are "paying tribute" to appease our enemies.

3. "The children of Israel secretly did against the Lord their God things that were not right.... They set up for themselves sacred pillars and wooden images" (2 Kings 17:9-10).

   The idolatrous gods of these nations, though slightly different in name, had the same focus of worship—sexual perversion. They are mentioned as early as Judges, the generation immediately following Joshua's death (see Judg. 2:13). It only takes one generation to be raised in a culture void of godly leadership to turn an entire nation away from God. America experienced this generation in the 1960s, dubbed "the sexual revolution" and "free love" society. The vacuum left by the absence of godly teaching was quickly filled with the casting off of restraint (see Prov. 29:18). This was what Israel did in Judges 2:13: "They forsook the Lord and served Baal and the Ashoreths." According to the commentary footnotes on this verse in the New Spirit-Filled Life Bible, "Baal was a fertility and nature god of the Canaanites...Ashtoreths were female deities, such as Ashtoreth (consort of Baal) who was the goddess of war and fertility."[1] Most Bible scholars and historians agree that the "sacred pillars" and "wooden images" referred to in Second Kings 17:10 were images of the male and female reproductive organs.

Although pornography in America is not new, it has exploded to levels of explicitness, depravity, and perversion never before experienced, and the floodgates of filth have been opened in magazines, books, movies, television, and most recently the Internet. "Lifestyles" came "out of the closet," and today, to speak out against this is considered hate speech, even "home-grown terrorism," and can be punishable by arrest and imprisonment.

4. Warnings from the prophets: "Turn from your evil ways, and keep My commandments and My statutes..." (2 Kings 17:13).

   The call to America for national repentance has been and continues to be loud and clear, from the early days of the late David Wilkerson to the current prophets, such as Rick Joyner, Bobby Conner, Bob Jones, Lou Engle, and others. The question: is the nation listening and responding? The answer for Israel was tragic: "Nevertheless they would not hear, but stiffened their necks..." (2 Kings 17:14).

I believe there is a groundswell of God's people in America who are awake and uniting in intersession for our nation. Don't stop! Our nation's future hangs by a thread!

5. "So they...worshiped all the host of heaven" (2 Kings 17:16).

    Astrology is satan's counterfeit to the prophetic word today.

6. "They caused their sons and daughters to pass through the fire..." (2 Kings 17:17).

    The images of some of these gods, especially Molech, were hollowed out so that wood fires could be built inside of them. When the metal turned red hot, they would place their babies onto the outstretched arms of the god, thus sacrificing to it and supposedly appeasing it. Since Roe v. Wade was passed in 1973, it is estimated that close to 53 million unborn babies have been aborted (killed, murdered) to the god of convenience. God have mercy on us! Lou Engle's ministry "The Call" is, in a large part, a call to national repentance over this very sin. God is responding! Mississippi recently reported there is only one abortion clinic left in the entire state! Don't stop crying out for those who cannot cry out for themselves! "Children are a heritage from the Lord; the fruit of the womb is a reward" (Ps. 127:3). A reward, not a burden!

7. "...practiced witchcraft and soothsaying" (2 Kings 17:17).

    This refers to casting spells and fortune telling. Seen any horror movies recently? Again, this is the satanic counterfeit of the word of knowledge and the prophetic gifts.

8. "...sold themselves to do evil in the sight of the Lord" (2 Kings 17:17).

    Prostitution is an acceptable, if not legal, lifestyle in some parts of the country.

Without national repentance, God won't have to judge America. The above are the seeds of moral decay that have and will crumble every nation. I highly recommend the book, *The Harbinger*, by Jonathan Cahn, a novel that describes nine "harbingers" or warnings based on Israel's response to an attack when God lifted His hand of protection from them because of the idolatry listed in Second Kings 17. Their response—arrogance—led to their demise as a nation. Cahn uses Isaiah 9:10 to illustrate Israel's response to being attacked by Assyria: "We've been attacked, but we will build back, stronger and better." There is no mention of God—only their self-sufficiency. No repentance or change of the lifestyles listed above. Cahn compares their response to America's following 9/11. The similarities are chilling.

When the Lord lifts His hand of protection off of a land or person, the enemy then has access to bring calamities and destruction. This is not judgment; it is the consequence of a people who do not fear the Lord. Can it happen to America? Isaiah 9:10 was read from the floor of the U.S. Senate on 9/12. The parallels Cahn speaks of in the book are astonishing.

Israel's end came as the king of Assyria carried Israel away captive and resettled the land with people from his cities. Yet the land was still God's. These people "...did not fear (revere) the Lord; therefore the Lord sent lions among them..." (2 Kings 17:25).

This is the kind of fear we must have. Bobby Connor devotes Chapter 1 in *Shepherd's Rod 2012* to this very topic. The fear and awe of God is the first step toward national repentance—the only thing that can save our beloved nation: "The fear of the Lord is the beginning of wisdom..." (Prov. 9:10). "The wicked shall be turned into hell, and all the nations that forget God" (Ps. 9:17). The church must lead the way to repentance, "For the time has come for judgment to begin at the house of God..." (1 Pet. 4:17).

Jeremiah and Daniel wept and confessed the sins of their nation, asking God to show mercy and forgive, including themselves in that call. Will we fear the Lord and do the same?

NOTE

1. Jack W. Hayford, ed., *New Spirit-Filled Life Bible* (Nashville, TN: Thomas Nelson Bibles, 2002), 316.

FEAR OF OTHER GODS

...You shall not fear other gods... (2 Kings 17:35).

Israel had it backward. Second Kings 17 is a narrative of Israel's history of turning from fearing the Lord to fearing other gods and their resulting depraved behavior that led to their national demise.

How does a nation birthed in covenant with a God who delivered them from slavery come full circle back to a place of bondage? Like the proverbial frog in the pot of water, it happens gradually, degree by degree. The principle applies to us individually as well as nationally. Reviewing America's last 50 years, we began "turning up the heat" in the early 1960s when the Supreme Court banned prayer in school. Ten years later, Roe v. Wade opened the door for the murder of 53 million of our unborn children. Along the way, it has become illegal to publicly display the Ten Commandments or nativity scenes, say invocations or benedictions, or pray using Jesus' name in public or even at military functions. All the while, we have found it necessary to re-define marriage.

The same can happen to us in our personal walk with God. Second Kings 17:35 warns of three gradual steps we can take that will result in turning our fear of the Lord to the "fear of other gods."

1. "Bow down to them."

   In his book, *Face to Face with God*, Bill Johnson says, "The enemy's agenda has always been to rob our destinies by getting us to worship anything but God." Why? Because, as Bill states, "(This) issue of worship is the defining issue of human history. We were made to worship the One in whose image we were created... we always become like whatever we worship...."[1] Since his rebellion in Heaven, satan has sought worship—even from Jesus (see Matt. 4:8-10). The word for *bow down* in our text means "to be prostrate in homage to royalty" (Strong's, H7812). We worship whatever (or whoever) ranks as top priority in our life. God's love for us is so intense that He wants to be our top priority because we are His! That was the reason He told us not to have any other gods besides Him (see Exod. 20:3).

Anything that becomes the central focus of our daily life becomes our god. Career, relationship, finances, entertainment, material possessions, etc. Fear of losing any or all of these things will elevate them to godhead status. We tend to worship what we fear losing, so we cling to it, thus "appeasing" the god. The cure? Adopt Abraham's attitude, which was a willingness to lay on the altar that which was most precious to him (Isaac), allowing him to die, if necessary. Reinhard Bonke recently said, "Every religion teaches that man must go after God and seek His approval. Christianity is the only religion where God pursues man for relationship."

2. "Serve them."

   Serve in the Hebrew means "to work for," but not as an employee. Strong's Concordance says it means "to enslave, be/keep in bondage" (Strong's, H5647). It is forced labor, not voluntary. For three years I served as a chaplain for the city rescue mission in Mobile, Alabama. My responsibility was to interview men who came to us to get into our Christ-centered drug and alcohol rehab program. I interviewed men from every walk of life, from doctors and psychologists to business owners and construction workers to high school dropouts and prisoners. Their circumstances and backgrounds were all different, but their bottom line was the same—they were serving (in bondage to) their addiction, whether prescription drugs, crack cocaine, or alcohol. "Other gods" are not respecters of persons; they all lead to broken lives and relationships. It was my privilege to introduce these men to the God who said, "Therefore if the Son makes you free, you shall be free indeed" (John 8:36). Those who were serious about changing their lives encountered a God who danced over them with joy (see Zeph. 3:17), broke the chains of their bondage, and invited them into a new level of relationship: "No longer do I call you servants...but I have called you friends" (John 15:15).

You and I have the same choice Joshua challenged Israel to make: "...choose for yourselves this day whom you will serve..." (Josh. 24:15). Joshua had already made his choice. So have I: "...But as for me and my house, we will serve the Lord" (Josh. 24:15). Have you?

3. "Sacrifice to them."

    Sacrifice, according to Strong's, means "to slaughter an animal (usually in sacrifice): kill, (do) sacrifice, slay" (Strong's, H2076). David refused to offer burnt offerings (sacrifice) "...with that which costs me nothing" (2 Sam. 24:24).

Two questions need to be asked: to whom are we sacrificing and what are we sacrificing? Are we sacrificing our tithes to the god of necessity (bills) and our offerings to the god of material things, comfort, and convenience? Maybe the god of time demands so much from us that we have little or none left for soaking in Papa's presence. The list goes on and on. I sense Daddy's call here is not as much a command as it is a plea. His love for us is so intense; He just wants to hang out with us. Did you know *He* wants to be in *your* presence more than we want to be in His? "O Jerusalem...How often I wanted to gather your children together, as a hen gathered her chicks under her wings..." (Matt. 23:37).

We have a tender, passionate, Song of Solomon love being offered to us that no other gods can match. The invitation is still open. Will you respond?

NOTE

1. Bill Johnson, *Face to Face with God* (Lake Mary, FL: Charisma House, 2007), 53.

NO FEAR IN OBEDIENCE

*Then you will prosper, if you take care to fulfill the statutes
and judgments with which the Lord charged Moses
concerning Israel. Be strong and of good courage, do not fear
nor be dismayed* (1 Chronicles 22:13).

David was coming to the close of his assignment on earth. The man after God's own heart had a lifelong dream—present his Lover-God with His very own magnificent house. But, alas, the Lord told David he could not build the house because his hands had shed blood in war, and hands of violence could not build a house of peace. A house or atmosphere of peace can only be established by one who is at peace, creating the atmosphere in which the Prince of Peace can feel at home.

So David called his son Solomon, which means "peaceable" from the Hebrew word *shalom* (see 1 Chron. 22:6-16). David relayed God's message to him and that the assignment to build the house of peace for the Prince of Peace would be given to Solomon, the man of peace.

For us, Paul reminds us that our body "...is the temple of the Holy Spirit" (1 Cor. 6:19). In this world of turmoil, people are desperate to find a haven of peace. Jesus promised He would leave His supernatural peace with us, and that peace would surpass all our understanding, guarding our hearts and minds through Christ Jesus (see John 14:27; Phil. 4:7).

I guess I'm drawn to this message of peace today, especially as news of a shooting massacre in a Denver, Colorado suburban theater comes across the wires. Twelve dead and fifty injured—many critically. A couple of days ago, a suicide bomber blew himself up on a bus crowded with Israeli tourists in Bulgaria. If the world ever needed a temple of peace it is now. That is our assignment. As we host His presence, we will speak, "Peace, be still," to the atmosphere and culture around us.

Our text today is David's advice to his son as he engaged in the phenomenal task of building God a habitation! He began by saying, "Then you will prosper." How would he prosper in this impossible assignment? By keeping and obeying the law of the Lord (see 1 Chron. 22:12). David re-emphasized that point in verse 13: "Then you will prosper, if you take care to fulfill the statutes and judgments with which the Lord charged Moses concerning Israel." *Prospering*, which means "to push forward" (Strong's, H6743), is a supernatural outflow of obedience.

What has Daddy asked you to do—speak or pray into the life of the Wal-Mart clerk, the doctor's receptionist, the stranger at the gas pump? You will prosper—*push forward* toward your destiny as you step out of your comfort zone in obedience to carry the Prince of Peace to someone who desperately needs Him today.

Confidence comes with obedience. David encouraged his son to "...Be strong and of good courage; do not fear nor be dismayed (1 Chron. 22:13). *Strong* there is an aggressive word meaning "to fasten upon, to seize." So our obedience to His assignment will produce a confidence in Him to aggressively pursue and advance His Kingdom.

Why would Solomon fear? Look at the task before him. David had provided all the materials for the temple. Now, like a bicycle that comes with 150 parts and an instruction sheet in Chinese, Solomon had to put together all the materials, making it into a house for God! Reason enough to be afraid? That was why he prayed:

> *Now, O Lord my God, You have made [me] king...but I am a little child; I do not know how to go out or come in. ...Therefore give to Your servant an understanding heart...* (1 Kings 3:7,9).

David told his son much the same thing that Mary said to the wedding attendants: "...Whatever He says to you, do it" (John 2:5). That's His message to us today. Relax. Rest in His peace and assurance of His presence. Whatever He says to you, do it. Feel like you're not qualified to do it? Bill Johnson says in his book, *Hosting the Presence*, "Being willing to do what you are not qualified to do is sometimes what qualifies you."[1]

Feeling unqualified? Congratulations! You're qualified! Just do whatever He says to you. Fear not!

NOTE

1. Bill Johnson and Heidi Baker, *Hosting the Presence: Unveiling Heaven's Agenda* (Shippensburg, PA: Destiny Image Publishers, 2012), 94.

FEAR OF BEING QUALIFIED

And David said to his son Solomon, "Be strong and of good courage, and do it; do not fear nor be dismayed, for the Lord God—my God—will be with you. He will not leave you nor forsake you, until you have finished all the work for the service of the house of the Lord" (1 Chronicles 28:20).

This was David's second encouragement to Solomon to "be strong and of good courage, and do it..." (building the temple). I must admit, I would probably need more than two encouragements from my father if I were facing a project of this magnitude! What about you? Has God given you a dream or vision so immense that you laugh when you think about it and view it as mere fantasy? My writing this book is an example. "Yeah, right! Me? A published author? With Destiny Image no less? Dream on!" Yet, here I am, being strong and courageous and doing it!

Jesus always challenged His disciples to do the impossible: "Oh, you want to walk to Me on the water, Peter? Sure, c'mon!" (See Matthew 14:22-32.) "Five thousand hungry men plus women and children? No problem. *You* give them something to eat!" (See Luke 9:10-17.) "Why did you have to wake Me up to calm the storm? Why didn't *you* say, 'Peace, be still'?" (See Mark 4:35-41.) On and on, Jesus challenged them:

...He who believes in Me, the works that I do he will do also; and greater works than these he will do, because I go to My Father (John 14:12).

Heal the sick, cleanse the lepers, raise the dead, cast out demons... (Matthew 10:8).

Solomon's assignment? Build a temple that would house the Shekinah glory of God! No wonder he needed multiple encouragements!

But there had to be more than a "Rah, rah, you can do it!" cheer of encouragement. There had to be something of substance in which Solomon could put his trust, something that gave him confidence that the task would be completed. Something beyond his own ability. So it is with us.

That something for Solomon (and for us) was Presence: "...for the Lord God—my God—will be with you." That's the calming, reassuring element that brings the impossible assignment into a completed destiny. It brings Heaven to earth, and He gets the glory!

After giving the disciples the impossible assignment of discipling nations, Jesus assured them, "...lo, I am with you always, even to the end of the age" (Matt. 28:20). Assurance of His presence makes all the difference! Jesus and Paul said the same thing on opposite sides of the coin. Jesus said, "...without *Me* you can do *nothing*" (John 15:5). Paul said it this way, "I can do *all* things *through Christ* who strengthens me" (Phil. 4:13).

In expanding that promise, David projected it into Solomon's future, stating that God's presence would not leave or forsake him: "...until you have finished all the work." Solomon stood at the threshold of his life, assignment in hand, overwhelmed by its magnitude. Knowing he was hopelessly unqualified, he desperately needed the assurance that He who gave him the assignment would be with him until it was finished.

Are you overwhelmed by the prophetic words that have been spoken about your destiny? Is your initial response, "No way! I'm not qualified to do that!" Neither was Moses, Joshua, Gideon, David, or Solomon. God loves choosing the unqualified but willing, equipping them with His passion and power and sending them out to do great exploits (see Matt. 10:1,7-8; Luke 10:1,9). Remember, the disciples became apostles, not because of education in religion, but because of having been with Jesus, in His presence! Acts 4:13 states of the Sanhedrin:

> Now when they saw the boldness of Peter and John, and per-
> ceived that they were uneducated (in Greek, illiterate) and
> untrained (in Greek, idiots) men they marveled. And they
> realized that they had been with Jesus (Strong's, G62, G2399).

So, if your critics call you *illiterate* or an *idiot*, rejoice! You're in good company! These everyday, blue-collar fishermen, tax collectors, and so on built quite a reputation. Because of their time with Jesus and being "endued with power from on high" (Luke 24:49), it is said of them that "these who have turned the world upside down have come here too" (Acts 17:6).

That's our impossible assignment, too—to disciple nations (see Matt. 28:19). In other words, turn your world upside down!

Throughout Scripture, whenever God called someone to accomplish the impossible, He always did so with the assurance He would be with them. That's His message to you and me today: "Fear not, for I will be with you. I will never leave you nor forsake you!"

FEAR OF ENGAGING THE ENEMY

You will not need to fight in this battle. Position yourselves,
stand still and see the salvation of the Lord, who is with
you, O Judah and Jerusalem! Do not fear or be dismayed;
tomorrow go out against them, for the Lord is with you
(2 Chronicles 20:17).

Aren't sermons and seminars on spiritual warfare wonderful? You leave them fired up and ready for war. But then something happens—reality! Monday, work, real crises. Suddenly you realize the battle has been engaged.

Diagnosis—cancer. Marriage—over. Job—lost. House—in foreclosure. Name your battle. And they always seem to suddenly happen just before or just after a great victory, like with Jesus. He was led by the Spirit into the wilderness to be tempted by the devil. This happened *immediately* after the Father spoke His approval and the identity of Jesus and the Holy Spirit descended and rested upon Him (see Matt. 3:16–4:1).

The story in First Chronicles 20 is probably my favorite because it so reflects our current culture and the promise of God's conditional intervention.

Judah was surrounded by the darkest evil of their society—the Moabites and Ammonites (see 2 Chron. 20:1). They were the descendents of the two cousins/half-brothers conceived out of an incestuous relationship between

Lot and his two daughters—*Moab* ("from our father") and *Ben-Ammi* ("son of my kin"). The depravity of these people evolved into worship of Baal and Molech (see Num. 25; Lev. 18–21). Both advocated, among other deviant sexual practices, the offering of their own children to these gods. And now they had come to surround the people of praise (Judah), threatening their annihilation.

It is in this setting that Jeshoshaphat ("whom Jehovah judges") responded in a way with which I can identify with. How about you?

1. He feared.

   There it is again. The natural response to an overwhelming enemy onslaught (see Isa. 60:2). That is not wrong, as long as we don't camp and live there. Notice the king's next, almost immediate response.

2. He set himself to seek the Lord.

   Divine strategy is needed. Jehoshaphat knew that if he didn't get God's strategy for this crisis, he and his people would be destroyed. Desperation drives us to Father—as it should. Children should run to Daddy (Abba) when threatened. *Seek* here means "to tread or frequent; usually to follow (for pursuit or search); by implication, to seek or ask; specially to worship" (Strong's, H1875). Do we frequent or tread like a familiar path toward His presence in worship? Then, to make sure his focus was on the One who had the answer:

3. He proclaimed a fast.

   Job said he treasured the words of God "...more than my necessary food" (Job 23:12). Have you ever been in a place of crisis where you didn't feel like eating because your only focus was getting God's answer? Fasting is not difficult then. "I have *got* to hear from God in this. Nothing else matters." We cry out with Jacob, "...I will not let You go unless You bless me" (Gen. 32:26).

Are you there now? Fear not! Daddy's answer is one soaking session away. Put on a soft worship CD and soak in His presence, blocking out all distractions. His presence will settle over you, bringing His peace and joy (see Isa. 26:3; John 14:27; Ps. 16:11).

4. He acknowledged his need of God.

    The king admits three things:

    a. "We have no power against this great multitude…"

    b. "…nor do we know what to do…"

    c. "…but our eyes are upon You."

The third one is most important, but the first two must be confessed in order to arrive at the third. If we think, "I can handle this," we won't look to Him.

In this humble and desperate attitude, God revealed the strategy for victory—and it worked. Setting worship in the front line (see 2 Chron. 20:21) brought God's response: "Do not be afraid nor dismayed…for the battle is not yours, but God's" (2 Chron. 20:15).

That's the message for you today. Fear may be your initial emotional response to the crisis, but settle yourself into worship, seeking Him and in His presence, He will quicken to your mind and spirit His strategy for victory! The crisis didn't take Him by surprise; neither should His answer surprise you! (See Isaiah 40:31; 30:21; Proverbs 3:5-6.)

FEARING GOD
FOR THE WRONG REASON

Then I would speak and not fear Him, but it is not so with me
(Job 9:35).

It was the night of our banquet for Mobile School of Supernatural Ministry. Students were pumped; the upperclassmen were serving the incoming students, giving them prophetic words, embracing and welcoming them. Tears of joy and excitement filled their eyes as Papa God's Presence overwhelmed them. The next week, at our first class, two of the students were conspicuously absent. In following up with one of them, we learned how all hell had broken loose since she was accepted into the school—her house flooded due to a water pipe rupture, vehicle breakdowns, illness, etc. She tearfully told us she had to withdraw from school to return to work to pay for all the resulting unexpected expenses.

Such is the case when we determine to sell out to God and pursue Him and all He has for us. That's not a negative confession; it's a spiritual principle. The enemy will attack our circumstances to intimidate and hinder us from our pursuit of God.

That's where we find Job in this narrative. Job was speaking to his friends (the likes of which I do not need!), trying to understand why all of this calamity had suddenly struck him (see Job 1 and 2). Even God had testified that "...there is none like him on the earth, a blameless and upright man, one who fears God and shuns evil" (Job 1:8). I believe He sees us the same way under the blood of the New Covenant. So, why calamity? Job's reasoning seems to follow this logic:

1. God is omnipotent and no one can stop Him from doing whatever He wants (see Job 9:1-13).

2. If I (Job) am innocent (see Job 9:21), then why is He crushing me like this (see Job 9:12,17)?

3. Conclusion: God must be angry with me (see Job 9:13,34).

It is that conclusion that led to his fear in verse 35. Human reasoning of God's ways will always lead to wrong conclusions. God said He would reveal His ways to us by His Spirit (see 1 Cor. 2:6-10). Bill Johnson says, "God doesn't hide things *from* us, but *for* us" (see Deut. 29:29). Sometimes, though, even in the new covenant, God doesn't explain to us the "why" of everything that enters our life. Again, Bill Johnson says, "I choose not to focus on what God has not done, but rather on what He has done."

We can eliminate Job's conclusion, though. God is *not* mad at us. He rejoices over us with singing and dancing, loving us with an everlasting love (see Zeph. 3:17; Jer. 31:3). Paul lists all the tribulations he was subjected to and considered it a privilege to suffer for Christ (see 2 Cor. 11:23-28; 12:10).

However, I am not saying when the enemy attacks our circumstances we should passively sit by and let him steal, kill, and destroy (see John 10:10). Because of the cross and resurrection, Jesus has given us all authority over the enemy (see Luke 10:19). Bill Johnson says if we have *all* authority, that means the devil has none! Paul teaches that "The weapons of our warfare are not carnal (natural) but mighty in God..." (2 Cor. 10:4). John reminds us that the One who lives in us is greater than the one who is in the world (see 1 John 4:4). We need to daily put on His armor (see Eph. 6:10-18) and walk as the "more than conquerors" (see Rom. 8:37) that we are, recognizing that it is "...God, who gives us the victory through our Lord Jesus Christ" (1 Cor. 15:57).

Fear of the Lord in Scripture refers to reverential awe, not a cowering fear of an angry God. His wrath over sin was satisfied at Calvary. Therefore, let's settle that issue here and now—my sin and yours have been atoned for. Paul states it is the kindness (goodness) of God that leads to repentance, not His wrath (see Rom. 2:4).

When Job finally did get his audience with God, the "why" of Job's calamity was never answered. God's message to Job was: "If I am big enough to have created all of this, am I not big enough to know what I'm doing in your life?" (See Job 38-41.) Job's response was acknowledgement of a personal encounter with God and repentance (see Job 42:5-6). That's the answer, my friend—encounter! Respond to Jesus' invitation in Matthew 11:28: Come to Him and He will give you rest. Does that sound like He is angry with you? Paul asked the Romans, "...If God is for us, who can be against us?" (Rom. 8:31). Paul wrote from the assumption that God is for us. Therefore, the answer to the question is obvious: no opposition is strong enough to overcome His alliance with us.

What I do in times of unexplainable calamity is declare Psalm 91 aloud, inserting my name and the names of those in my family, then declare Romans 8:31-39. Declaration speaks the truth of His Word, coming into agreement with God. Then I put on a worship CD, crawling up on Daddy God's lap, getting lost in His presence, because, In His presence is fullness of joy (see Ps. 16:11), not fear!

THE FEAR THAT SIN BRINGS

Then surely you could lift up your face without spot; yes, you could be steadfast, and not fear (Job 11:15).

I have to be real careful here. Job's friends really get my indignant juices flowing.

On the one hand, I don't want to belittle the truth that when we allow wickedness to dwell in our tents, we have reason to fear a holy God (see Job 11:14). David spoke from personal experience when he said, "If I regard iniquity in my heart, the Lord will not hear" (Ps. 66:18).

Isaiah said, "But your iniquities have separated you from your God; and your sins have hidden His face from you, so that He will not hear" (Isa. 59:2). As I have shared earlier, I have been in that place. It is a dark and lonely place to live. In that context, Job's friend Zophar's way out is accurate (see Job 11:13-14). It is similar to God's statement to Israel at the dedication of Solomon's temple in Second Chronicles 7:14. So, if there *is* sin in your life, follow Zophar's (and God's) counsel in these two passages and you will not need to fear His presence.

On the other hand, I see and have experienced sin used by the church as the universal cause for the Christian who struggles with their breakthrough.

"There must be sin in your life," they say. How many Zophars do you have in your life? I seem to be surrounded by them.

You see, Zophar's whole premise was wrong. There was no sin in Job's life. The more he contended that, the more they accused him of arrogance. Sound familiar?

Unlike Job, there *was* sin in my life. I had multiple affairs with women in the churches I pastored; I was hooked on pornography and preaching holiness while living a secret life in a cesspool of moral failure. When, after 11 years, God in His merciful discipline (see Heb. 12:5-11) exposed the sin, I was broken, repeatedly crying out David's confession of Psalm 51. But rather than assure me that God had heard my repentant cry and that He had not only forgiven my sin but would restore what the cankerworm had eaten (see Joel 2:25), I was told that I had disgraced the ministry, brought shame to the cause of Christ, and would never be useful in ministry again. The resulting depression was overwhelming, bordering on suicidal.

The facts are these: Yes, David had sinned (so did I). But along with his cry for forgiveness was one for restoration (see Ps. 51:12). Under the new covenant, His blood washes and cleanses from *all* sin (see 1 John 1:7). I'm sure you've heard the play on the word *justified*—"just-if-I'd never sinned." God does say, "...I will forgive their iniquity, and their sin I will remember no more" (Jer. 31:34).

If past sin disqualifies us for Kingdom usefulness, then Abraham, Moses, Samson, David, Peter, Paul, and many others would have faded into oblivion rather than become fathers of our faith. Indeed, it was Paul who wrote, "There is therefore now no condemnation to those who are in Christ Jesus..." (Rom. 8:1).

May I encourage you to do what I have done? Refuse to listen to the Zophars in your life, and instead read chapter 8 of Romans every day until it explodes in your spirit that *you* are the subject of chapter 8! Then play a soaking worship CD, crawl up on Daddy's lap, and let Him love on you.

I'll meet you there!

A LESSON FROM THE HORSE

He mocks at fear, and is not frightened; nor does he turn back from the sword (Job 39:22).

Job was getting a lesson on the character of God from the nature He created. The Teacher? God! I guess when God is teaching you about Himself, it might be a good idea to pay attention! And Job is. In this passage (Job 39:19-25), God spoke of the horse prepared for battle—his strength and tenacious, fearless courage as he charges into war (see Job 39:21).

I want to move away from God's lesson to Job here to focus on the characteristics God lists for the horse in battle, as they might pertain to us.

First comes the obvious—there is war. That's the setting in which his courage and bravery stand out. It is only in the heat of battle that what is in us will come forth. Will it be courage or cowardice?

The blood of the New Covenant does not exempt us from war—it equips us for it. Jesus said He has given us all authority over all the power of the enemy (see Luke 10:19). To have authority *over* the enemy speaks that we are engaging in confrontation *with* the enemy.

Paul uses warlike language: "For we do not wrestle against flesh and blood..." and, "For the weapons of our warfare..." (Eph. 6:12; 2 Cor. 10:4). Realize that our spiritual life is one of warfare. We are on one side or the other. You might say that when we embraced Christ, we defected from one army to the other. Peter says He "...called you out of darkness into His marvelous light" (1 Pet. 2:9).

So, the horse is in a war. So are we. Now what? If we follow the analogy through—if we are the horse in battle—then we must possess his attributes as well.

First, God asks Job, "Have you given the horse strength?" (Job 39:19). *Strength* here can be translated the "force (and) power (that propels to) victory." It speaks of aggressively advancing toward the enemy rather than running from him in fear (see Job 39:20). We have cited multiple references to God's encouraging statement, "Be strong and of good courage..." (see Josh. 1:6-7,9). Our favorite Psalm says that even when we walk through the valley of the shadow of death, we will fear no evil. Why? Because, "...You are with me" (Ps. 23:4).

That's it! Presence! "In His presence is fullness of joy..." (Ps. 16:11), even in the midst of the battle! Cultivate daily encounters in His presence; *host* His presence, as the title of Bill Johnson's book intimates.

Second, God calls the horse majestic, which means "royally glorious" (see Job 39:20). Battered down by attacks of the enemy, I have spent most of my Christian life seeing myself as much less than royally glorious. It wasn't until I took a course called "Who I Am in Him" that I began to realize how God saw me, and it was totally different from my view. I began to make a list:

- I am a new creation (see 2 Cor. 5:17).
- I am more than a conqueror (see Rom. 8:37).
- I am a friend of God (see John 15:14-15).
- I am loved by God (see John 15:9).
- I am God's son (He also has daughters) (see Heb. 12:5).

On and on the list goes. As you meditate in His Word, ask Holy Spirit to quicken to you who He says you are to Him. Start your own list. Declare

150

each one aloud. Gideon did not see himself as a "mighty man of valor" but God did (see Judg. 6:12). Ask Him, "Daddy, how do You see me?" You will never bow in shame before the enemy again, but stand majestically, royally glorious, washed in His blood, clothed in His righteousness, unafraid in battle! Job 39:22 says, "He mocks at fear." It literally means he "playfully laughs" at fear. There is a place of rest in God where our peaceful confidence in His presence totally eliminates all fear (see Heb. 3:11–4:1).

This entire devotional is summed up in Psalm 27. Every pronoun "I" or "my" is not just David—it is you; it is me. Read Psalm 27. Let His Word be final.

Nothing needs to be added.

THE DESTRUCTION OF FEAR, PART 1

Though an army may encamp against me, my heart shall not fear; though war may rise against me, in this I will be confident (Psalm 27:3).

Okay. I admit it. It was a set up. I left you with the assignment to read Psalm 27. And, like a good student, you did, didn't you? Now, here we are, in Psalm 27.

I call this the "overwhelming" psalm. David celebrates overwhelming victory in partnership with an overwhelming God with whom he has an overwhelming, intimate relationship. In this unbeatable combination, there is no room for fear; it cannot exist here any more than a snowball can exist in fire.

We are facing seemingly overwhelming evil today, from government corruption to terrorism to world economic collapse to child pornography and human trafficking. Watching the news one day often throws me into depression for a week.

The secret to living in victory as overcomers lies in this psalm, so I will devote several days to it.

We could start and end our discussion with the first two words: "The Lord." When He is present, what else needs to be said? Nothing, but David goes on to identify who God is to him. First, he declares, "The Lord is my light..." (Ps. 27:1). Jesus said, "I am the light of the world..." (John 8:12). Most children are afraid of the dark. The solution? Dad comes in and turns on the light. Darkness and fear vanish. Fear, as an initial response, is not bad. It is our response to it that is important. Invite Daddy into the room (your circumstance) and His light (peace) will dispel the darkness (fear). This is the confidence-building foundation upon which every victory over the enemy is launched. He is the Commander in Chief. He doesn't come to take sides. He comes to take over!

Secondly, David says the Lord is his "salvation" (Ps. 27:1) which is the Hebrew word *Yesha*, from which is derived the name *Yeshua* (Joshua and Jesus in Greek). It means "liberty, deliverance, prosperity, safety." David was prophetically saying, "The Lord is...Jesus"! His personal pronoun *my* said the Lord was *his* savior (salvation)! *Wow!* He is the One who frees me from the bondage of the enemy, delivers me from his control, and keeps me safe (see Ps. 91)! That's why David confidently asks, "Whom shall I fear?" (Ps. 27:1). If the Lord's light—His presence and glory—rests upon us and He is our salvation and protection, really, who do we have to fear? Um...I can't think of anybody, can you?

Oh, but David is just getting started. This boy is pumped! This is an example of how David was able to encourage himself in the Lord (see 1 Sam. 30:6 KJV). He ramps it up to the next level, stating, "The Lord is the strength of my life" (Ps. 27:1). *Strength* here means, "a fortified place, a defense, a fortress, a rock, a stronghold." *Wow*—again! The Lord is our fortified place. He is our fortress or stronghold. We usually think of strongholds in the negative sense with Paul's reference to "pulling down strongholds" (see 2 Cor. 10:4). But David is saying God is his fortified place. He is the One to whom I run when I'm under attack. A fortress is a place of safety and protection, designed to withstand an enemy's onslaught. Too many times I try to deal with enemy attacks using my own strength, resolve, wisdom, and emotion, resulting in wrong decisions, emotional and spiritual burnout, depression and defeat. How about you?

I just realized something else. David says, "the Lord is the strength of my *life*." Our life is every day, not just in times of crisis. We are currently preparing for a possible hurricane here in Mobile, Alabama. Lines have formed at gas stations and grocery stores as we prepare for the storm. David made the Lord the strength of his life in the ordinary, mundane days of his life. That prepared him for the storms that would inevitably come. And the more determined you are to pursue, reach, and fulfill God's destiny for you, the more inevitable and intense the storms will be (see Mark 5:35-41). Get your storm supplies stored up so that when the storm strikes, you can speak, "Of whom shall I be afraid?" (Ps. 27:1), drawing from the supply of His peace that you have stored up from soaking in His presence in the uneventful days.

David's storm did come, as he knew it would. But preparation brings a different outcome:

1. "They stumbled and fell" (see Ps. 27:2).

2. David's heart did not fear (see Ps. 27:3).

3. He was confident (see Ps. 27:3).

My wife and I stocked up on food, water, and gas; we secured the house and outdoor items in preparation for the storm. We were ready; therefore, we were confident and unafraid. As it turned out, the storm never developed as predicted. You might say it stumbled and fell. By the way, the storm was named *Isaac* (which means "laughter"). I think it was prophetic, as the storm baffled the forecasters with all their computers and satellites. I think God was having fun with them; every time they said it was about to become a hurricane, dry air would get drawn in from somewhere and make their dire prediction look foolish. "Has not God made foolish the wisdom of this world?" (1 Cor. 1:20). He sure did this time! "He who sits in the heavens shall laugh…" (Ps. 2:4).

The storm that was predicted to cause widespread damage brought refreshing showers, cooling breezes, then sun. The storm stumbled and fell. So will yours! What the enemy intended for evil (your destruction) God meant for good (see Gen. 50:20; Rom. 8:28). If you have prepared for your storm as David did, I dare you to name it *Isaac*; laugh at it and it will stumble and fall before you, refreshing instead of destroying you!

THE DESTRUCTION OF FEAR, PART 2

Though an army may encamp against me, my heart shall not fear; though war may rise against me, in this I will be confident (Psalm 27:3).

Instead of fear destroying you, how would you like to destroy fear from your life, especially in these uncertain days? What would it be like to live our lives totally absent of fear? David found the secret to such a lifestyle. I believe the days that lie ahead will be the fulfillment of Jesus' statement, "men's hearts failing them for fear..." (Luke 21:26). We don't have to be one of them if we follow David's model of living: "*One thing* I have desired of the Lord, that will I seek..." (Ps. 27:4).

Singleness of purpose. David didn't desire a big ministry, wealth, fame, or even doing great things for God. He had only one passion: "...that I may dwell in the house of the Lord all the days of my life, to behold the beauty of the Lord" (Ps. 27:4). Living in God's presence was his only life passion. And while in His presence, in intimate fellowship with Him, he would "inquire in His temple" (Ps. 27:4).

According to David, there is a natural progression into the supernatural. It begins with *desire* (Ps. 27:4). The word literally means, "to ask, inquire, request, pray, desire, wish for, demand" (Strong's, H7592). It is the same word used in Psalm 122: "*Pray* for the peace of Jerusalem..." (Ps. 122:6). David seems to be saying that he was asking, praying, even *demanding* that he live his life in God's Presence. The word *dwell* there means, "to sit down in quiet, remain, to settle, *to marry*" (Strong's, H3427). David wanted to live his life sitting down in quiet, soaking in God's Presence.

From personal experience, my spiritual and emotional stability is directly proportional to the amount of time I spend resting quietly in His Presence (with a worship CD playing) at the start of my day. David didn't have worship CDs, but he did have a harp. Make your own music with God. Love on Him and let Him love on you. Can there be any better start to your day?

Next, David cited two specific purposes for his desire to live in God's presence. First, "to behold the beauty of the Lord" (Ps. 27:4). David uses a wildly descriptive word in *behold*. Listen to this: "to gaze at, mentally to perceive, contemplate (with pleasure); specifically to have a vision of" (Strong's, H2372). In the '60s, we had an adolescent phrase for this kind of look: "have a crush on." It was when I got that starry-eyed look toward a girl. I contemplated with pleasure what it would be like for us to be an item, having a vision of us walking down the street together, hand in hand. David wanted to just hang out with God—not on the level of a teenage crush, but on the level of marriage. David wanted to be married to God! Everything that applies to the covenantal relationship in marriage applies here. Can I revert to my teen years for a moment? God has a crush on you! There's that starry-eyed look in His eyes every time He looks at you. When Jesus stretched out His arms to you at Calvary, it was more than forgiveness of sin that He was after. It was a marriage proposal!

David's second purpose for wanting to live his life in God's presence was "...to inquire in His temple" (Ps. 27:4). *Inquire* literally means "to plough, break forth, to inspect, admire, care for, consider, search or seek out" (Strong's, H1239). David wanted to learn more and more about the One he loved, searching out the secrets of His heart (see Deut. 29:29; 1 Cor. 2:9-10). When Lori and I were dating, I could tell you some information about her.

But now, we have spent the last 41 marital years searching out and admiring the secrets of one another's heart.

Do you know what's in God's heart? The secrets He longs to share with you? Is His passion your passion? Have you shared your heart and passion with Him? Bill Johnson says, "If it matters to you, it matters to Him." This level of intimacy can only be experienced by a lifetime, marital relationship with Him. He longs to share the secrets and passions of His heart with you. Will you let Him? I'm going to give you the same advice as an old-time television commercial about a product that would ease indigestion: "Try it. You'll like it!"

THE DESTRUCTION OF FEAR, PART 3

Though an army may encamp against me, my heart shall not fear; though war may rise against me, in this I will be confident (Psalm 27:3).

Many times when I was hired for a job, I was told, "It comes with benefits." What are the benefits of living in Psalms 27:4? They are listed in verses 5 and 6.

1. "...He shall hide me in His pavilion" (Ps. 27:5).

   The verse begins with, "For in the time of trouble." That statement, first of all, assures us that there *will* be times of trouble. It's not a matter of if, but when. Second, it assures us of the immediate protective response of Father for His children. *Hide* literally means "to hide by covering (see Ps. 91:4); to deny (access to), to protect." Living in His presence protects us, not *from* attack, but from becoming a casualty *of* the attack. This *pavilion* is described in Strong's Concordance as an entwined or fenced-in hut or lair, like a lion's. God's Presence is a fence inside of which we live protected from the spiritual, emotional, and physical effects of the enemy's onslaught. Psalm 91 protection is still in force, regardless of economic collapse, political upheaval, or religious persecution.

2. "...In the secret place of His tabernacle He shall hide me; He shall set me high upon a rock" (Ps. 27:5).

Here David says, or at least implies, that God will not only protect us, but make us a showcase to the enemy, as He did with Job: "Have you (satan) considered My servant Job...?" (Job 1:8). *Tabernacle* here means "a tent (as clearly conspicuous from a distance)" as we can see in the next phrase: "He shall set me *high* upon a rock." Dwelling in the secret place of His Presence sets us above the reach of the enemy. He can't get to us. He's like a child trying to reach the plate of cookies he sees on the table. He sees them, but he just can't reach them! God has you hidden in His Presence. Satan sees you there but he can't get to you. This picture is of us being raised and set securely on a high cliff by God, completely out of the reach of the enemy, as is repeated in verse 6. Is this not a clear picture of God's covering protection over His children (see Matt. 23:37)? Is this not reason enough for us to *fear not* and rest in His Presence?

David's conclusion goes beyond rest. Listen: "Therefore I will offer sacrifices of joy in His tabernacle; I will sing, yes, I will sing praises to the Lord" (Ps. 27:6). Realizing God's personal intervention on his behalf, David responded with breakthrough worship and praise.

But he defined his joyous breakout as being a *sacrifice*, which literally means "the slaughter of an animal." Joyous praise does not come naturally, especially in the middle of a storm. It is an act of the will; we literally sometimes have to make ourselves worship and praise Him. David says *I will*— that is intentional. If we wait until we feel like worshiping, which usually depends on our circumstances, satan will make sure it never happens. He fears nothing more than true intimate worship. *He* wants worship; therefore, he will go to any extent to prevent your worship of God. So we must worship with the same resolve as Habakkuk:

Though the fig tree may not blossom, nor fruit be on the vines; though the labor of the olive may fail, and the field yields no food; though the flock may be cut off from the fold, and there be no herd in the stalls—yet I will rejoice in the Lord, I will joy in the God of my salvation (Habakkuk 3:17-18).

Using agricultural terms, Habakkuk said that when everything went wrong and failed, he would still rejoice and joy in the Lord, because the source of his joy was not his circumstances but in "the God of my salvation." That's the essence of sacrifice: "Even though...yet I will." Praise is not emotion; it is a decision.

I was amazed to find that David used two different Hebrew words translated as *sing* in this verse. The first one means, "a strolling (traveling) minstrel." To me, that means that praise must go beyond the church service. It must travel with us wherever we are. Do my co-workers, friends, and family see me as a worshiper, even when I'm going through difficult times? The second *sing* means, "striking with the fingers; to touch the strings or parts of a musical instrument, and play upon it; to make music, accompanied by voice; hence, to celebrate in song and music" (Strong's, H2167).

We all have worship CDs of our favorite artists. It is not optional; it is essential that we bathe ourselves in worship daily and carry it with us throughout the day. That is what envelops us in His presence and becomes the pavilion or tabernacle that surrounds, covers, and protects us from the enemy attack so that we may never have to fear, but can find our joy in the "God of our salvation."

FEAR OF CATASTROPHIC CALAMITY

God is our refuge and strength, a very present help in trouble.
Therefore, we will not fear, even though the earth be removed,
and though the mountains be carried into the midst of the sea
(Psalm 46:1-2).

As I write this, news stories today are reporting at least 50 dead, hundreds injured, and thousands of homes destroyed by a series of earthquakes in China, while minor tremors were felt this morning in southern California. Mississippi and Louisiana continue to clean up after hurricane Isaac, while fires continue to rage and destroy homes in the western U.S.

On the economic front, the European Union's currency and economies are in the midst of collapse, while here in the U.S., 23 million Americans are unemployed, gas is approaching or has reached 4 dollars per gallon, and food prices have risen 15 percent in the last six months. The government's answer? Print more money, further devaluing the dollar while taxes are due to increase dramatically. Foreclosures are at an all-time high.

No, no, no! Don't run out and stand in front of that bus! There is hope. Whew—you had me worried there for a second.

We are not the first generation to face political and economic upheaval, natural disasters, or persecution for our faith (see Job 1–2; Matt. 5:10-12; 2 Cor. 6:4-10; 7:5; 11:23-28).

David's list was pretty catastrophic as well. I don't think he was referring only to a major earthquake or tsunami. I believe he was talking about life. When everything we thought was solid and dependable—career, health, marriage, church, etc.—is violently shaken until it disintegrates.

For over a year, I knew God was telling me to take an early retirement. I also knew that to do that would cut my income by more than 50 percent. It defied all logic. Of course, God's math always does. But David was not talking about early retirement; he was saying when the bottom drops out of your life in every area (remember Habakkuk 3:17-18?), here's the involvement you can expect from Papa God. Ready? This is going to be an awesome ride, so make sure you're strapped in good and tight.

David said God is a very present help in trouble. What is *trouble*? I looked it up in Strong's Concordance, and ladies, you're going to love this one! It says, "tightness, a tight place, translated as a female rival or adversary." Remember when you had that crush on the high school quarterback and he started to pay attention to you, and the captain of the cheerleaders swooped in and...? Oh—you were the cheerleader? Sorry I brought it up. Anyway, I believe David, in choosing this word, was referring to anything that competes with our intimate relationship with God. By definition, that thing, whatever it is, is an *adversary*, causing "adversity, anguish, distress, and tribulation." Jesus said we can't serve two masters; we will love one and hate the other (see Matt. 6:24). He even said if we love family more than Him, we're not worthy of Him (see Matt. 10:37). Joshua, Elijah, and others called Old Testament Israel to choose who they would serve (see Josh. 24:15; 1 Kings 18:21).

Competition for affection is the trouble David was referring to. Are you in trouble? Relief begins with a choice. Your "Isaac" (and mine) must be put on the altar, offered to God. He may give it back to us as He sees our willingness of heart, or He may ask us to plunge the knife into it and let it die so He can resurrect it supernaturally in His time. Either way, He loves us too much to tolerate a "female rival"—whatever that may translate into—competing for our love.

Now we go to the big stuff—the earth being removed (Ps. 46:2). To *remove* here means "to alter (change); to barter or dispose of" (Strong's, H4171). This, I believe, speaks of major changes or upheavals in our life. Lori and I moved from upstate New York to Alabama in 2000. I was 50 years old and not very thrilled about uprooting and starting over, leaving a ministry and going to…well, nothing. I was kind of like Abraham—without the faith. That's why you won't find my name in Hebrews!

We all go through foundation-shaking upheavals—loss of a spouse through death or divorce, death of a parent or child, broken relationships, loss of job or career, serious health issues, etc. As Job asked, where is God in this?

Wherever He is, that's where we should be. Verse 1 says "God is our refuge," which literally means "a shelter, a place of hope or trust." It comes from a root word meaning "to flee for protection" (Strong's, H4268, H2620). We were given a puppy last year. (Okay, so I begged my wife like a kid.) Abby ("source of joy") was eight weeks old and very skittish, especially of sudden noises. She was four months old when the New Year's firecrackers were set off by every human being in our subdivision. Besides peeing and pooping all over our carpet, she fled to her room, under our bed, between our legs—any place she sensed protection—trembling in terror. She is one year old now and still hides behinds us when there's any loud noise or a stranger comes to the door. If we're outside, she'll make a beeline for the house at the pop of fireworks. She is seeking refuge—the place of protection, safety, and trust.

Where or who is *our* refuge? It is in learning to live in His Presence (see Ps. 91:1) that we can take that deep spiritual breath and know that Daddy will protect us and take care of us:

Casting the whole of your care [all your anxieties, all your worries, all your concerns, once and for all] on Him, for He cares for you affectionately and cares about you watchfully (1 Peter 5:7 AMP).

A refuge is a place of safety (see Prov. 18:10). He is not only our place to hide, He is our *strength* or our "forceful power or security" (Strong's, H5797). When the enemy floods your life with overwhelming circumstances, in an attempt to distract you from your affection toward God by making you pay attention to him and his attack, God rises up and rushes to your side to be strong on your behalf (see 2 Chron. 16:9). If, when the bottom drops out of your life, you spend more time rebuking the devil than worshiping God, the enemy has succeeded in winning your "affection." Remember, he wants to be the center of attention—to be worshiped. Don't give him the satisfaction. Call Daddy to your side through worship and satan will back down.

When I was in high school, I once had a crush on the head cheerleader—and she was friendly to me! I took that as a signal, so I flirted with her. Suddenly, from the pit of hell appeared our star quarterback—with biceps set in concrete. With a sheepish Elmer Fudd smile, I drew on my own athletic ability—track. I think I set a new world record for the 100-yard dash! That's the picture you need to have of satan's response to Daddy showing up as your strength. To be "a very *present* help" literally means, "to appear, to come forth, to meet or be present." So when satan overwhelms your circumstances, Daddy shows up and shows off. This word *present* means all you have to do is make a formal introduction.

"Oh, hi satan. I'd like you to meet my Daddy, God. Oh, you've already met? Great! I'll leave you two alone so you can talk about old times. I'd tell you to have a nice day, but somehow I don't think that's going to happen."

Then step back, smile, and watch the Lion tear up the wolf. It'll really be a fun day for you!

FEAR OF MAN

In God (I will praise His word), in God I have put my trust; I will not fear. What can flesh do to me? (Psalm 56:4)

People can be intimidating, especially for those of us with introverted or shy personalities. Anyone with a strong, aggressive personality can be intimidating to me. They don't even have to try. Timothy seemed to struggle with this, too (see 2 Tim. 1:7). *Fear* in that verse can be translated "timidity."

This writing is highly personal for me. I have spent most of my life struggling with the fear of man. Need for affirmation and acceptance developed a lifestyle of anxiety over what people were thinking of me. The truth was, most of the time they weren't!

What about those who can bring harm, physical or otherwise, to my life? As I write today, on the eleventh anniversary of 9/11, riots are breaking out against our embassies in several Middle Eastern nations. The U.S. ambassador, along with three of his staffers, has been killed as threats against the U.S. mount. An Iranian pastor was just released after three years in prison under a daily threat of execution. A literal *miracle!*

At least two pastors that I know of here in the U.S. sit in jail today. Their crime? Conducting Bible studies in their homes without a permit!

When David wrote Psalm 56, he was running from Saul, who was trying to kill him. He fled to the Philistine city of Gath (Goliath's hometown). Because of what he had done to their "outstanding citizen," he was not well received. So now not only was Saul after his life, his enemies didn't want him around (see 1 Sam. 21:11). You know you're having a bad day when the devil doesn't want you!

David's list of opposition to him in Psalm 56 is quite overwhelming:

1. "Man would swallow me up" (Ps. 56:1)

2. "Fighting (against me) all day" (Ps. 56:1)

3. "He oppresses me" (Ps. 56:1)

4. "My enemies would hound me all day (Ps. 56:2)

5. "All day they twist my words" (Ps. 56:5)

6. "All their thoughts are against me for evil" (Ps. 56:5)

In addition, verse 6 pictures them corporately planning to destroy David's life through slanderous destruction of his reputation.

Remember, all David was trying to do was fulfill his destiny in God. He was anointed to be the next king of Israel. He didn't seek the position. It was his assignment. Has God given you an assignment? Do you feel like you are alone on the planet pursuing it, with every other human being seeming to actively oppose you? Has it left you in fear—fear of your own survival financially, or perhaps even physically? Hey David, is there room in the cave for one more? We have a new member!

At one point in the story, David had to pretend he was insane to protect himself from being harmed. It caused his enemies to dismiss him as not worthy of bothering with. Have your critics asked you, "Are you crazy? You're not qualified to do this." Cool! They have played right into God's hand!

David, surrounded by enemies, overcame his fear with one action word—trust. "Whenever I am afraid, I will trust in you. ...In God I have put my trust; I will not fear..." (Ps. 56:3-4). *Trust* here means "to be confident, sure, bold, secure" (Strong's, H982).

We are living in frightening times. All-out war has been declared on Christians, both inside and outside of this nation. Our trust, confidence, and security can no longer be in our finances (world economies, including ours, are collapsing), careers (unemployment is at depression-like levels), OR possessions (foreclosures are at a record high). God said He would shake everything that can be shaken so that only that which cannot be shaken will remain (see Heb. 12:26-28). It's happening. Yet like David, we can say, "I will not fear. what can flesh do to me?" (Ps. 56:4). Why could he declare that? Because his trust, his confidence was in a Person. Is yours? He promised He would prepare a table of provision before you *in the presence of your enemies* (see Ps. 23:5). That speaks not only of provision, but peace—your enemies are still there, but He and you are sitting down for a romantic candlelight dinner for two!

He is our only Anchor; the only Solid Rock in which we can trust. Anchor yourself in Him through intimate, joyous worship, and you will live in peace in the midst of the storm.

GOD'S LEADING DISPELS FEAR

And He led them on safely, so that they did not fear; but the
sea overwhelmed their enemies (Psalm 78:53).

In this psalm, David was recounting Israel's history and God's faithfulness in song. Here, he was referring to God leading the Israelites through the wilderness after the miracle of the Red Sea. You could probably write this chapter yourself, the life application being so obvious. So let's look at God's encouraging words for us today.

First of all, "He led them." To *lead* means "to guide or even transport." So Israel, fresh off the Red Sea miracle, was now in the wilderness, knowing they were supposed to end up in the Promised Land but having no idea how to get there. Fortunately, they had their GPS: "God's Place of Safety." So do you!

Our journeys, though starting together at the cross, will lead us individually in diverging paths according to the particular Kingdom assignment we've been given. As with Israel, that path will lead into uncharted territory.

Without our "GPS," we will get hopelessly lost along the way, much like the couple who rode through the countryside for hours looking for their friend's home. The wife, admitting they were lost, begged her husband to stop and ask directions.

"We're not lost!" he snapped. "Look there. I recognize that tree."

"You should," the wife retorted. "It's the fourth time we've passed it."

But even when we depend on Daddy's guidance, we sometimes don't understand the path (see Ps. 32:8; Prov. 3:5-6). He lead Israel from the miraculous deliverance through the Red Sea into the wilderness. David was led from anointing for royalty to the wilderness caves for 10 to 13 years. Jesus was led by the Spirit from the baptismal declaration, "This is My beloved Son," into the wilderness confrontation with satan (see Matt. 3:17–4:1). *Wow!* Three cases of being led from miraculous anointing to wilderness, not ministry. I'm beginning to see a pattern here, aren't you? If you feel like, after your supernatural encounter with Him where your destiny is revealed, you are then led into a spiritual and emotional wilderness where nothing seems to be happening, be encouraged—you're in good company!

After my moral failure, God worked on restoring my relationship with Him and my wife and children. I went through deep depression, guilt, and shame. No one was there to assure me that I was still His son and that His calling on my life was irrevocable (see Rom. 11:29). That wilderness experience lasted for 20 years, rejected by man and, I thought, by God. I was wrong!

There is one word in this verse that quiets all the questions of His leading us into this wilderness experience. That word is *safely*. According to Strong's Concordance, it means "a place of refuge or safety, both the fact (security), and the feeling (trust)" (Strong's, H983). Wherever He is leading, the fact is we are secure, safely sheltered in His arms, and we can relax in confidence and trust. Fact and feeling—they go together. Anything other than a fact is a lie. So what lies are you being told in your wilderness experience? How about:

1. "I don't feel His presence. He must not be pleased with me." *Lie!*

Truth:

But Zion said, "The Lord has forsaken me, and my Lord has forgotten me." Can a woman forget her nursing child, and not have compassion on the son of her womb? Surely they may forget, yet I will not forget you. See, I have inscribed [literally, "tattooed"] you on the palms of My hands; your walls are continually before me (Isaiah 49:14-16).

2. "The economy is collapsing. I am going to lose everything." *Lie!*

Truth:

Though the fig tree may not blossom, nor fruit be on the vines; though the labor of the olive may fail, and the fields yield no food; though the flock may be cut off from the fold, and there be no herd in the stalls—yet I will rejoice in the Lord; I will joy in the God of my salvation. The Lord God is my strength; He will make my feet like deer's feet, and He will make me walk on my high hills (Habakkuk 3:17-19).

3. "We are losing our freedoms in America, especially to worship God. We can be jailed for publicly expressing our faith." *False fear* as a result of true facts.

Truth:

Blessed [happy, fortunate, well off] are those who are persecuted for righteousness' sake, for theirs is the kingdom of heaven. Blessed are you when they revile and persecute you, and say all kinds of evil against you falsely for My sake. Rejoice and be exceedingly glad, for great is your reward in heaven... (Matthew 5:10-12).

That must be the process for us in today's God-hostile environment—embrace God's truth and reject the lie. Bill Johnson has said, "Believing a lie empowers the liar." Once we embrace His truth, the feeling (the confident trust in His faithful care) will come.

The result of acknowledging His leading us in safety, even when it takes us into the wilderness experience, is expressed in the next phase of the Psalm: "...so that they did not fear" (Ps. 78:53). This is a natural, supernatural outflow of confidently trusting His leading.

We must understand that His leading is not to keep us *from* the wilderness, but to manifest His supernatural care *in* it. It says, "Yea, though I walk *through* the valley" (Ps. 23:4). Not around!

In another psalm, David encourages us to, "Cast your burden on the Lord, and He shall sustain you; He shall never permit the righteous to be moved (shaken)" (Ps. 55:22). Listen to the glorious meaning of *sustain* from Strong's Concordance: "to maintain, nourish, provide food, bear, hold up, protect, support, defend; to supply the means necessary for living" (Strong's, H3557). Incredible! God's tender care for His children leaves no stone unturned. When the burden of cruel treatment is too hurting to endure, Daddy is there to scoop us up, bind up our wounds, heal our heart, and set a table before us in the presence of our enemies (see Ps. 23:5). No human, no matter how close, can lead us as safely as Father can. His peace that passes all understanding will guard our hearts and minds through Christ Jesus (see Phil. 4:7).

I believe that is the only thing that will carry us victoriously through these trying times. Spend time soaking in His presence; rest in Him and be refreshed. Experience His *shalom*, and *dwell* in that secret place (see Ps. 91:1). That's where you'll find me. Join me—there's always room for one more!

WHOSE SIDE ARE YOU ON?

The Lord is on my side; I will not fear. What can man do unto me? (Psalm 118:6)

"Tony...over here."

"Frank...you're with me."

"John..."

And so it went. Every gym class the same. Two captains appointed by the teacher, while the rest of us stood in line—waiting to be picked. Of course, all the athletic jocks were picked first. Then it went down the line to the rest of us. Hopeful, I wondered whose side I would be on. I would size up the teams as to which looked stronger, hoping to be chosen on that one. Finally, as in every class, there was only one left unchosen—me. The captains would look at each other with the look of, "You take him!" Finally, one would say, "Okay, Pileggi, I guess you're over here. Go stand in right field—and stay out of the way!" By then, it didn't matter whose side I was on—I wasn't going to contribute, so who cares? For some strange reason, I just didn't feel a part of the team.

Have you ever been there? Wondered whose side you were on and if anybody else cared? To that question, David gave an awesome answer: "The Lord is on my side." Actually, his answer reverses the question. It's not, "Whose side am I on?" but, "Who is on *my* side?" When finally I was picked and on a team, I would look around, hoping the best athlete in the class was on our team so it would give us the best chance of winning. When I look around at my life and see that the Lord is on my side, I can more than *hope* for victory, I am *assured* of it!

The reason David needed that assurance is revealed in verse 5: "I called on the Lord in distress." *Distress* here means, "something tight; trouble." It comes from a root word that means "to malign, stab with words" (Strong's, H4712, H6895, H6896). My wife and I are experiencing this right now in the church—from leadership!

Maligning, stabbing words. It has happened throughout our Christian walk of ministry, pastoring, and leadership. Like a physical stabbing, the pain is excruciating. It is difficult to hold back the tears even as I write this. When those with whom you co-labor turn on you and viciously attack you, using the pulpit as their whipping post, it hurts! How do you respond? There are only two options—bitterness and offense, or David's: "The Lord is on my side; I will not fear. What can man do to me?"

You see, David chose the latter. He *chose* the Lord instead of bitterness. I have often made the wrong choice here. I will not do so this time. I will pray God's blessing on my brother and move on. I have wasted too many years wallowing in bitterness, unforgiveness, and self-pity. The times in which we live are too crucial to waste any more time wounding one another with friendly fire. The church has lost her focus and purpose (bringing Heaven to earth in the love and power of Father) by shooting at each other rather than at the enemy. We make satan's job easier. While we're fighting with each other, a world looking for something real bypasses us as being irrelevant and latches onto a false supernatural power—the counterfeit. I refuse to go there anymore.

David went on to say that when he called upon the Lord in his distress (tight place of trouble), "The Lord answered me and set me in a broad place"

(Ps. 118:5). This is literally "a large, open place of liberty." Do you see that contrast? Distress—tight place. Broad place—large, open. *God* will reverse the curse! He will turn what was meant for evil into good! Having experienced God's turnaround in his life, David's conclusion was: "It is better to trust in the Lord than to put confidence in man" (Ps. 118:8).

Wherever there is a vacuum, something will rush in to fill it. Where there is an absence of trust (see Ps. 118:8-9), fear will rush in (see Ps. 118:6). If we, by an act of our will, choose to trust Him in the pain and hurt, that trust will empty the fear of man from our emotions, as well as any bitterness and unforgiveness, and replace it with a rush of His peace (see John 14:27). Peace is from the Kingdom of light. Fear, anger, bitterness, and unforgiveness come from the kingdom of darkness. Light and darkness can't co-exist. A room is either light or it's dark. It can't be both. So it is with our heart. We can't have both. I know it hurts. I'm hurting right now. But I will take David's counsel that it is better to trust in the Lord than to put confidence in man.

Will you?

FEAR OF SUDDEN TERROR, PART 1

*Do not be afraid of sudden terror, nor of trouble from the
wicked when it comes; for the Lord will be your confidence,
and will keep your foot from being caught* (Proverbs 3:25-26).

If this one is not appropriate for today's world, I don't know what is. Ever since September 11, 2001, *terror* has become one of the most common words in our language. Out of sheer demonic hatred, total destruction and death is threatened of any nation or people whose faith lies in the Judeo-Christian ethic/religion.

As I write this, U.S. embassies continue to be under attack by radical extremists while our government negotiates with known terrorists. The president of Iran promises to "wipe Israel off the face of the earth" (little satan), then promises to come after the U.S. (big satan). He believes the only way their "messiah" can appear is for Israel to be destroyed and the world to be thrown into total chaos—sudden terror. As a result, many (including Christians) live in fear of another terrorist attack as well as global economic collapse—sudden terror. In the midst of the current political, economic, and global chaos in which we live today, how are we, the church, to stand above it all as a beacon of refuge and hope, inviting the terrorized to come and live in the victory of Romans 8:31-39?

The first thought I have in answer to that is where we keep our focus. In our School of Supernatural Ministry class last night, the DVD was on "The Importance of Rest" with Bill Johnson speaking. In that lesson, Bill said:

- Awareness of God's presence is a huge part of rest. Do not let any situation, such as something on the news, become bigger than your awareness of God's presence. If we focus on dilemmas, we become anxious. Do not dwell on anything for which you do not have answers.

I am a news-a-holic and lately have been fighting anxiety and depression as I watch the world sink into deeper end-time turmoil. I realize now that the remote has an off button and God is not going to use it for me. It is not sticking my head in the sand, ignoring what's going on in the world. But it is choosing where my focus will be—the forces of darkness or the lordship of Jesus. If you, too, are battling this priority choice, come with me on this journey to the One who is still in charge.

The first thing the Lord is telling me is, "Get My perspective back." He brought Psalm 2 to mind:

> *Why do the nations rage, [literally: "throng tumultuously"], and the people plot a vain [literally "worthless or empty"] thing? The kings of the earth set themselves, and the rulers take counsel together, against the Lord and against His Anointed, saying "Let us break Their bonds in pieces and cast away Their cords from us."* **He who sits in the heavens shall laugh**; *the Lord shall hold them in derision* (Psalm 2:1-4).

Strong's Concordance defines *derision* as "to deride; by implication to speak unintelligibly (as if imitating a foreigner); have in derision, laugh (to scorn), mock, stammering" (Strong's, H3932). Now, that's not very politically correct. While all this is going on, God and Jesus are up there belly-laughing, mocking and mimicking their language. I'm sorry if that offends you in this politically correct world, but I'm just telling you what the word means. I'm not saying we should mock anyone. I'm just saying we need to get God's perspective of world events. He doesn't seem to be troubled in the least. He's assuring us He is still in charge and always will be, as we can see in His response in the rest of Psalm 2—please read it!

Oh, by the way. I turned my television off and have a worship CD playing. What a difference! Peace has settled over me; even Abby, our sheltie, is sleeping!

The point is, we must choose where we will live—either in anxiety and panic from the world events or in His peace—yes, and *joy*. Tomorrow, we'll return to our Proverbs text and be further encouraged and settled as we look at Papa God's personal involvement, concern, and care for His children. Take a deep breath, relax, and find your rest in His presence, because in His presence is fullness of joy (see Ps. 16:11). It really works!

FEAR OF SUDDEN TERROR, PART 2

Do not be afraid of sudden terror, nor of trouble from the
wicked when it comes; for the Lord will be your confidence,
and will keep your foot from being caught
(Proverbs 3:25-26).

When I first read, "Do not be afraid of sudden terror," I thought, "Yeah, Lord. Easy for *You* to say!" The meaning of *sudden terror* in the original Hebrew sounds like a summary of today's news:

1. Sudden: instantly; from a root meaning to open the eyes, a wink; moment, quickly or unexpectedly, at an instant (Strong's, H6597).

2. Terror: a sudden alarm, dreadful, great fear; from a root meaning to be startled (by a sudden alarm); hence to fear in general, make to shake (Strong's, H6343).

God is telling us not to fear when a sudden, dreadful event happens in a moment—something that startles us and causes us great fear. In a post-9/11 world, that sounds eerily like a terrorist attack. We now live in general fear each day, fearing the news of another attack. But God is telling us *not* to fear, even when trouble *does* come from the wicked (the King James says, "desolation"). This takes it one step further. Not only are we to not fear at the *threat* of sudden terror, but we are not to fear when it actually happens! How is that possible? I remember the church staff with whom I worked seated in the conference room on 9/11, watching the Twin Towers crumble. That hollow knot in my stomach mixed with tears for my country and fear of what was happening to us are fixed in my memory forever.

Never stop praying Second Chronicles 7:14 for our nation. Intercede for her! Call her back to God! Ask God to spare her as Abraham did for Sodom. Ask for mercy instead of judgment as we repent for the sins of our nation as Jeremiah and Daniel did for Israel. Remember and review this paragraph as we go to the next verse of our study.

The reasons for us to not be afraid in these times is found in verse 26: "for the Lord will be your confidence." The word for *confidence* there means, "Fatness, silliness, trust; from the root to be fat, silly, or foolish" (Strong's, H3689). Our trust in Him is to be so solid that it makes us giddy with joy to the point of silliness! There has been much criticism of the laughter revival in Toronto and elsewhere. But it's scriptural! Did you know that some form of the word *joy* appears in Scripture 70-80 times more than any form of *weeping* or *sorrow*? Maybe God is trying to tell us that we should laugh 80 times more than we cry! This is what is meant by the "fullness of joy" (see Ps. 16:11; John 15:11; 16:24).

We saw God laughing at the turmoil of nations in Psalm 2. Now He's saying, "You do it, too!" Again, we don't carelessly laugh when people are dying; it is the perspective of a child who believes his Daddy can knock out any bully who threatens him and so he gets giddy as he thinks, "I can't wait to see how Daddy takes care of this!" It is an extreme confidence in Daddy's control over every crisis situation—that it is going to turn out all right. That is how we must live in these days of peril.

I don't care how badly Israel is outnumbered—she always *has* been. She will *not* be wiped out! Get ready for supernatural intervention from her Daddy! That's the second part of verse 26: "…[the Lord] will keep your foot from being caught." *Caught* means "to capture with a noose, to catch in a net, trap, or pit" (Strong's, H3921).

My favorite psalm of all time says, "You shall not be afraid of the terror by night, nor of the arrow that flies by day" (Ps. 91:5). God is active in the affairs of man; He is not neutral. Listen to His promise to us in Isaiah 43:

> *When you pass through the waters [literally, "floods"], I will be with you; and through the rivers, they shall not overflow you. When you walk through the fire, you shall not be burned, nor shall the flame scorch you. For I am the Lord your God...* (Isaiah 43:2-3).

Notice, He doesn't say *if* you pass through but *when*. The American church, because of our national freedoms guaranteed by the Constitution, has not endured the persecution and martyrdom Christians have faced in most other nations. I believe very difficult times are ahead for believers in this nation and we are going to need to know, through God encounters, the truth of His promises spoken here. There are two ways to know God: "I have *heard* of You by the hearing of the ear (intellectually), but now my eye *sees* You (encounter)" (Job 42:5). With what is coming, only an ongoing God-encounter lifestyle will enable us to live in peace, power, and joy as multitudes come to us looking for refuge, their hearts "failing them from fear" (Luke 21: 26).

Did you say "peace" in these times? Yes. Look at the verse just prior to our text: "When you lie down, you will not be afraid; yes, you will lie down and your sleep will be sweet" (Prov. 3:24). Jesus was sound asleep in the boat in the midst of a storm that frightened seasoned fisherman! Bill Johnson comments: "The only storm you have authority over is the storm you can sleep in."

There is that place of rest into which we all can enter (see Heb. 4:9-11). The invitation is still open; this hotel still has vacancy (see Matt. 11:28-30).

The best part is, the cost has been paid; you are a guest, and you don't have to leave; you can take up residence there (see Ps. 91:1).

Before you go to bed each night, declare these verses over you and your family:

> *I lay down and slept; I awoke, for the Lord sustained me. I will not be afraid of ten thousands of people who have set themselves against me all around* (Psalm 3:5-6).

> *I will both lie down in peace, and sleep; for You alone, O Lord, make me dwell in safety* (Psalm 4:8).

It is not a formula; it is a lifestyle, the only lifestyle that will sustain us in the days that lie ahead.

FEAR OF EVIL PLANS

"Take heed, and be quiet; do not fear or be fainthearted..."
Thus says the Lord God: "It shall not stand, nor shall it come
to pass" (Isaiah 7:4,7).

Somebody tipped you off. Maybe it "slipped" during conversation. Maybe it was intentional—a friend's warning. But you were informed—your close friend or relative has teamed up with your enemy to bring you down, get you fired, ruin your reputation, spread malicious gossip.

This was what Ahaz, king of Judah, was facing. Rekah, king of Israel, Judah's brothers, conspired with Rezin, king of Syria, to join forces to "make war against it" (Isa. 7:1).

My wife and I are walking through a similar situation right now. A pastor with whom we have been partnering in ministry has abruptly joined forces with another ministry and now verbally attacks us, noting how useless our ministry is. Needless to say, we are reeling from this sudden turn of events and feel like we've been punched in the stomach. So this chapter, at least for Lori and me, is not a history lesson—it is a description of our current path. I can easily identify with the king's emotional response: "So his heart and the heart of his people were moved as the trees of the woods are moved with the wind" (Isa. 7:2). The word *moved* here has a wide range of meanings, including "to waver, reel, shake, stagger" (Strong's, H5128).

When David's own men turned on him, wanting to kill him, David had to encourage himself in the Lord (see 1 Sam. 30:6). At Jesus' most crucial hour, Mark says all of his disciples "forsook him and fled" (Mark 14:50). There is a time for all of us, especially those in leadership, when we will stand alone. All those we disciple and count on will forsake us and flee, for whatever reason.

In his book, *Strengthen Yourself in the Lord*, Bill Johnson says David faced "...the deepest and most betraying rejection of all...his mighty men—those whom he'd persevered with for years...talked about stoning him."[1]

The Bible is a book of reality, not of superheroes. First Samuel 30:6 starts by admitting that "David was greatly distressed." This human emotion is a common reaction to a great disappointment, not only in circumstances, but also when those you thought would be loyal to you turn on you instead. It was in that devastating moment that David drew from the intimacy that had developed in the years of the shepherd fields, alone with his harp and his God. We must have that intimacy to draw on in the times of great betrayal. Bill Johnson states it this way:

- God knew David would succeed as a leader because he took the initiative to seek Him in the secret place. This is the same quality of maturity that He is looking for in us...those who seek God's face and pursue His destiny for their lives when no one is around, are the people who possess the initiative required to strengthen themselves.[2]

Bill's statement that jumped off the page at me was:

- ...God brings moments into our lives when we have to stand alone in difficulty and testing. God will even blind the eyes and deafen the ears of our closest friends in those moments so we can learn to minister to ourselves.[3]

That's where Lori and I are now. We also cling to God's promise made to the king of Judah in our text: "It shall not stand, nor shall it come to pass" (Isa. 7:7). Joseph also made the statement to his brothers that what they intended for evil, God meant for good (see Gen. 50:20).

I strongly sense there are many reading this who have been deeply wounded by those to whom you were closest. They laid plans, joining with an adversary whom at one time you both fought against, side by side. The wound is deep, the tears many (see Ps. 56:8), the sleepless nights constant. Are your heart and emotions wavering as the trees in the woods (see Isa. 7:2)? Jesus said that His anointing was, in part, to "heal the brokenhearted" (see Isa. 61:1). That describes me right now; does it describe you? Then join me with Mary at Jesus' feet, soaking in His presence, letting His words heal our hearts. Among those words is His promise, "It shall not stand, nor shall it come to pass."

Remember His words spoken over you prophetically. Retrieve and re-read them. They are as true now, in this hour of disappointment, as they were the day He first spoke them. Bill Johnson concludes that David's ability to "strengthen himself" in the Lord became his "breakthrough (that) kept him standing in front of an unseen door that was just about to open—the door to the throne room."[4] The battle that David was rejected from fighting in was the battle in which Saul was killed, which ushered David into his destiny as king.

Stand strong, my friend. You and I, as we strengthen ourselves in Him, will not see the evil plans laid against us come to pass, but rather the door to the throne room will open up as we step into our destiny and promotion!

NOTES

1. Bill Johnson, *Strengthen Yourself in the Lord* (Shippensburg, PA: Destiny Image Publishers, 2007), 22.

2. Ibid., 28.

3. Ibid., 29.

4. Ibid., 24.

BRIDGE OVER TROUBLED WATERS

Do not say, "A conspiracy," concerning all that this people call
a conspiracy, nor be afraid of their threats [terror or fear],
nor be troubled (Isaiah 8:12).

This is almost the same message as yesterday, except that it is taken to the next level. Now, the attack against God's people is called a *conspiracy*. By definition, a conspiracy is "an evil alliance" (Strong's, H7195). It involves the same enemies listed in our last chapter, but their plans are now revealed as being more sinister. A group of nations was forming an alliance to coordinate a plan to destroy Judah.

A friend who turns on you is hurting enough. If they join your mutual enemy, that is even more devastating. But when you learn that they have formed a group which has as their goal to totally destroy you, that is the epitome of evil.

Your fellow employees have banded together and gone to your supervisor to complain about you, or worse yet they have circulated a petition to get you fired. Whatever the circumstance, it seems like the world is against you. You are overwhelmed by the opposition and slander. How do you respond? Vindication or revenge come to mind, as David often pleads in the psalms. But God instructs Isaiah—and us—quite differently.

Isaiah began by saying, "The Lord spoke thus to me with a strong hand, and instructed me..." (Isa. 8:11). The picture here is that of a parent loudly calling to their child as they run toward a busy street: "No, no, no! Don't go there!" *Instruct* there literally means, "to chastise with blows or words" (Strong's, H3256). It is an urgent warning against a particular action. What was God warning Isaiah not to do? "...That I should not walk in the way of this people" (Isa. 8:11).

God is emphatically calling us to a higher level of response. Don't stoop to their level. Don't coordinate your own conspiracy to vindicate yourself from theirs. I know Jesus taught about forgiving those who sin against us (see Matt. 6:14-15), but why was God speaking in such an urgent tone here? I believe the writer of Hebrews answers that question best: "...lest any root of bitterness springing up cause trouble, and by this many become defiled" (Heb. 12:15). It literally means "poison that contaminates the whole." There are so many Christians who have allowed offense to poison their spirit with bitterness to the point where it has contaminated their whole Christian walk. Have you ever met someone (or are you that someone) who is so bitter about a hurt that they are negative about everything? No matter what topic or person you bring up, they can only complain or speak negatively about it.

"Look at how God blessed you. You found ten hundred-dollar bills in your front yard!"

"Yeah, they're probably counterfeit."

God is warning us that this is a very slippery slope. Anger and unforgiveness toward those who have wronged us will slip us into a state of bitterness where we seek to even the score with them as our primary goal of life. There is no joy, peace, or compassion. Our intimacy with Father is lost as we become convinced that life, if not God, has dealt us an unfair hand.

I spent years bitter with a pastor who dressed me and my wife down from the pulpit without mentioning our names. Everyone knew who he was referring to. We left the church, refusing to return even though he came to our home, confessing and begging for our forgiveness. It was years before

I allowed God to deal with my heart and forgive him. By that time, he had moved on and was pastoring across the country. I was attending our fellowship's annual conference one year when someone tapped me on the shoulder. I turned to see that pastor and he bear-hugged me before I had a chance to run away! That day, God in His grace and mercy brought us together to give us opportunity to restore fellowship. I have never seen him again since. That was probably 25 years ago now. I shudder to think that I could still be carrying that root of bitterness around with me today.

With God's urgency, I would plead with you—if you are in a similar place, release that person to God's grace and pray:

> Father, I forgive *(their name)* for *(what they did or said)*. I release them now to Your grace and mercy, and I bless them in Your name. I repent of and renounce the spirit of bitterness that I have allowed to rule my mind and heart. I close that door now and ask for Your blood to cleanse and wash it away. I receive the infilling of Your Spirit in its place, complete with Your love, joy, and peace. I welcome You, Holy Spirit, and ask that you take up residence in me and guard my heart and mind. Thank You for setting me free and healing my broken heart.

Now, that door is closed. Jesus said He would shut doors no man can open (see Rev. 3:7). Do not go back and open it. You are free! Stay free!

As the old television infomercial says, "But wait, there's more!" He charges Isaiah to not "...be afraid of their threats, nor be troubled" (Isa. 8:12). We are not to panic, fear, or live in anxiety of what their slander or conspiracy may do. This is the bridge or transition—from the warning against getting even to God's solution. This bridge is to not live in fear of what their threats may do to you physically, financially (law suits), or reputationally (false accusations). The word *troubled* here literally means "to live in dread." How do I do that? How do I live in a state of peace, unconcerned about the raging storm of threats, loss of job, or any other consequence of their evil plan?

Philippians 4:6-8 has been my bridge, taking me from seeking vengeance to God's answer. If I replace anxiety with thankful prayer, I experience His peace, and that peace sets a guard over my mind so I can fill it with thoughts of verse 8.

The foundation for that peace is rooted in knowing who my Abba (Daddy) is: "The Lord of hosts" (Isa. 8:13). The commentary in the New King James Bible for this term says: "A title for *Yahweh* used over 50 times by Isaiah and more than 200 times in the Old Testament, it signifies He is the Deliverer surrounded by hosts of heavenly power" (footnote on Isaiah 6:3).

"...Him you shall hallow [sanctify, set apart as holy]; let Him be your fear[reverential awe], and let Him be your dread [the One you are in awe of]" (Isa. 8:13). Children are in awe of their dad. He can do anything, fix anything, and buy anything! We must recapture the awesomeness of our omnipotent Father. Then we can look across the bridge and compare that to the sudden puniness of the conspiracy being planned against us.

"He will be as a sanctuary..." (Isa. 8:14). Strong's Concordance defines *sanctuary* as "a consecrated thing or place, especially a palace of Jehovah; an asylum, chapel, hallowed part, holy place" (Strong's, H4720). Living in His presence is the safe place, like a palace. Of course! We've been adopted by the King. Where else would we live?

Have you crossed the bridge from the land of vengeance to view the awesomeness of your Father and see how completely He manages the protection of His children? Are you living in the palace of His presence, at peace, knowing you are safe in Him? Well if not, I invite you to cross that bridge—the palace door is open. Dad is waiting at the door to welcome you. You even have your own room! Your own private place of safety where you and Papa God can spend time together while He takes care of everything that's going on—on the other side of the bridge!

MOVING FROM FEAR TO STRENGTH

Strengthen the weak hands, and make firm the feeble knees.
Say to those who are fearful-hearted, "Be strong, do not
fear! Behold, your God will come with vengeance, with the
recompense of God; He will come and save you" (Isaiah 35:3-4).

To live in fear is to live in weakness. Fear paralyzes. Taken to its extreme, it can lead to panic attacks, high blood pressure, strokes, and worse. Emotionally it leads to hopelessness and depression. I know. I've been there. There must be hope as we face these perilous times. Where will that hope come from? David asks the question, "And now, Lord, what do I wait for?" then answers, "My hope is in You" (Ps. 39:7). Is yours?

Today our president, in a speech to the United Nations General Assembly, made the statement: "The future must not belong to those who slander the prophet of Islam." Does that mean that we who embrace Jesus Christ, and not the prophet of Islam, do not have a future on this planet? Does it then follow that if we take that stand, our future (life) is being threatened? Are we ready to take that stand? We have never had to in America—yet—and I fear because of that many will lose hope when (not if) we are faced with this level of persecution.

In that light, today's chapter becomes much more than a mere source of inspiration and encouragement to get us through a tough day at the office. It becomes essential to our very spiritual existence. So let's take our time and hear what Father wants to say to us.

Isaiah 35 begins with the promise of the manifestation of "the glory of the Lord" (Isa. 35:2). It is a prophetic picture of both Christ's first and second comings. But it follows the judgment of the nations in chapter 34, which you must read to understand the context in which God speaks to His people.

He encourages us to "Strengthen the weak hands..." (Isa. 35:3). God uses the same word here (*strengthen*) that is used with two other Old Testament patriarchs. He charged Joshua, "Have I not commanded you? Be strong..." (Josh. 1:9). It's the same word. It is also used of David: "...But David strengthened himself in the Lord his God" (1 Sam. 30:6).

It occurs to me that God doesn't give us a command He hasn't already equipped us to fulfill. Nehemiah said, "...The joy of the Lord is your strength" (Neh. 8:10). That's why He could challenge Joshua to be strong and David could strengthen himself. I am convinced, in this chaos we call the world today, that it is no longer optional whether we live in a supernatural lifestyle of power that flows out of intimacy with the Father. Those who choose to live in an American comfort zone of church attendance as the sole source of their spiritual strength, *will not stand* in this hour when we, even here in America, may be commanded to renounce our faith in Jesus Christ so that we don't "slander the prophet of Islam."

What turned the disciples from cowards who ran from the mob in the Garden of Gethsemane to the power-filled apostles who "turned the world upside down" (see Acts 17:6)? One event that became a lifestyle—the power of the Holy Spirit (see Acts 2:1-4). Forget the controversy about speaking in tongues. That's *not* why the Spirit was given. "You shall receive *power* when the Holy Spirit has come upon you..." (Acts 1:8). It is not about tongues, it's about power!

The apostles faced everything from the demonic to governmental opposition and *still* the church expanded. She was birthed in the Acts environment and she will thrive and expand today in that same environment: "...the kingdom of heaven suffers violence, and the violent take it by force" (Matt. 11:12). The lines in our world have now been drawn. There is no middle ground. We must, with Joshua, "...choose for yourselves this day whom you will serve.... But as for me and my house, we will serve the Lord" (Josh. 24:15).

On what basis can we, as the body of Christ, lock arms with one another and "Strengthen the weak hands, and make firm [literally, make alert in courage] the feeble knees" (Isa. 35:3)? We are also told to "Say to those who are fearful-hearted, 'Be strong do not fear!'" (Isa. 35:4). That is the message of this book. My heart is to encourage you to always remember, "...He who is in you is greater than he who is in the world (1 John 4:4).

There are three closing statements in Isaiah 35:4 that serve as the reasons why we can be strong and not fear:

1. "Behold, your God will come with vengeance..."

    Vengeance means "revenge." God keeps excellent records. Without repentance comes judgment. We are His children. He is a protective Father. Persecution of His children does not go unnoticed—or unpunished. Whether in this life or in eternity, the scales of His justice will be balanced.

2. "...with the recompense of God..."

    Recompense is "treatment of someone according to what they deserve." Can we have enough confidence in our God that, as we stand in the joy of His strength in this evil day, He will reward man's activity according to what they deserve—whether judgment or mercy? I believe that's why Jesus could admonish us to "...pray for those who spitefully use you and persecute you" (Matt. 5:44). We don't need to balance the scales. We need to be intercessors for them, "…knowing that the goodness of God leads [them] to repentance" (Rom. 2:4), and leave the scale-balancing to Him.

3. "…He will come and save you."

    We have already seen that *save* in the Hebrew is a form of *Yeshua*, meaning "to open wide or free, safe." At the center stage of our mind and heart must be the fact that Yeshua (Jesus) is our protection and salvation, not government or the world system.

It's all about who is the focus of our day, every day. And who is the Source of our strength? In challenging us to don "…the whole armor of God," Paul prefaces it by encouraging us to "…be strong in the Lord and in the power of His might" (see Eph. 6: 10-11).

All the satanic chaos engulfing the world today becomes microscopically puny when placed alongside Paul's victorious declaration:

> … *He raised Him from the dead and seated Him at His right hand in the heavenly places,* **far above** *all principality and power and might and dominion, and every name that is named, not only in this age but also in that which is to come. And He put all things under His feet…* (Ephesians 1:20-22).

Paul then adds that God "…raised us up together, and made us sit together in the heavenly places in Christ Jesus" (Eph. 2:6).

An old chorus I grew up with comes to mind and I leave it with you. Let the words be your focus and confession at the beginning and ending of each day:

- Turn your eyes upon Jesus. Look full in His wonderful face. And the things of earth will grow strangely dim in the light of His glory and grace.

THE OVERWHELMING PRESENCE

Fear not, for I am with you; be not dismayed, for I am your God. I will strengthen you, yes, I will help you, I will uphold you with My righteous right hand (Isaiah 41:10).

The overriding principle God has established throughout this book—the common thread linking every *fear not* verse—has been: His presence overwhelms fear, melting it away like snow before a strong spring sun. This verse centers on this truth and lists Father's activity on our behalf as a result of His abiding presence. We can actually see three aspects of our relationship with Father—His presence, His identity, and His activity.

1. HIS PRESENCE.

The first and most important reason God gives for us not to fear is that He is with us. When He says He is with us, He is saying He is equally involved in our life situation, accompanying and walking alongside of us. Sometimes that presence is tangible; we sense the electricity of His power surging through us. But more often it is a walk of faith in His declaration that He is with us. We accept the truth of His statement because He said it, not because we feel it. Jesus left His disciples with that statement (see Matt. 28:20). I wonder if they always felt His presence when they were beaten and imprisoned for their witness. The writer of Hebrews quotes from Deuteronomy 31:6,8 and Joshua 1:5 to remind us "I will never leave you nor forsake you" (Heb. 13:5). His daily presence is more than a promise; it is a statement of fact.

2. HIS IDENTITY.

He identifies Himself twice as the I AM, the same identity He gave to Moses in answer to his question, "Who shall I say sent me?" (see Exod. 3:13-14). Think of that. That same God who met Moses at the burning bush and accompanied him to Egypt, overturning a demonically inspired government to deliver His people from bondage, is the God who now meets us with the same identity and promise of His presence.

He further personalizes His identity to us as *your God*, using *Elohim*, the plural term in describing Himself. In other words, the fullness of the Godhead—Father, Son, and Holy Spirit—is accompanying us in our daily life journey, whatever that may entail. He who spoke the universe into existence, which is still being expanded, is actively engaged in your life on the speck of dust called earth. Kind of overwhelming, isn't it? But He prefaces that identity with *your*. This omnipotent Creator is not just God—He is *your* God. As much as you identify your possessions—my home, my car, my television, etc.—God is reminding us we have one possession we often overlook: "Hey guys. Remember Me? You *own* Me! I am *your* God, *your* possession. You use your car to get to your destination. Won't you use Me to get through the difficult times to your destiny?"

I once saw two pictures of the earth in space. The first showed the earth by itself—a beautiful blue globe suspended in space. The second picture superimposed the sun behind the earth. Suddenly, the earth became almost an indiscernible tiny black spot against the backdrop of the sun. Now, place yourself on that little black dot and superimpose the *Son* behind the sun! Now, how do the world's crises and yours measure up in comparison? It's all in the perspective, isn't it?

3. HIS ACTIVITY.

There are three interventions God promises us:

1. "I will strengthen you."

   He is saying, "I will show you what to do in the physical realm and give you courage for anything that comes in the mental and spiritual realms." In other words, wisdom and knowledge (see Josh.1:7; Eph.1:17, James 1:5). Not only will you have supernatural boldness (courage) to face the crisis, but the gifts of the Spirit (words of wisdom and knowledge) will be in operation in you to bring divine solutions.

2. "I will help you."

   The word for *help* there means "to surround; to protect or aid" (Strong's, H5826). Do you feel surrounded by the enemy in your circumstances? It reminds me of the story in 2 Kings 6 where Elisha's servant got up one morning, went outside, and saw that they were surrounded by the enemy. He panicked, ran to Elisha and said, "Look! What are we going to do?" (see 2 Kings 6:15). Elisha prayed that his servant's eyes would be opened. They were, and he saw "...the mountain was full of horses and chariots of fire all around Elisha" (2 Kings 6:17). The enemy that surrounded the men of God was itself surrounded by the heavenly host. Elisha's observation was, "Do not fear, for those who are with us are more than those who are with them" (2 Kings 6:16). God is saying to us in this time of global turmoil, "I have surrounded the enemy that has surrounded you, and I have surrounded you with My protection" (see Ps. 91).

3. "I will uphold [sustain] you with My righteous right hand."

   The right hand is the hand of power and authority. He is there to sustain us for the long term. This is not just a good church service, where we go home feeling good. It is a day-to-day, month-to-month, enduring strength obtained, as Bill Johnson says, through "extravagant worship." It is intimacy—a life partnership with the I AM, where we say with Moses, "If Your Presence does not go with us, do not bring us up from here" (Exod. 33:15). We rest where He rests; we move where He moves. In that divine bubble of His protective presence, we have no fear of whatever enemy may surround us, because *He* surrounds *them*!

FLUSH!

For I, the Lord your God, will hold your right hand, saying to you, "Fear not, I will help you" (Isaiah 41:13).

It is one of the first basic lessons taught to every newly-married man by his beautiful, sweet bride. She takes him by the hand and leads him into the bathroom and does a show and tell class with him: "See this handle? Flush, then, seat down! Now you try it." It is one of the more quickly learned lessons of marriage. Can I get a witness out there guys?

Yessiree Bob. We're quick learners. But, how about Israel in this verse? It seems verse 13 is almost a repeat of verse 10. There are some subtle differences here, though, that I believe will further encourage us to *fear not*.

The first one is God's identity. In verse 10, He identifies Himself, "I am your God." Here, He expands His identity to "I, the *Lord* you God," adding *Jehovah* to *Elohim*. *Jehovah* means, "the Self-Existent One" (Strong's, H3068). It emphasizes the strength that is defending us. He is saying, "I, the Self-Existent Father, Son, and Holy Spirit will hold your right hand." *Wow!* What a statement! What other allies do we need? No wonder Paul's conclusion was, "If God is for us, who can be against us?" (Rom. 8:31).

In Isaiah 41:10, God said He would uphold us with His righteous right hand. Here He says, "I...will hold your right hand" (Isa. 41:13). Remember, the right hand represents strength and authority. He is promising to be that for us. I guess you might say God's favorite Beatles song is "I Wanna Hold Your Hand"! I'm just saying! God then repeats His promise from verse 10, "I will help you."

But my attention was drawn to verses 11 and 12 as the reason why God said verse 13. God is letting us know the end result of the enemy who seeks to steal, kill, and destroy our lives (see John 10:10). If you have opposition—people or circumstances—that falls into any of these categories, you need to list them now and say the title of this chapter after it—*aloud*.

Ready? (See Isaiah 41:11-12.)

> *"All those who were incensed against you shall be ashamed and disgraced."* Flush!
>
> *"They shall be as nothing."* Flush!
>
> *"And those who strive with you shall perish."* Flush!
>
> *"You shall seek them and not find them."* Flush!
>
> *"Those who contended with you. Those who war against you shall be as nothing."* Flush!
>
> *"As a nonexistent thing."* Flush!

Ah, that feels better. As these events come into our lives, we need to do this daily. There is something to be said about regularity—but I won't say it. I'll let Paul say it. In his farewell message to the elders of the Ephesus church, Paul said about all of the opposition he endured for his stand for Christ, "But none of these things move me..." (Acts 20:24).

As our focus remains on Him and we carry His Presence, we will also be unmoved by any opposition and persecution aimed at us. We will be able to say the same words Paul said and then—*flush!*

WHO IS THAT IN THE MIRROR?

"Fear not, you worm Jacob, you men of Israel! I will help you," says the Lord and your Redeemer, the Holy One of Israel (Isaiah 41:14).

I was highly offended when I first read this. *God is calling me a worm? I* thought. Can't be. God only says good things about us. This must be a wrong translation of the Hebrew. So, I looked it up in Strong's Concordance. I shouldn't have. The meaning of *worm* is "a voracious maggot" (Strong's, H8438). Now I'm really offended! "God, you called me a voracious maggot! What's up with that?"

I sensed Him tell me to go into the bathroom.

"But I don't have to go," I protested.

"Go anyway," I felt Him say.

So I reluctantly obeyed. When I arrived, I felt Him instruct me to look in the mirror.

"Describe to Me the person looking back at you."

Suddenly, it all came together.

"I simply called you by the name you gave yourself. That is how you see yourself. Now go back and read the next line of that verse. It reads, *You men of Israel!*" God then emphatically said, "That's how *I* see you."

Then God reminded me of the meaning of the names *Jacob* and *Israel*. *Jacob* means "deceiver;" *Israel* means "prince." *Man* literally means "adult, full-grown, mature." Suddenly, I saw the whole picture: "Fear not, you voracious maggot deceiver. You adult princes." What a contrast. I realized I had come to believe the lie of the enemy—the first statement, that I am a worthless sinner. This was *not* God's statement; it was my self-evaluation based on the lie of the enemy. God sees me as an adult prince!

It reminds me of the "mirror" the 10 spies looked at when they gave their report of the Promised Land: "There we saw the giants...and *we were like grasshoppers in our own sight...*" (Num. 13:33). Look into the mirror and what do you see? A grasshopper? A voracious deceiving maggot? Who does Father see? An adult prince. *Identity determines destiny.* What you observe, you become. We must adopt His eyesight to see ourselves as He sees us, because His perspective is the reality.

Why does satan sell us this perspective? Well, a maggot is no match for a military enemy; a prince is. A maggot feeds on death; a prince represents his Father, the King, and advances the Kingdom wherever he goes. Which one of those presents a threat to the enemy? Will you be motivated to fight an enemy if you see yourself as a grasshopper—or maggot—in comparison? How about if you know your family lineage—as a prince who carries the unlimited authority of his Dad, the King? Do you see now why you're being lied to?

The reason God says to *fear not* is because you are not a worm, you are a prince. The enemy knows that as such, you carry all the King's royally delegated authority to overturn his kingdom and advance your Father's! If he can make you believe a lie as to your identity, he knows you won't use that authority against him—because you don't realize *you already have it* (see Luke 10:19; Matt. 28:18).

The next point the Lord showed me was that He made the statement, "I will help you" for the third time (see Isa. 41:10,13). Bill Johnson has said that when the Lord gives you the same word several times, it is not because it is more important than the ones He says only once. It is because He knows the resistance against it will be greater in the enemy's attempt to cause you to doubt it, so He reinforces it through repetition. He wants us to be assured, beyond any doubt, that in these difficult times He *will* be present to help us. We can rest in that promise. He knows what we have need of (see Matt. 6:32). We can trust His Word. He has said that He watches over His Word to perform it (see Jer. 1:12). David went so far as to say, "...For You have magnified Your Word above all Your name" (Ps. 138:2). Now, if He has been given "...the name which is above every name" (see Phil. 2:9), and He magnifies (literally "makes large") His Word even above that, do you think we can trust that Word?

His final word in verse 14 is to further expand His identity as He did in verses 10 and 13. Here He adds "Redeemer" and "Holy One of Israel." As Redeemer, He is our "next of kin and as such qualified to buy back a relative's property, marry his widow, etc" (Strong's, H1350). Satan claimed ownership of us through sin. Jesus paid the price—it cost Him every drop of His blood—and bought us back. We now operate under new ownership!

He, the Holy (Sacred) One of Israel, has identified Himself with us, His not-so-perfect children. As He, the Holy One, identifies our body as His temple, He comes in and dwells in us and His holiness becomes our holiness. What a divine setup! He has left no room for the accuser. To attack our holiness is to attack His holiness. It also makes him a trespasser on God's property.

That's how we must address him when he comes with his fear: "You are trespassing on God's property. Leave *now*, in Jesus' Name and by the authority He has given me by my position as an adopted child of the King—a prince (or princess) representing His Kingdom. I know that's who I am because I've looked in the mirror!"

UNDER OMNIPOTENT OWNERSHIP

But now, thus says the Lord, who created you, O Jacob, and he who formed you, O Israel: "Fear not, for I have redeemed you; I have called you by name; you are Mine" (Isaiah 43:1).

Who owns you? Somebody does. We hate to admit it. Sounds too much like slavery to be "owned" by someone. We like to consider ourselves as free, independent agents. What right does God have to claim ownership of us? There are several ways one can claim ownership:

1. "CREATED"

The Lord identifies Himself as the One who created you. It seems kind of basic, but when you create or build something, doesn't that make you its owner? The only way you can surrender ownership is through gift or sale to someone. You built it—you own it.

God's first claim to ownership is creation. We are His idea. But we are not an ornamental creation. Although we were created for His pleasure, we were also to partner with Him in advancing His Kingdom (see Rev. 4:11; Eph. 2:10).

2. "FORMED"

Not only did He create us, He formed us into His image (see Gen. 1:26). This is a particular kind of creation. It is creating from a blueprint rather than randomly. *Form* means "squeezing into shape; to mold into a form, especially as a potter" (Strong's, H3335). This personalizes creation. He had a unique mold in mind when He thought of you. You went from idea to being because He wanted fellowship with a particular person—*you*. He formed your personality uniquely, your likes and dislikes, your gifting—all that makes you uniquely you. He squeezed all that into His mold—you! That's what makes you uniquely special to Him. He is jealously protective of you and says "...he who touches you touches the apple of His eye" (Zech. 2:8).

I just sense Father wants me to ask this question here: "Have you been or are you now being abused—physically, sexually, verbally, emotionally?" If so, especially if it involves a family member or spouse, you may feel (or have been told) you must stay in the situation. Or, you may be angry at God for "allowing" it to go on. Please hear me—that is *not* God's will or destiny for you. Remove yourself from that situation immediately. Get help to do it—from a pastor, friend, or counselor. There are discreet shelters where the abuser cannot find you. But know God did *not* approve of it. You are the apple of His eye, and He wants to bind up your wounds and reveal how special you are to Him (see Isa. 61:1-2). He rejoices over you with singing and dances over you with joy (see Zeph. 3:17). Anything else you've been told is a lie, and believing the lie empowers the liar. You are worth every drop of blood that Jesus shed—that makes you of the highest value in all of creation. So don't let anyone tell you that you are worthless. You were formed in His image; you look just like your Daddy!

3. "REDEEMED"

This is the third claim to His ownership of you. Adam and Eve surrendered ownership of the human race to satan. But God still considered us His, and so He and His Son came up with a plan to buy us back—redeem us in order to restore us to the Rightful Owner. Value is determined by the price one is willing to pay, such as for a family heirloom in order to reclaim its ownership. The owner shouldn't have to pay anything for the heirloom—it was his in the first place. But because of its intrinsic value, he is willing to pay any price to reclaim it. That's the picture of our value to the Father and Jesus. He was willing and *did* pay the ultimate price—for you and me.

4. "NAMED"

About a year ago, Lori and I brought home a new little bundle of joy—an eight-week-old Sheltie puppy. The first thing we did was give her a name—Abby ("source of joy"). It confirmed ownership; she was now ours. If you have children, I'm sure you chose a name for them soon after or even before they were born. (If you didn't, don't tell them; it could traumatize them!)

In our Western society, we usually name our children the most popular, trendy, or personal favorite name at the time. In the Bible, names carried meaning—usually a character description. So when God said, "I have called you by your name" (Isa. 43:1), He was not only confirming ownership, He was describing character. So what is your name? Like yesterday, notice again that God calls His people first by the name given by man—Jacob (deceiver). Then He refers to them by the name *He* gave them—Israel (prince). There is a stark contrast between the way man sees you and the way God sees you. Since God is declaring ownership, whose opinion are you going to believe—man's (deceiver) or God's (prince)? Who are you anyway?

5. "CLAIMED"

"You are Mine" (Isa. 43:1). As used here, *mine* is the greatest possessive pronoun in the language! It is absolute. It leaves no doubt. It is the signed adoption papers identifying in whose family we now belong. When you pay off your house or car note, you have a deed identifying you as its owner. This is God's title deed to us. He is declaring to us and the kingdom of darkness: "I have paid the price. I have bought him or her back. I have legally changed their name. Here is the title deed." He takes it, stamps it in His blood, shows it to the devil, and then hands it to us. In crimson red, the stamp reads: "You are Mine!"

YOU ARE NOT ALONE!

*Fear not, for I am with you; I will bring your descendants
from the east, and gather you from the west* (Isaiah 43:5).

I solation. It's terrible to feel all alone, whether it's from a broken relationship
or taking a stand for your convictions. And today, taking a stand for biblical morality and righteousness may very well require you to stand alone in
this anti-God environment.

God's message here is to remind us that even when we pass through the
waters, He will be with us (see Isa. 43:2). As in previous verses we've looked
at, God's number-one reason for telling us to *fear not* is because "I am with
you" (Isa. 43:5). His presence is the key and the only requirement for victorious supernatural living. Living in and carrying His presence wherever we go
is living the supernatural lifestyle.

Like viewing a diamond from different angles, we are given many beautiful aspects of the fruit of living without fear. Israel was facing captivity and
deportation—the end of their existence as a nation (similar to us today).
Amidst that terrifying threat, God promised His presence; then "turned the
diamond" and revealed the sparkling hope of future restoration. They would
not remain isolated and alone as God's people (see Isa. 43:5-7). Furthermore,
the restoration would be complete: "*Everyone* who is called by My name…"

(Isa. 43:7). Unity will come to the body of Christ when our focus becomes singular and universal—His Presence.

David declared, "*One thing* I have desired of the Lord, that will I seek..." (Ps. 27:4). That desire was to live life in His Presence, behold His beauty, and commune with Him. When the body of believers has nothing else to fall back on, then passion for His Presence will become our only focus. Result—*unity!* It will be the answer to Jesus' prayer in John 17: "that they all may be one, as You, Father, are in Me, and I in You; that they also may be one in Us, that the world may believe that You sent Me" (John 17:21).

The reason God is going to bring us together as a mighty army, never to feel isolated or alone, is described in verse 4. It is how He feels about us! Listen to these three love statements from Daddy God to us, the apple of His eye:

1. "Since you were precious in My sight" (Isa. 43:4).

    Precious there means "to be heavy (with value); to make rare (and thus valuable)" (Strong's, H3365). This is when you feel all alone—the only believer—like Elijah did: "...I alone am left; and they seek to take my life" (1 Kings 19:10). God is saying you are precious because you are a rare breed and thus very valuable, like a one-of-a-kind diamond. Being rare is not necessarily a bad thing. After all, aren't we "a new creation" in Christ (see 2 Cor. 5:17), "his own special people" (see 1 Pet. 2:9)? He is saying, "I have made you to stand out; you are special, set apart to carry My glory." What a privilege! As such, we may stand alone as salt and light that others can see, taste, and follow.

2. "You have been honored" (Isa. 43:4).

    Honored also means "heavy," but in the opposite way of *precious*. It means "heaviness through abundance, numerous, rich" (Strong's, H3513). We house the abundance of God's glory, presence, and power that the world is so desperately seeking. We may be rare, as a set-apart vessel, but in that vessel rests the abundance of God's glory. God is saying to you, "You are special, set apart for Me, and you carry the abundance of My glory."

3. "And I have loved you" (Isa. 43:4).

   Strong's Concordance describes this love as "having affection for (sexually or otherwise)" (Strong's, H157). It encompasses love at all levels, from friendship to marital intimacy. Do you realize that He is drawn to you, attracted to you? Sorry guys—you are *attractive* to Him.

These three statements from God to us are what Valentine's Day cards are made of. Have you ever made any or all of these statements to your spouse or fiancée? (If you haven't, shame on you!) "You are so precious to me, Honey." "I honor you." "I love you."

Because of how He feels about us, He makes an even greater promise: He will bring our descendants—our sons and daughters—from the ends of the earth back to Him. Do you have children away from God? Wherever they are geographically and spiritually, He has promised He will gather and bring them back. He has heard the intercessory cries of mothers and fathers for their children. Now declare it to the four winds: "Give them up! Do not keep them back!" (see Isa. 43:5-6). They are not only yours, they are His. There is a multitude, a great end-time harvest being gathered in "the valley of decision" (see Joel 3:14).

We are *not* alone!

FEAR OF MISSING HIS BLESSING

Thus says the Lord who made you and formed you from the womb, who will help you: "Fear not, O Jacob My servant; and you, Jeshurun, whom I have chosen" (Isaiah 44:2).

I cannot count the number of times I have become depressed or even angry at God as I have seen God pour out blessings on other believers, especially in the area of finances. "What about me?" I would whine. "I've been faithful in giving and tithing, and yet we continue to struggle financially. When is it going to be our turn?"

Sound familiar? Or am I the only "sucking your thumb" 50-year-old Christian? My complaints extended to spiritual blessings as well—in revival meetings where it seemed everyone else was laid out on the floor, laughing or crying or experiencing gold dust or some other manifestation, while I stood there feeling and experiencing nothing.

Getting beyond the childish whining, there was something deeper to my frustration—hunger for Him. I so wanted to experience intimacy with Him that went beyond the religion of performance—reading X number of Bible chapters a day or praying X number of hours per day, etc. I could not meet the performance levels religion required and so, as a result, felt God was disappointed in me and withheld His blessings from me. If you add to that my personal and moral failures, you can understand why I chose to take up residence in the house of hopelessness.

Today's text blows that house into splinters! God reminds us who we are in relation to Him as we discussed in previous chapters:

1. He made us.

2. He formed us.

3. He will help us.

4. We are His servant.

5. He chose us for intimacy.

He expands on a couple of these to emphasize how personally involved He is in our life. For example, this time when He says that He formed us, He adds "from the womb." He wants us to understand He was intricately involved with us *before* we were born. It is as He said to Jeremiah, "Before I formed you in the womb I knew you; before you were born I sanctified you…" (Jer. 1:5). The process of that intricate involvement in our formation is detailed by David in Psalms 139:14-16. Such personal attention must elevate our value to Him immeasurably.

He also says He has *chosen* us. That word means "to try or select" (Strong's, H977). It speaks of a free-will selection. He didn't have to; He *wanted* to. His relationship with us is one of *His* choosing because of His love and passion toward us.

But the most important message of His *fear not* in verse 2 is actually verse 3. It seems from the context that, because of their sin and resulting judgment, Israel feared they had permanently forfeited God's blessings on them and their future generations. This is the fear God addresses when He promises to "…pour water on him who is thirsty" (Isa. 44:3). The picture here is melting a solid into a liquid and then pouring it out into a mold, allowing it to harden into that image. Water in Scripture always refers to the

Holy Spirit. God's promise is to pour out His Spirit on us to mold us into an image, that image being of Jesus: "...being transformed into the same image from glory to glory, just as by the Spirit of the Lord" (2 Cor. 3:18). There is only one requirement for God to fulfill this promise—thirst (see Matt. 5:6).

He also posts a flash flood warning for dry ground. Life has a tendency to dry us out spiritually and emotionally. In 2010 and 2011, we suffered through extreme drought here in southern Alabama. We averaged between 15 and 20 inches below normal in rainfall each year. The ground was like concrete. Gardening without irrigating was useless. That condition has also frequently described my spiritual status. Does it yours? It is in those times that Father promises to flood us with His presence for refreshing new life. When He says, "I will," no further discussion is necessary.

Finally, His promise of blessing extends to our offspring (the next generation) and descendants (unlimited future generations). God's Spirit, literally His "exhaled breath," is promised to our future generations, and His blessing (literally, "benediction or prosperity") is upon our children. He leaves no one out. Our circumstances or our children's current spiritual condition may scream out against these statements. But our choice is clear. We can believe the truth, the "I wills" of God's promises, or believe the lies of our feelings or circumstances. The only thing that gives power to a lie is believing it. I don't know about you, but I refuse to believe the lie.

I invite you to declare with me His truths over us, our families, and future generations:

I declare today that because I am thirsty, the water of His Spirit is poured out on me, molding me more into His image every day. I am flooded by His presence when my ground is emotionally and spiritually parched. His blessing rests upon my children, and His Spirit will be poured out without measure upon my grandchildren and all future generations.

It is I AM who has declared these "I wills" over me, and therefore I come into agreement with Heaven, allowing the angels to fulfill their assignment, and I will declare them daily because "All the promises of God in Him are Yes, and in Him Amen, to the glory of God through us" (2 Cor. 1:20).

FEAR OF CONFLICTING PROCLAMATIONS

Do not fear, nor be afraid; have I not told you from that time, and declared it? You are My witnesses. Is there a God besides Me? Indeed there is no other Rock, I know not one
(Isaiah 44:8).

We live in the age of instant and continuous information—the Internet, multiple 24-hour news networks, talk shows, etc. There are literally thousands of voices out there proclaiming the state of the world, economy, politics, etc. Based on those proclamations, declarations of what is coming are made. Most are dire, even frightening. Many are contradictory, leading to confusion.

As I write this, we are five weeks from our presidential election. The voices are deafening, each with their own set of promises and predictions, each backed by their own set of statistics and facts. The all-important question is: Which voice am I to believe?

This is the choice Israel faces in this text. They are hearing proclamations and declarations that don't line up with what God has declared over them (see Isa. 44:1-5). Now they must choose whose voice they will heed. So must we.

Before I believe a politician, preacher, salesman, etc., I want to know their credentials—their background, character, and track record. God hands Israel His "resume" in verse 6, reminding them of His identity and credentials.

How about this for a resume?

1. "The Lord"—Jehovah, the Self-Existent or Eternal One

2. "King of Israel"—reigning royalty

3. "Redeemer"—the next of kin who buys back a relative's property or marries their widow

4. "The Lord of hosts"—(see number one above) over a massive army organized for war

5. "The First and the Last"—the Head or Beginning, first in place, time, or rank; at the same time, hindermost

Here is what I believe He is saying to us today in these tumultuous times:

> My child, I know there are so many voices out there speaking what is and what is to come. These voices have troubled you and brought fear as they predict and threaten what is coming. I, too, have a voice in these matters, but I want to identify whose voice this is so that you may have confidence to embrace My message to you. I am the Self-Existent Eternal One, your reigning King, but also your next of kin who has bought you back and married you as My bride. I lead a massive angelic army organized for war on your behalf, and I have always been in charge, the Head of all things from before the beginning of time, and I will be the One who will wrap everything up at the end. I am the Father, the Son, and the Spirit. You need to look to none other for safety and provision, for there is no other.

Is He all that to you today? If not, He wants to be. We cannot live these days in peace, power, and joy until we identify this Voice and embrace Him.

Since there is no other God, the next logical question is "Who can proclaim as I do?" (Isa. 44:7). If another voice *is* out there, "...let him declare it and set it in order for me" (Isa. 44:7). In other words, "Okay, you think you know better than I do? Go ahead, state your case and set Me straight. Correct Me and show Me where I'm wrong, "since I appointed...the things that are coming and shall come" (Isa. 44:7). Do I sense a little sarcasm here?

One of the things I'm seeing as I write this devotional is that God never tells us to *fear not* without telling us why, as He has done here. Now He can again encourage us not to fear or be afraid (see Isa. 44:8).

We as children become frightened when scary things happen. When our children were young, we took them with us to a church-sponsored haunted house for Halloween. I won't get into the obvious theological contradiction there, but it so terrified my five-year-old son that we had to leave and subsequently deal with nightly nightmares, despite our reassurances.

God is reminding us of His reassurances in scary times. "Have I not told you from that time, and declared it? You are My witnesses" (Isa. 44:8). "I've told you not to fear, remember? You were there—you witnessed it."

As a statement of finality, He asks a question He already answered in verse 6. "Is there a God besides Me? No, I already told you that." He reinforces that answer now by saying, "Indeed, there is no other Rock; I know not one" (Isa. 44:8).

Do you? We need to quiet ourselves with a divine filter of worship that drowns out all the other voices of proclamation and learn to "lean into God" (Bill Johnson's phrase) and hear only His voice. I'll bet, as we do, we'll hear, "Peace be still!"

FEAR OF THE REPROACH OF MEN

Listen to Me, you who know righteousness, you people in
whose heart is My law: Do not fear the reproach of men, nor
be afraid of their insults (Isaiah 51:7).

Kids and teenagers are especially sensitive about their self-image. They crave acceptance by their peers. They can also be the cruelest toward those they don't accept.

I hated school for that reason. I was on the receiving end of the cruel mocking and name-calling from the cool crowd. Growing up in a strict Pentecostal holiness family, I was not allowed to participate in school activities like dances or sports. That labeled me as a holy roller, square, and geek, to name the kinder ones. As I moved into junior high school, I developed a severe case of acne. That earned me the title "Zit-face." Whoever said, "Sticks and stones may break my bones but names will never hurt me," must have grown up in the forest with Bambi. I grew to hate myself and avoided being around people. I was a loner—and enjoyed it. I developed a love for weather-watching, a solitary hobby that needed no other participants.

Names *do* hurt, especially for children who are developing their self-image and trying to learn where they fit in this world. For most of my adult life, I believed I was ugly and inferior. The craving for acceptance eventually produced moral failure that, when discovered and exposed, spiraled my emotional and spiritual life downward into a suicidal hopelessness. With virtually no counseling, it took me 20 years crawling out of that hole. If I had been exposed earlier to the teachings of Bill Johnson and the culture of honor out of Bethel Church in Redding, California, who knows? Maybe... just maybe.

We are living in an age today where the insults and name-calling far exceed what I faced in school. It is now national, political, even worldwide. Today, we who stand for righteousness are labeled homophobes, racists, dangerous, and anti-abortionists, to name a few of those that are printable.

Father encourages us not to fear "...the reproach of men..." (Isa. 51:7). I looked up *reproach* both in Strong's Concordance and the New World Dictionary of the American Language. I was shocked at the depth of evil this word encompasses. You might not want young children to read this definition due to its explicitness. The combined definition of reproach is: "abuse; haughty and contemptuous rudeness; insulting and humiliating treatment or language; scornful insult; something to be ashamed of; the external genitals of either sex."

Have you ever been subjected to this level of insult and/or name-calling? I have. It's not only hurtful; it is intimidating. Christianity is at the center of this attack. Take a stand for righteousness and you will be labeled every vile name in the book. Attempts to silence us are under way by listing as *hate speech* any stand against behavior Scripture labels as *sin*.

It is under these relentless attacks and threats that Father tells us to fear not. He is talking directly to us, His children: "Listen to Me, you who know righteousness, you people in whose heart is My law..." (Isa. 51:7). Why should we not fear? The answer is: "For the moth will eat them up like a garment, and the worm will eat them like wool..." (Isa. 51:8).

The moth and worm eating them up speaks of how temporary our accusers are and how insignificant their attacks. Yet under the New Covenant, Father's heart is for them, not against them. He asks us to "...bless those who curse you, do good to those who hate you, and pray for those who spitefully use you and persecute you" (Matt. 5:44). That is impossible to do if we attempt it as merely dutiful obedience to a command. We must pray in the Spirit, for the Spirit prays the heart of the Father. We must ask Father for His heart toward these accusers. His compassion is overwhelming, and His heart breaks for them. So must ours—on both counts.

In our text, Father states that His righteousness is forever and His salvation is from generation to generation (see Isa. 51:8). Life is temporary, but Father lives in eternity. Evil attacks against His children are temporary and will end, but He has prepared eternity for us and our future generations. Peter expressed the heart of the Father when he said Father was "...not willing that any should perish but that all should come to repentance" (2 Pet. 3:9). Jesus wept over the city of Jerusalem, the very people who would soon cry, "Crucify Him!" and call for a murderer to be freed rather than Jesus (see Matt. 23:37). Since we already have the mind of Christ, we must also have His heart (see 1 Cor. 2:16). When He was abused, His response was "Father, forgive them, for they do not know what they do" (Luke 23:34). When we have His heart, we will pray likewise toward those who reproach us. It is then, and only then, that the goofy quote I wrote earlier will become true: "Names will never hurt me."

FEAR OF SHAME FROM THE PAST

Do not fear, for you will not be ashamed; neither be disgraced, for you will not be put to shame; for you will forget the shame of your youth, and will not remember the reproach of your widowhood anymore (Isaiah 54:4).

I have told you my story already—standing before my congregation reading my resignation due to moral failure. That is the definition of *shame*. You may have your own. The shame became so overwhelming that it led me to the brink of suicide. It was at that point that precious Holy Spirit brought me to this verse, and I felt something break in me. Hope began to rise up in me for the first time in years and I remember thinking, "Yes, maybe there *will* be a tomorrow." (Title of my next book? Hmmm.) So this one is highly personal to me.

What about you? What part of your past has formed a ball and chain around your ankles that you are dragging around with you? Please, I beg you—let Holy Spirit apply His healing salve to your wounds. How long will you allow your past to rob you of the joy of His presence (see Ps. 16:11)? If you have repented of it, it is already forgiven and forgotten by God (see Jer. 31:34; Ps. 103:12). You say there is nothing to be joyful about? What about your salvation or your strength to daily live for Him (see Ps. 51:12; Neh. 8:10)? Satan has robbed me of joy over long-ago forgiven sin that was removed from my life by Jesus' blood. I am counting on God restoring the years of joy the enemy has stolen (see Joel 2:25). When do you want your payback? How about starting today?

To do that, we must follow Father's instructions in this text. His first words are, "Do not fear." I believe He is saying to us, "You are in relationship with Me now. That means you are in a safe place. Your forgiveness is so complete, shame cannot enter. I am not ashamed of you. I am proud of you. Why do you choose to remember that which I choose not to? As long as you are in My family, you will never be ashamed" (see Isa. 54:4).

He also says we will not be *disgraced*. That word means "to wound, taunt or insult." Let's face it, in some people's minds you'll never be restored. "You might be forgiven," I was told, "but you'll never be used in ministry again." That's being disgraced. Father says there is no disgrace in His house. You are "accepted in the Beloved" (Eph. 1:6). You can't be accepted and disgraced at the same time.

Next, Father refers to the future with Him. How will our relationship with Him proceed from here? Will Father throw our past in our face if we fail Him some time in the future? *No!* "You will (future tense) not be put to shame" (Isa. 54:4). Maybe you've been in a relationship where, in the heat of an argument, the person brought up a past offence you thought was taken care of—forgiven and forgotten. And it was thrown in your face, reopening the old wound. It will *never* happen in Father's family.

Once we've embraced that statement, we can flow into Father's next one: "…you will forget the shame of your youth" (Isa. 54:4). I was unfaithful to my wife the first 11 years of our marriage. I carried the shame of that sin for the next 20 years. The tragic thing that I now understand is that I didn't have to. Doing so retarded the restoration of my relationships with both God and my wife. The greater the sin we've committed, the greater the subconscious need to punish ourselves and grovel in shame. We feel unworthy of instant forgiveness. What that does is cheapen the blood of Jesus—His sacrifice wasn't good enough. I see some of you living in a cesspool of shame and Father is saying, "I have removed the cover. You are free to come out and leave the cesspool of your youth behind." In Christ, you are a new creation (see 2 Cor. 5:17); baptism is a prophetic statement that we have died to the past and live in "newness of life" (Rom. 6:4).

Finally, Father also prophesies over us that we "will not remember the reproach of your widowhood anymore" (Isa. 54:4). For *reproach*, look at yesterday's definition. *Widowhood* speaks of separation from your spouse. Father is saying, "That which separated you from Me will no longer have any effect on our relationship. Intimacy has been restored. I don't want you to remember what caused our separation anymore. It's over, gone; we are back together!"

If there is any separation in our relationship with Father, it is because we have a memory problem—we are remembering what we should have forgotten. God also has a memory issue, but it's not a problem. He always seems to forget what He has forgiven. He is inviting us to do the same!

FEAR OF OPPRESSION AND TERROR

In righteousness you shall be established; you shall be far from oppression, for you shall not fear; and from terror, for it shall not come near you (Isaiah 54:14).

We have talked about terror on the international stage (see days 54 and 55). I believe here God is encouraging us not to fear these things as they come against us *personally*. Psychologists call them *phobias*. God calls them *oppression* and *terror*.

Whatever we don't have faith for, we fear. There is an old joke that goes, "He told me, 'Cheer up. Things could be worse.' So, I cheered up; sure enough, things got worse." Well in response to that, God does not say oppression and terror will not come. His message to us is, "you shall not fear" when it does come. Why does He say that?

Before we discover the answer to that, what does He mean by *oppression* and *terror* that would cause us to fear? I was surprised to discover that oppression here means "injury, fraud, distress, unjust gain, extortion, a thing deceitfully gotten" (Strong's, H6233). To me, this speaks directly to economic issues—distress caused by being defrauded in business.

Several years ago, my wife's car broke down and had to be towed. I had met a mechanic briefly when he was working on my neighbor's car across the street from me. I called him and he said to have the car brought to his shop. He quickly "diagnosed" (by looking at it) that the engine was blown and it would cost between $800 to $900 to fix. He needed $500 up front so he could purchase the engine. Four weeks later and after numerous phone calls, I angrily told him the car would either be done by the end of the week or I would take him to court. That Friday, I went to pick it up, paid him the balance, and drove it home, upon which the engine stalled permanently again as I pulled into my driveway. As I quickly "lost my salvation" and called him, he said he would be right over to look at it. Several hours later, he showed up, said it needed such and such; he would go pick up the parts and be right back. That's the last time I ever saw him. I won the small claims court case—where he did not show up—in the amount of $936, which has never been collected. All follow-up addresses and phone numbers have proven to be bogus. Do you think that might fit the description of "oppression" here? I'm sure you could tell me some horror stories of your own.

Terror here means "dissolution, ruin, consternation, destruction, dismaying" (Strong's, H7288). Webster's New World Dictionary defines *consternation* as "great fear or shock that makes one feel helpless or bewildered." That was me, if you add "angry." It refers to financial ruin as a result of being defrauded in business. That can range from being ripped off by paying twice as much for something to being defrauded in an illegal or unethical business deal. I think we've all had experience in this arena at some time. It does make you feel hopeless. But that's where God's encouragement comes in. He said we would not have to fear these things because He would keep them far from us. Well, they sure have come close to me! I told you about one; there have been many more. So it seems God has not kept His promise to me.

So in asking Daddy why, I immediately saw a common thread in all of the incidents that happened to me: I never once prayed for guidance or revelation in making *any* of these business decisions! This was true in everything from home-based businesses to major purchase decisions. They all seemed obvious or common sense decisions to me. Maybe in an honest world where you can take people at their word, that would be true. But, in today's world, where identity theft is a multi-billion dollar business, we need divine wisdom and guidance more than ever before we sign a contract, make a purchase, or start a business.

Proverbs is the book of wisdom, much of it to do with business: "Dishonest scales are an abomination to the Lord, but a just weight is His delight" (Prov. 11:1). "The rich rules over the poor, and the borrower is servant to the lender" (Prov. 22:7). These are just two of many examples. God instructs us to "...lean not on your own understanding; in *all* your ways [decisions] acknowledge Him, and *He shall direct your paths*" (Prov. 3:5-6).

God's promise is that when we ask Him for His opinion *first*, that's how He will keep these things far from us. When David's enemies attacked Ziklag, stealing his and his men's wives and children and burning their city, David "...inquired of the Lord, saying, 'Shall I pursue...?'" God answered, "Pursue" (1 Sam. 30:8). Indeed, this was a major decision, involving the lives of hundreds of people. The instinctive response would have been, "Let's go after them," but David suppressed his emotions, and inquired of the Lord. And that is the secret to keeping oppression and terror far from us. Father will do His part if we will do ours. He will not impose His will or counsel upon us, but leaves an open invitation for us to come to Him (see Prov. 3:5-6; James 1:5). Then, through His wise counsel, He will steer us around the grenades of business and financial terror that permeate our society today. *That's* His promise!

FEAR OF NOT BEING RESTORED

"Therefore, do not fear, O My servant Jacob," says the Lord,
"nor be dismayed, O Israel; for behold, I will save you from
afar, and your seed from the land of their captivity. Jacob
shall return, have rest and be quiet, and no one shall make
him afraid" (Jeremiah 30:10).

After I resigned my church in disgrace, I spiraled into the blackness of depression, shame, and guilt. My wife was on the verge of an emotional breakdown, our marriage on the brink of dissolution. I knew it was my fault—and my counselor emphasized that in no uncertain terms. But what really angered me was that my wife's counselor told her it was all *her* fault! What? "If you had been a better wife to him, he wouldn't have strayed." *What?* If there has ever been a "perfect" wife on this planet, it is Lori. If she had a fault, it was that she was too trusting of me. The mother of our three children, a pastor's wife, never entertaining a twinge of temptation to be unfaithful, a professional nurse, and a gorgeous woman, what man could ask for anything more? And yet it was *her* fault?

Because of those conclusions, we were told we would probably never be restored to ministry. Have you suffered loss and been told that God may forgive you, but would never restore you?

This is where Israel was. In captivity because of their own sin, they had lost hope of ever being restored to their homeland. Indeed, their captivity lasted a full 70 years—an entire generation. But here in Jeremiah 30, God brought a message of hope to Israel and to us. Let's look at it.

God's first instruction to Jeremiah was to "...write in a book for yourself all the words that I have spoken to you" (Jer. 30:2). Do you journal? You should. Lori and I record all prophetic words spoken over us as well as personal words He speaks to us during our quiet time. A written word seems to establish what He has spoken and offers something to fall back on when circumstances seem to contradict what was spoken. I have a prophetic word spoken in 1984 that I still have and refer to. That word kept hope of restoration alive in me in the dark years of the '80s. Keep a journal!

The message God wants written down is: "...I will bring back from captivity My people...and I will cause them to return to the land..." (Jer. 30:3). There it is; the message of restoration! So in our text, He encourages His people to not fear or be dismayed, because He will carry out His promise to restore them to their land (see Jer. 30:10). Our confidence, even while we are in the captivity of loss, must rest in His promise of restoration: "...I will save you from afar" (Jer. 30:10). He will *save* me—bring me back to my God-ordained destiny. He told Jeremiah earlier, "...I am ready to perform My word" (Jer. 1:12), and His word to those of us who have suffered loss due to our own sin is this: "I will bring you back and restore what the cankerworm has eaten" (see Joel 2:25).

Second, God not only promises to restore to us what the enemy has stolen, but to our children as well: "I will save...your *seed* from the land of *their* captivity" (Jer. 30:10). Do you have children in the captivity of addiction, sickness, bitterness, etc.? You've been praying for them to return to the Lord for years but they seem as far away from God today as ever. You have not seen any movement; they're still in captivity. Latch onto this promise today—journal it! He will save your seed from the land of their captivity!

The end result of God's restoration for us and our children is threefold—return, rest, and quiet (see Jer. 30:10). To *return* means to go back to the starting point. To *rest* means to be still or idle. To be *quiet* means to be peaceful. To embrace God's promise of restoration will result in reinstating us in the area that was lost, be it ministry, career, marriage, relationship, physical, emotional or spiritual health. "For the gifts and the calling of God are irrevocable" (Rom. 11:29). He cannot revoke what He has given us—*He will* restore it! "He who calls you is faithful, who also will do it" (1 Thess. 5:24).

So *rest*: "Be still, and know that I am God..." (Ps. 46:10). His invitation to enter His rest (see Heb. 4) still stands: "Come to Me, all you who labor and are heavy laden, and I will give you rest" (Matt. 11:28).

And finally, be *quiet*—peaceful: "In returning and rest you shall be saved; in quietness and confidence shall be your strength..." (Isa. 30:15).

Friends, God is our loving Father. His dreams for us are good (see Jer. 29:11; Eph. 3:20). Jesus took our punishment—there is no punishment in grace. It is His *goodness* that leads us to repentance (see Rom. 2:4). Repentance brings restoration! So we can rest in *His* peace—and we don't have to be dead to rest in this peace! Restoration is assured. Fear not!

FEAR OF FATHER'S DISCIPLINE

"Do not fear, O Jacob My servant," says the Lord, "For I am with you; for I will make a complete end of all the nations to which I have driven you, but I will not make a complete end of you. I will rightly correct you, for I will not leave you wholly unpunished" (Jeremiah 46:28).

I thought of skipping this one. I figured you would, so why bother writing it? No one likes to address or submit to discipline. So maybe you will skip it. I pray you won't. I am a product of Father's discipline. Without it, I probably wouldn't be alive today—no exaggeration.

Discipline is not a fun topic, whether it concerns bratty children in Wal-Mart, rebellious teenagers at home, or ministers gone morally astray. If we are the disciplinarian, we are not popular. If we are the disciplined, we avoid it or endure it unhappily. Where do we begin our discussion? Okay, Lord, You take over. We want to *really* hear Your heart on this.

1. The necessity for discipline

    Any discussion on discipline must begin here. The purpose of discipline is to correct, not punish. To inflict pain in anger is abuse, not discipline. That's a strong statement, but it's true, and punishment is not the Father's heart. The punishment for our sin was taken by Jesus on the cross. Discipline is reserved for family members, and only when and as needed.

My son, do not despise the chastening of the Lord, nor detest His correction; for whom the Lord loves He corrects, just as a father the son in whom he delights (Proverbs 3:11-12).

Notice, this is a "family meeting." He addresses us as "My son." (Ladies, that's literally, "My child.") Beyond that, He identifies us as "whom the Lord loves" and "the son in whom He delights." Discipline is an act of love because He delights in us.

This passage is quoted in Hebrews 12. There, the author expands the idea, saying that "without chastening" we are "illegitimate and not sons" (Heb. 12:8). Discipline is a mark of family identity.

2. The limits of discipline

    "I will not make a complete end of you" (Jer. 46:28). Destruction is not the purpose of discipline. Proverbs says, "Foolishness is bound up in the heart of a child; the rod of correction will drive it far from him" (Prov. 22:15). Father's heart for us is to correct foolish attitudes and behavior. It is not to end our dreams and dismantle our destiny, but rather to enable us to fulfill and reach both.

After resigning my church for moral failure, I had lost the very thing for which I was put on this planet. But ministry had become my god, and my behavior had become undisciplined. After 11 years of Holy Spirit wooing me in an attempt to bring me to repentance, the time for discipline had come. But I saw the discipline of Father as that which destroyed my destiny. That view was enhanced by others in ministry, and so hopelessness set in. That was never Father's heart for me. Neither is it for you. His discipline may seem severe, but it serves as a refining fire (see Mal. 3:2-3). Its purpose is to purify, not destroy.

3. The goal of discipline

> "I will rightly correct you…" (Jer. 46:28). A question a judge must ask before passing sentence is: "Does the punishment fit the crime?" That's what Father is saying to us here. Correction is needed, but it will be only that which fits the particular issue at hand. We can trust Him to correct from a love motivation, not anger.

I have walked through the furnace of Father's disciplinary, refining fire. As much as I would have preferred to blame God or others for its pain, I knew it was of my own doing. Eventually, I changed my thinking (called *repentance*) and agreed with David in praying Psalm 51 for myself, especially, "Do not cast me away from Your presence, and do not take Your Holy Spirit from me" (Ps. 51:11), as well as Job's acknowledgement that "He knows the way I take; when He has tested me, I shall come forth as gold" (Job 23:10).

With all humility I can tell you that Father has not cast me away from His presence and has not taken His Holy Spirit from me. He has walked me through the refiner's fire, and by His grace and to His honor and glory I am coming forth as gold!

If you are going through the fire of discipline, allow Father to bring the cleansing and purifying He intends so that He can propel you to your destiny as you are held up as a trophy of His grace who will encourage many others to engage.

> *Why are you cast down, O my soul? And why are you disquieted within me?* ***Hope in God, for I shall yet praise Him for the help of His countenance*** (Psalm 42:5).

DADDY'S RESPONSE

*You drew near on the day I called on You, and said,
"Do not fear!"* (Lamentations 3:57)

There is so much in this and the surrounding verses that we could camp here indefinitely. Maybe it's because verses 55-57 seem to describe so much of my life and reveal His tenderness as my Father. I pray He reveals the same to you.

"I called on Your name, O Lord, from the lowest pit" (Lam. 3:55). Is that where you are right now? What is your lowest pit? A devastating divorce? Bondage to addiction? Terminal illness? Tragic loss of spouse or child? It is a pit so low no one can reach. No encouraging words from a friend, uplifting sermon from a pastor, nothing. The depression is crushing, the feeling of hopelessness overwhelming. I've already told you what my pit was—the humiliating loss of ministry and possible disintegration of my marriage. For Jeremiah, it was watching the destruction of his nation and enslavement of his people. It was more than he could bear. Joseph, David, Daniel, Paul, and Silas all had their *pits*. The question is: when we are in that position, what is our response? To whom do we call for help? For Jeremiah, there was only One: "I called on Your name, O Lord." The psalmist said, "Out of the depths I have cried to You, O Lord" (Ps. 130:1). David said that the Lord heard his cry and brought him "up out of a horrible pit" (Ps. 40:1-2).

Jeremiah said that his *position* was the *pit*. His response was his *petition*. He said he called on the name of the Lord. Verse 56 tells us what he said: "You have heard my voice: 'Do not hide Your ear from my sighing, from my cry for help.'"

When I was in the depths of my depression, I couldn't formulate long, flowing, articulate, hour-long prayer sessions. All I could cry out between sobs was, "God, please have mercy on me!" I couldn't even call Him "Father" at that point. All Jeremiah could do was to call out for help. Is that where you are today?

A toddler falls into deep water. Her panicked cry, "Daddy, help!" is all she can say. A flowery, polite request for assistance is not necessary. Immediately, Daddy is there reaching his strong arms into the water and lifting his precious child out. That's the picture here.

From the position in the pit comes the petition for help and the response is immediate—Daddy's proclamation: "You drew near on the day I called on You, and said, 'Do not fear!'" (Lam. 3:57).

From our *pit* comes our *petition* and the immediate response is Daddy's *proclamation*: "Do not fear." You must embrace this—Daddy's response is *always* immediate to the cry of His child. As Isaiah said, "...before they call, I will answer; and while they are still speaking, I will hear" (Isa. 65:24). He answers with the strength of His Presence because He knows that is what we need most. The manifestation of deliverance from your pit may delay, but His presence will not. Daddy is present—now, always.

I have quoted Isaiah 43:2 and Psalms 23:4 before. Review them, write them on index cards and carry them around with you or commit them to memory. They are His loving words of promise that He is by your side. Slip your hand into His in worship and He will walk you through the deep waters and lift you out of the pit of despair, because in His Presence is fullness of joy (see Ps. 16:11).

FEAR OF MINISTRY OPPOSITION

Like adamant stone, harder than flint, I have made your forehead; do not be afraid of them, nor be dismayed at their looks, though they are a rebellious house (Ezekiel 3:9).

I have been in or associated with ministry in some form or another for over 40 years. I can easily confirm the word to Ezekiel here. The minister's greatest opposition is usually from those in the church, the so-called children of God. Church splits, obstinate board members, and offended believers are the daily challenges faced by a pastor. Having pastored four churches in my lifetime, I can verify that the greatest opposition to God's vision and message has always come from within. I could write a book—oh, I *am* writing a book. Well, my next book may be *Save 'em and Shoot 'em*. Too strong? How about *Memoirs of a Crusty Old Preacher*? Still have to work on the title, but you get my drift.

Ezekiel was being called into the ministry. God here was specifying the people to whom he would minister. He was not being sent to a people of "unfamiliar speech," but to the house of Israel (see Ezek. 3:6-7). Today, it would sound like, "I am not sending you to the lost, but to the church." That would seem like an easy assignment, but it wasn't. History hasn't changed much. Let's look at Ezekiel's call and compare it to today's.

Probably the most important ingredient in God's call to ministry is that we have His word for the hour. God told Ezekiel to "eat this scroll" (Ezek. 3:1). We must have God's Word in us as more than head knowledge only. Digestion makes the food we eat a part of us. We must have God encounters as a lifestyle of experiencing His Word. We cannot give what we do not possess. Otherwise we have no life-giving message.

After Ezekiel had God's Word in him, he received his assignment: "go to the house of Israel" (Ezek. 3:4). The message may vary, depending on the group to whom we are speaking. Believers can receive words of encouragement, exhortation, or warning. Unbelievers usually hear of God's love, His sacrifice, and His salvation. Ezekiel was sent with a hard word for Israel that dealt with their rebellion.

I think all of us wonder how our message will be received as we begin our journey into ministry. We have high hopes of it bringing impact and changes to our culture. Yet statistics show that 80 percent of ministers quit within the first five years. Disillusioned, wounded, and often bitter, they leave never to return to the divine call on their life. Well with Ezekiel, God left no doubt as to the outcome: "the house of Israel will not listen to you, because they will not listen to Me..." (Ezek. 3:7). Now, *that's* discouraging! To make matters worse, God added, "...had I sent you to them[the lost—the people of "unfamiliar speech"], they would have listened to you" (Ezek. 3:6). How would you like God to guarantee you that absolutely no one will listen to your preaching, but He wants you to go anyway? Guaranteed failure. Or is it? If we base successful ministry on the number of converts, then Ezekiel was an abject failure. But if we measure it by his obedience, then he was a smashing success. It is a lesson to us.

I know I have often felt a failure in ministry because I have not impacted great numbers of people. Have you? Now let's evaluate our obedience. Lori and I have moved from upstate New York to New Jersey to Pennsylvania to New York City, back to New Jersey, back to upstate New York, and eventually to Alabama. Sounds like a 40-year wandering through the wilderness, doesn't it? How about you? Have you been obedient to go wherever you felt God sent you, regardless of sacrifice or tangible results? Obedience was God's bar of measurement for success. It must be ours.

Because God knew Ezekiel would face vehement opposition, He equipped him with a crusty armor that would immunize him from it. He would make Ezekiel's forehead like an "adamant stone" which is like a prickly thorn bush. This is God's symbolic defense of Ezekiel's mind so that the destructive words that would be hurled at him throughout his life would not be able to penetrate his mind and discourage him.

Father has provided similar armor for us. We have the helmet of salvation, a mighty weapon through which we can bring down thought strongholds into submission to Christ, and a list of thoughts to counter the evil spoken of us (see Eph. 6:10-18; 2 Cor. 10:4-5; Phil. 4:8; Col. 3:2). Couple these with our immediate obedience to Father's directives and success is guaranteed.

That's why God could tell Ezekiel, "do not be afraid of them, nor be dismayed at their looks…" (Ezek. 3:9). *Wow!* Even their facial expressions would contort into scowls of hatred. Sound familiar, men and women of God?

The ministry is not to be a popularity contest, tickling the ears of our hearers (see 2 Tim. 4:3), but a faithful execution of our Father's commission (see Matt. 28:19-20; Mark 16:15-18). Opposition is becoming fiercer every day, even here in America. Silencing prayer and any reference to God is now a focus of our government, while in other nations many "Ezekiels" are being tortured and martyred for their obedience to the call.

In his book, *The Ultimate Treasure Hunt,* Kevin Dedmon says, "The Greek word for witness is martus, from which we also get the English word martyr."[1] Father is equipping us with armor to deflect the fear of rejection by consuming us with His passion for the ultimate treasure—people. Armed with His passion, our "forehead" (mind) becomes "harder than flint" toward opposition, and our goal is simply to become His love and leak it onto all with whom we come into contact (see 1 John 4:8). Success in ministry is not measured in numbers; it is measured in faithful, determined obedience.

That may not be measured here; it will be accurately measured and rewarded in Heaven. Let Paul's exhortation to the Galatians be ours: "Let us not grow weary while doing good, for in due season we shall reap if we do not lose heart" (Gal. 6:9).

Amen!

NOTE

1. Kevin Dedmon, *The Ultimate Treasure Hunt* (Shippensburg, PA: Destiny Image Publishers, 2007), 151.

FEAR OF PRAYERS
NOT BEING ANSWERED

Then he said to me, "Do not fear, Daniel, for from the first day that you set your heart to understand, and to humble yourself before your God, your words were heard; and I have come because of your words" (Daniel 10:12).

Daniel was desperate. He, along with his nation, was suffering in bondage under Cyrus, king of Persia. He wanted to know God's plan for His people. Would they ever be freed from their slavery? If so, when? And what was Israel's ultimate destiny? Daniel's heart cried out for God's response. Verse 2 says Daniel mourned for three weeks before Gabriel arrived with the answer. Why did it take so long? What was going through Daniel's mind while he fasted, prayed, and wept over his nation? I wonder if he ever, at some point, asked himself, "Why is God not answering me?" In my opinion, being human, he must have. But he did not question enough to cause him to stop praying. That is the key.

Uncontrolled, our mind can run wild with thoughts of doubt when we've been praying for so long, perhaps years, for something and still have seen no breakthrough. We examine ourselves, our motives, everything, to see if something—sin, unforgiveness, etc.—might be blocking the answer.

The Holy Spirit shows us nothing. So what is it? Not praying long or hard enough? Not fasting enough? Not declaring enough? Not enough faith? Is unbelief negating the prayer? If there is a "yes" to any of these questions, Holy Spirit will show us and we can correct them. But what if "no" is the answer to all of the above potential problems? When we've exhausted all possibilities, the question remains, "Why is God not answering?"

There has been a popular teaching in the church for years that God has three answers to prayer—yes, no, and wait. I used to teach it. But unless God specifically speaks "wait" into your spirit, I don't believe that any longer. I believe it has become a convenient cop-out for unanswered prayer. I believe the answer given to Daniel in this text is true more often than we care to admit.

The spiritual (invisible) world is more real than the material (visible) world. It was the spiritual world that spoke the material world into existence (see Gen. 1–2). The interaction between these two worlds is constant. I submit to you that, after examining yourself, if Holy Spirit does not reveal any area of lack mentioned above, perhaps Gabriel's answer to Daniel may explain our delayed answer as well: "...from the first day that you set your heart to understand...your words were heard; and I have come because of your words. But the prince of the kingdom of Persia withstood me twenty-one days..." (Dan. 10:12-13). There are several outstanding and encouraging truths to point out in Gabriel's words.

First is "from the first day." This seems to confirm Isaiah 65:24 quoted earlier that "before they call, I will answer." God's heart is *for* us, not against us. Jesus told us that if we abide in Him and His words abide in us, "...you will ask what you desire, and it shall be done for you" (John 15:7). If we ask according to His will, I believe He responds immediately as any loving father would. Then, why do we not see the answer? Could it be opposition from the kingdom of darkness?

Second, Gabriel said, "your words were heard" (Dan. 10:12). The only thing I know that causes God to not hear us is sin (see Ps. 66:18). If Holy

Spirit does not reveal anything, then be assured your words were heard, with or without material manifestation of the answer. Again, Isaiah 65:24 assures us, "while they are still speaking, I will hear." You can trust His word because God is not a man that He should lie (see Num. 23:19).

Third, Gabriel continued, "I have come because of your words" (Dan. 10:12). God responds to you. Let me say that again: *God responds to you!* Hear Father's word to you. You are discouraged. You've begun to believe the lie that God doesn't care, because you prayed for X and nothing has happened. There is a reason why the answer hasn't arrived, but it's not because God doesn't care. Have you considered Gabriel's next statement as your possible reason for delayed answer?

"The prince of the kingdom of [darkness] withstood me..." (Dan. 10:13). Could it be possible that your answer has been hung up in the second heaven in spiritual warfare? Need Scriptural proof? Okay:

> *We do not wrestle against flesh and blood, but against principalities, against powers, against the rulers of the darkness of this age, against spiritual hosts of wickedness in the heavenly places* (Ephesians 6:12).

Daniel did not know what the reason for the delay was. He didn't know why any more than we do. But rather than whine, complain to God, or give up, he did the only thing he knew to do—persist in prayer until the answer came. We must do the same. We can do nothing else. Jesus taught us to pray, "Your will be done..." (see Matt. 6:10). If we are praying His will, answers can be delayed but not refused. Beni Johnson instructs her student intercessors to pray until the burden of the issue lifts. It is then that you know there has been a breakthrough in the spirit realm. It is then that we turn to rejoicing. I believe many of us are overdue for some rejoicing. The enemy has been set to flight and we're still fighting! It's time for victory declarations like Romans 8:31-39 and First John 4:4.

Persist, then rejoice and *see* the salvation of the Lord!

DRAINED OF ALL STRENGTH

And he said, "O man greatly beloved, fear not! Peace be to you; be strong, yes, be strong!" So when he spoke to me I was strengthened, and said, "Let my lord speak, for you have strengthened me" (Daniel 10:19).

Daniel's vision had overwhelmed him, and when Gabriel came to explain it to him, Daniel admitted to Gabriel that he had no strength or breath left in him (see Dan. 10:16-17). Daniel asked, "...how can this servant of my lord talk with you, my lord?" (Dan. 10:17). He didn't even have enough strength to converse with Gabriel.

Awful scenarios have been forecast by politicians and economists as to what may be coming if the election (25 days away at this writing) goes the "wrong" way. Many Christians feel overwhelmed by the flood of evil being unleashed, and the loss of speech and religious freedoms we may be facing. Truly, like Daniel's, a terrifying vision. The anxiety can sap the strength from us if we allow it to. Will we?

It happened to Daniel, a man who survived Nebuchadnezzar and the lion's den without fear. He was now overwhelmed by an end-time vision. Are we? I must admit, more than an hour of television news or radio talk shows and I can feel the anxiety and anger rising in me. Time to turn it off and draw on the same antidote offered to Daniel from Gabriel (see Dan. 10:19).

1. "O MAN GREATLY BELOVED"

That statement seemed to have nothing to do with Daniel's vision and resulting weakness. But it had everything to do with it. Daniel was told that he was greatly beloved. He was reminded that God was delighted in him. The same is true of you (see Rom. 1:7). The first strengthening factor when we feel overwhelmed by life or world events is to remember that we are loved by God (see Jer. 31:3). Knowing that fact refocuses our priority on truth, rather than facts. You and I are greatly beloved. That forms the basis of our confidence: "Cast your burden on the Lord, and He shall sustain you; He shall never permit the righteous to be moved" (Ps. 55:22). That's us!

2. "PEACE BE TO YOU"

This is the *shalom* of the Old Testament, which includes all of the following: "safe, well, happy, friendly, welfare, health, prosperity, and peace" (Strong's, H7965). Gabriel spoke this as a declaration over Daniel. Father speaks it over us today (see John 14:27). But He said that peace was available only *in Him* (see John 16:33). His first words to His terrified disciples after His resurrection were, "Peace be with you" (John 20:19). Paul left no doubt as to the source of our peace: "For He Himself is our peace..." (Eph. 2:14). It certainly isn't world circumstances. Jesus was called the Prince of Peace (see Isa. 9:6), and He came preaching a message of peace: "He came and preached peace to you..." (Eph. 2:17). What did Jesus say to the storm? "Peace, be still!" (see Mark 4:39). It was Gabriel's message to Daniel; it was Jesus' message to His disciples; it was Paul's message to the church; and it is still His message to us today. The world political landscape in every above-mentioned case was not friendly toward personal freedom. Daniel was under the thumb of the ruthless Persian Empire. Jesus and Paul ministered under the Roman Empire. The point is, can we advance God's Kingdom and experience personal peace in an adverse political climate? Scriptural evidence seems to indicate *yes* on both counts. Philippians 4:6-8 is the key to living in the peace Jesus made available to us.

3. "BE STRONG"

Gabriel encouraged Daniel to fasten himself on God (the meaning of *strong*). Focus on the Source of your strength, not on the vision. "Be courageous, Daniel. God is with you." I have previously referred to David strengthening himself in the Lord (see 1 Sam. 30:6). That's why he could write, "...The Lord is the strength of my life; of whom shall I be afraid?" (Ps. 27:1).

A weight lifter does not know how strong he is until he goes to the gym and begins lifting the barbells. It is the resistance of the weights that builds the muscles, increasing strength and endurance. It is easy to be strong in the Lord in a revival atmosphere. But it is through the resistance of persecution and tribulation that we are trained in war to be "strong in the Lord and in the power of His might" (Eph. 6:10).

Jesus told Paul, "My grace is sufficient for you, for My strength is made perfect in weakness." So Paul concluded, "...For when I am weak, then I am strong" (2 Cor. 12:9-10). If we feel weak, we're in good company. Jesus' message to Paul is His message to us. It is His strength, not ours, that moves us in victory through difficult times (see Rom. 8:37). Clothing ourselves in His presence clothes us with His strength.

Knowing who we are (His beloved) and experiencing His peace and strength will produce the same results as they did in Daniel: "...So when he spoke to me I was strengthened, and said, 'Let my lord speak, for you have strengthened me'" (Dan. 10:19). We certainly need strength to advance His Kingdom in these tumultuous times. As we keep our focus in Him, His presence will ensure us the daily strength we need to live in victory. Our choice is simple—live in fear or live in His strength. I choose Gabriel's message to Daniel: "Fear not, be strong." How about you?

RESTORING OUR LAND

Fear not, O land; be glad and rejoice, for the Lord has done marvelous things! (Joel 2:21)

Our land, America, is suffering. In nature, the Midwest has suffered through its worst drought since the 1930's "Dust Bowl." The far West has endured the worst wild fire season on record, scorching millions of acres and destroying many homes. Other parts of the country were hit by tornadoes and devastating floods.

Joel's account in chapter 2 describes the devastation brought by a plague of locusts on Israel's land (see Joel 1:4–2:11). Their destruction of the land sounds like the news we heard this past summer: crops destroyed resulting in skyrocketing food prices and shortages of animal feed. Wildfires scorch forests and pastures alike (see Joel 1:19-20). The parallels between Joel's description of Israel's land and what transpired in America this year are amazing.

National sin affects the literal land as well as its people. God mentioned drought, locusts, and pestilence in Second Chronicles 7:13 just before He gave the antidote we all know in verse 14. Second Chronicles 7:13 happened to Israel in Joel 1. The antidote in verse 14 is detailed in Joel 1:13-14 and 2:12-17. It is a call to national repentance with fasting and weeping. It is a call to "Return to the Lord your God" through prayer: "Spare Your people, O Lord, and do not give Your heritage to reproach..." (Joel 2:13,17).

At this writing, America is 24 days from the 2012 presidential election. Several weeks ago, many national Christian leaders—including Max Lucado, John Hagee, Lou Engle and others—called the American church to 40 days of fasting and prayer leading up to the election. It is the enactment of Second Chronicles 7:14 along with Joel 1:13-14 and 2:12-17. To do this means God will respond as He promised (and did) with Israel. Beginning with our text in Joel 2:21, God spoke to the land, the animals, and the people, promising full restoration, blessing, and abundance for all that was lost, including spiritual revival and the supernatural manifestation of His power that would result in a great harvest of souls. There is no reason to believe that if we, as a nation, follow the same pattern God laid out for Israel, we won't get the same result. He is no respecter of persons or nations.

Notice that in both Second Chronicles and Joel, God's call is to *His* people, not the unbeliever: "If *My* people who are called by *My* name..." (2 Chron. 7:14). We are called to do four things (which were done in Joel 2) in order for God to bring restoration to the land—humble ourselves (literally "to bend the knee, humiliate;" Strong's, H3665), pray, seek His face, and turn from our wicked ways. This is what we, as American believers, are doing these 40 days before the election—repenting for our personal and national sin. We are crying out for God to spare His people and our nation (see Joel 2:17).

The *fear not* of this text is God assuring Israel (and us) that our repentance will bring His restoration: "...I will hear from heaven, and will forgive their sin and heal their land" (2 Chron. 7:14). In Joel 2:21, it is described as "the Lord has done marvelous things!" The following verses detail those things—pastures spring up and trees return to bearing their fruit, rain returns to replace drought, crops are abundant and ready for harvest, and there is a full restoration of all that had been destroyed (see Joel 2:22-25).

Every literal narrative in Scripture has a personal, spiritual application for us. I have for many years declared Joel 2:25 over myself, to restore to me the years the enemy stole from me through my moral failures—20 years to be exact. I have asked God to add 20 years to my life so that "the glory of this latter temple shall be greater than the former..." (Hag. 2:9). He is doing it! We are in the third year of our school of supernatural ministry; I am traveling to the nations, and now writing this book!

What has the enemy stolen from you? Time? Relationships? Money? Ministry? Isn't it time to get it back? The process is still the same—repentance, declaration, then restoration. Then we can be *glad*. Listen to what this term means in Hebrew: "to spin around (under the influence of any violent emotion), usually rejoice" (Strong's, H1523). Zephaniah 3:17 uses this word to describe what Father does when He rejoices over us with singing. He also commands us to *rejoice* ("to brighten up;" Strong's, H8055).

Under the thumb of the Roman Empire and enduring the hatred of the Pharisees, Jesus was said to have been anointed with the oil of gladness more than His companions (see Heb. 1:9; Ps. 45:7). Our joy results from restored fellowship with the One who rejoices over us with singing and dances over us with joy (see Zeph. 3:17).

God's promise to us is:

> *You shall eat in plenty and be satisfied, and praise the name of the Lord your God, who has dealt wondrously with you; and My people shall never be put to shame* (Joel 2:26).

That is my goal—to live in verse 26. If it requires daily repentance and declaration to get there, then so be it. For my nation and for me, I will settle for nothing less. Will you join me?

IS IT EVER GOING TO GET BETTER?

In that day it shall be said to Jerusalem: "Do not fear; Zion,
let not your hands be weak" (Zephaniah 3:16).

Long-term trouble can weaken the strongest Christian's resolve. The great preacher Charles Spurgeon fought deep depression. Smith Wigglesworth ministered through the agonizing pain of kidney stones. On and on the list goes. Enemy opposition to the fulfilling of our call can take a toll on our resolve and persevering spirit. Are you tired of the fight, asking the title question above? So am I.

But there is good news for the righteous remnant who hold to their integrity. They will be able to "...feed their flocks," pursue their calling, "...lie down, and no one shall make them afraid" (Zeph. 3:13). This is a picture of peace as a lifestyle while Father acts as our Protector, keeping away those who would instill fear and terror through intimidation and threats. Hear Father's words to us, His children: "...*no one* shall make them afraid." It gives us reason to "Sing… shout…be glad and rejoice with all your heart…" (Zeph. 3:14). These are all very active words. Strong's Concordance defines these words as follows:

- *Sing*—"to emit (a shrill or chirping) sound, to shout for joy" (Strong's, H7442)

- *Shout*—"to split the ears with sound" (Strong's, H7321)

- *Be glad*—being "gleeful" (Strong's, H8056)

- *Rejoice*—"to jump for joy" (Strong's, H5937)

If you did any of these in most church services in America today, you would have ushers "usher" you out the door. This is not God commanding us to do this reluctantly. He is saying, "You have *reasons* to sing, shout, be glad, and rejoice." What are those reasons? I'm so glad you asked! Zephaniah 3:15 lists four that, when taken together, should make us giddy:

1. "The Lord has taken away your judgments…"

   That literally means Father has "turned off your verdict." Under the Law, we were judged guilty. Under the Blood, we are *declared* innocent. Christ's death turned off the guilty verdict of our sin! "As far as the east is from the west, so far has He removed our transgressions from us" (Ps. 103:12). Once we have repented and asked Father to forgive us of our sin, we are to respond by doing Zephaniah 3:14. To hold onto the guilt of our past is saying Jesus' blood was not enough to remove our sin. It is the ultimate form of pride.

2. "He has cast out your enemy…"

   Father stands between us and the adversary we hate (satan) and casts him out. He is the wall that barricades the enemy from getting to us. Another reason to do Zephaniah 3:14.

3. "The King of Israel, the Lord, is in your midst…"

   Strong's Concordance defines *midst* as "the nearest part, the center." Until recently, as a parent, teacher, and minister, I counseled people to put God first in their life. This gives the picture of a list of life priorities and we are to place God at the top of that list, Number One. Then I heard a different descriptive picture. It was that of an old prairie covered wagon wheel with numerous spokes coming out from the central axle. Rather than God being number one on our daily to do lists, He is to be the *center* or *axle* of our life. Then all the other priorities of life—marriage, children, relationships, career, church, etc.—are the spokes flowing out from the center, the axle—living intimately in Father's presence. That's what "in your midst" signifies. The hub, the center, the axle of our existence is "the King of Israel, the Lord!" Paul declared, "For in *Him* we live and move and have our being..." (Acts 17:28). With His presence at the center of our existence, isn't that enough to rejoice in?

4. "You shall see disaster no more."

The King James Version accurately says *evil* instead of *disaster*. Had enough bad things happen to you? Financial setbacks, relationships, etc.? It is time to declare with Father, "*No more!*" I challenge you to obey the Lord in these four areas of verse 14. Sing, shout, be glad, and rejoice. James exhorts the church to "submit to God. Resist the devil and he will flee from you" (James 4:7). We submit and resist by doing the four things listed in Zephaniah 3:14. The fleeing part will follow automatically, we will not fear, and our hands will no longer be weak (see Isa. 40:31).

FEAR OF LOST GLORY

According to the word that I covenanted with you when you came out of Egypt, so My Spirit remains among you; do not fear! (Haggai 2:5)

Do you ever get tired of having our "seasoned citizens" talk about the good old days? Especially Christians. They speak of the days of old-time Pentecost, when the Spirit *really* moved—the days from Smith Wigglesworth to Oral Roberts. Now *those* were the days of *real* revival.

I don't know about you, but those statements always left me longing for those days to return. Why can't we experience the move of God I heard my grandparents talk about? I carried that ache in my spirit with me to Bible school. I asked if I could open the chapel for open prayer for revival to anyone who desired. I was given permission and so submitted a bulletin announcement for prayer in the chapel after the supper hour during free time each evening. It started enthusiastically, with over 30 in attendance, but soon dwindled to a handful. We continued to meet, and the day before Thanksgiving break, God visited us powerfully in the morning chapel service that lasted all day, canceling classes. But upon returning from break, everything returned to normal. My hunger was not satisfied and a few of us continued "tarrying."

One March chapel service, our theology professor spoke. He was as boring in chapel as he was in class. When he sat down, no one stood to dismiss us to class. It was hushed—a holy hush. Then we heard a girl start sobbing quietly, then another and another. One by one, students came to the platform and asked to confess sins—everything from cheating on tests to immoral behavior to gossip. After two days of repentance, the power of God fell for two weeks with healing miracles, Holy Spirit baptisms, calls to ministry, and more. I had experienced a taste of the good old days.

Frustration has been the byword ever since. Except for occasional mini-moves of God in my ministry, I seemed to miss all the major revivals like Toronto and Pensacola. When God graced Mobile, Alabama with the "Bay of the Holy Spirit Revival" (2010-2011), I was finally immersed in His River while being introduced to Bill Johnson's culture of revival in Bethel Church in Redding, California. Thanks a lot, God! That just made me hungrier and thirstier! I continue to pursue Him, knowing that this is a *new* day, better than the good old days!

This is where Israel was in our text. Returning home from 70 years of captivity, they found that their precious temple, which Solomon had built to house God's glory, had been reduced to a pile of rubble, burned to the ground. God commissioned them to rebuild it, but they soon became discouraged at the enormity of the task and so left the temple in ruins and returned to building their own homes. The result was, God sent drought in the land and called them to return to what He called them to do—rebuild His house—which they did (see Hag. 1).

In Haggai 2, God addressed those who had seen the first temple and were discouraged at its current replacement, which paled in comparison (see Hag. 2:3). He called them to stop comparing and living in the past and focus on what He was doing now: "...be strong, all you people of the land...and work; for I am with you" (Hag. 2:4). In other words, "Don't quit! I have big plans! I promised you when you came out of Egypt that I would be with you, and My Spirit remains among you" (see Hag. 2:5). God says, "No need to fear. I haven't left you. Nothing has changed; I'm still here!" In fact, His conclusion is awesome: "The glory of this latter temple shall be greater than the former...and in this place I will give peace" (Hag. 2:9).

Faithfulness is the requirement that brings the greater glory. Faithfully build what He has given you as your assignment—even in obscurity, even if you feel what you are doing for Him is an inferior temple compared to the great revivalists you have read about. Today's move of God is eclipsing anything the world has ever experienced. There are documented creative miracles of eyeballs appearing in empty eye sockets, limbs growing out from stubs, auditory canal bones appearing in children born without them. Salvations in the Muslim world number over 1 million from just *one* missionary's report. Sadam Hussein's palace swimming pool is now being used as a baptismal tank, and the list goes on.

It is time to get our eyes off the sin-marred temples of our past and be strong and work, because He has declared over us: "My Spirit remains among you..." (Hag. 2:5). He has not taken His Spirit from us. He has equipped us for the task, not with less glory but with more (see Hag. 2:9). The glory is greater in us because the Greater One lives in us and has given us power to disciple nations (see 1 John 4:4; Acts 1:8; Matt. 28:19). So do not fear, because it is "not by might nor by power, but by My Spirit" (Zech. 4:6).

The bottom line is, as we face so many in fear of what is transpiring in today's world, we face them not with less glory, but greater glory. It is the anointing of Isaiah 61:1-2 and "...the zeal of the Lord of hosts will perform this" (Isa. 9:7).

REVERSE THE CURSE

And it shall come to pass that just as you were a curse among the nations...so I will save you, and you shall be a blessing. Do not fear, let your hands be strong. ...So again in these days I am determined to do good to Jerusalem and to the house of Judah. Do not fear (Zechariah 8:13,15).

The world does not understand how much Father loves them. The church has presented the gospel as religion—a set of rules and regulations rather than relationship. We have told the world how evil they are and everything they can't do and must do if they come to Christ. Consequently, they have been turned off to that brand of Christianity while picking up on the failures and hypocrisy of some. That scenario, coupled with the politically correct environment being advanced—and to a degree enforced by government— has opened the gates for believers to be vilified (made the villain), which is what *curse* means in our text. So believers are being called racists, homophobes, home-grown terrorists, dangerous, and on and on.

Everything from sidewalk preaching to home group Bible studies are being outlawed and their leaders in some cases jailed. Prayer, evangelism, and public displays of the Ten Commandments and nativity scenes are also illegal in many American cities. Vilified—cursed. We're there; it's happening. What does God have to say about this? "Woe to those who call evil good, and good evil; who put darkness for light, and light for darkness; who put bitter for sweet, and sweet for bitter!" (Isa. 5:20). That's His response to the nations. What is His response to us? "I will save you, and you shall be a blessing...I am determined to do good..." (Zech. 8:13,15). It is a picture of God speaking well of those who faithfully represent Him.

But it is our assignment not only to represent Him but to "re-present" Him. Rather than point out unbelievers' darkness, which they are already well aware of, we are to ask Holy Spirit to show us the "gold" that lies hidden in them and bless them with that revelation. What is their potential, their destiny, their childhood passion that has not yet been fulfilled? That's their gold. When God reveals it to us and we speak it into their life, this shows them a God who has specifically identified them as His treasure. We are to reveal God as a Father who is in a *good* mood, not angry and ready to punish. It is the goodness of God that leads to repentance (see Rom. 2:4).

I believe when people are shown God's goodness and how special they are to Him, the curse will be reversed and they will open up to receive His blessing. In being carriers of His presence, we are transmitters of His blessing to those who are living under their own personal curse. You can only impart what you have. They curse because that's all they've known in life. God has said to us in our text that He is determined to do good to us, and as a result "...you shall be a blessing" (Zech. 8:13). A blessing to whom? To the nations (literally, "heathen, unbelievers"). Beginning with Abraham, God has always had a reason for blessing, and that's so that we can be a blessing to others. So the next time you are checking out at Wal-Mart, the Dollar Store, Target, or the bank, ask Holy Spirit, "How can I bless him or her?" Let Him give you a word of knowledge, encouragement, or a simple compliment for them. You will make their day, and reverse the negative opinion (curse) they have of God and/or Christians.

Bless somebody today with Papa God's blessing that He has given you. It'll make your day, too!

FEAR OF CONTINUING TO CARRY OUT GOD'S PLAN

But while he thought about these things, behold, an angel of
the Lord appeared to him in a dream, saying, "Joseph, son of
David, do not be afraid to take to you Mary your wife, for
that which is conceived in her is of the Holy Spirit"
(Matthew 1:20).

The plans were set. The wedding date was on the calendar. The invitations had been sent out by camel mail. Responses were coming in. The week-long festivities would arrive before Joseph knew it. He hurried to finish the house he was preparing for them—a true honeymoon cottage.

Suddenly, everything changed. That little bump in Mary's belly seemed to be growing. Joseph had thought it was all the extra carbs Mary had been eating recently. But the bump never went away. In fact, it was getting bigger. No, it couldn't be. Not Mary. She would never...cheat? What other explanation could there be? A tumor? Mary hadn't shown any signs of being sick, except maybe a little nausea in the morning—nausea in the morning? *Oh, no!*

I don't know if that's the way it went down or not. All Scripture tells us is that Mary was "found with child" (Matt. 1:18). As if she didn't offer the information, it was found or discovered. Uh-oh. Trouble in paradise. I imagine at some point in time, one of them had to work up enough nerve to confront the other, hearts pounding.

"Mary, are you…?"

"Yes, Joseph. I am."

"How could you? We're engaged! With who? I mean, who….who's the father?"

"The Holy Spirit, Joseph."

"The Holy what? Holy…you expect me to believe that? You have to come up with something better than that. You're starting to show. What am I going to tell my friends? Heck, what am I going to tell the Pharisees? I can hear it now: 'Hey, Joe. I see you couldn't wait. Not cool, Bro!' And, I'll have to say, 'No, I'm not the father, the Holy Spirit is.' After they stop laughing, they'll start picking up stones wanting to know where you are. Do you realize what you've done, Mary? The wedding is off. Forget it."

"But, Joseph, it's true. I'm still a virgin."

"C'mon, Mary. I hated school, but *that* Biology class I did not skip!"

"Joseph, it is the Messiah I'm carrying, not just any child. It was prophesied in Isaiah, and the angel told me I was chosen to be that virgin" (see Isaiah 7:14).

"Look, Mary. Let me sleep on it. Tomorrow I will take you to the authorities and we will secretly annul our betrothal so you won't be publicly humiliated. I do still love you that much" (see Matt. 1:19).

You could probably create your own dialogue between them, but that basically sets the stage for Matthew 1:20. A sudden and seemingly-tragic event changes everything. Plans can't go on. God's plan for my life is over. Now what? Joseph's emotions must have been tumultuous, raging between heartbreak and anger.

"How could she have done such a thing?" he must have thought. "Mary has always been so tender toward God. She was always so careful not to do anything to displease Him. This is so unlike her. Could it be…could what she's saying be true?" He slept. He dreamt. The answer came. Then it all fit together. Suddenly it all made sense. No change of plans were necessary, because this *was* the plan—His plan.

Have you been or are you there now? Marriage plans, career plans, ministry plans. Then the bomb drops and everything changes, or so you think. Suddenly you're single and pregnant, your spouse is unfaithful, and your ministry and marriage crash and burn simultaneously. Or worse yet, you get the phone call no one wants to receive—your spouse or child has been killed in an accident and your world collapses around you. When your suddenlies come, can God's plan for your life still be fulfilled? Do life's "Job" experiences necessitate altering God's plan? Yes to the first question, no to the second.

Gabriel told Joseph not to be afraid to take Mary as his wife because what she told Joseph was true. From the scriptural fathers of the faith to my own story, the testimony is consistent that seemingly-negative life-changing events of our life actually lead to fulfilling—not altering—our God-ordained destiny. There are multiple Scriptures coming to my mind right now, so let me finish by leaving them with you. Wrap each one around your broken heart. Write them on index cards and place them under your tear-stained pillow and allow Papa God to hold you in His arms and sing them as a lullaby to you tonight.

> *But as for you, you meant evil against me; but God meant it for good, in order to bring it about as it is this day, to save many people alive* (Genesis 50:20).

> *For I know the thoughts that I think toward you, says the Lord, thoughts of peace and not of evil; to give you a future and a hope* (Jeremiah 29:11).

And we know that all things work together for good to those who love God, to those who are the called according to His purpose (Romans 8:28).

A man's heart plans his way, but the Lord directs his steps (Proverbs 16:9).

You number my wanderings; put my tears into Your bottle; are they not in Your book? (Psalm 56:8)

The steps of a good man [or woman] are ordered by the Lord, and He delights in his way. Though he fall, he shall not be utterly cast down; for the Lord upholds him with His hand (Psalm 37:23-24).

Delight yourself also in the Lord, and He shall give you the desires of your heart. Commit your way to the Lord, trust also in Him, and He shall bring it to pass (Psalm 37:4-5).

Cast your burden on the Lord, and He shall sustain you; He shall never permit the righteous to be moved (Psalm 55:22).

Keep me as the apple of Your eye; hide me under the shadow of Your wings (Psalm 17:8).

For thus says the Lord of hosts: "He sent Me after glory, to the nations which plunder you; for he who touches you touches the apple of His eye" (Zechariah 2:8).

Good night. Sweet dreams, you little apple, you!

THE PRICE OF THE
SUPERNATURAL LIFESTYLE

*Therefore do not fear them. For there is nothing covered
that will not be revealed, and hidden that will not be known*
(Matthew 10:26).

It should be easy. The gospel is such a message of love, you would think everyone who hears it would embrace it and we would all live happily ever after. So why is there so much resistance, even opposition, to the message and the Person of the message.

The easy answer is the age-old war of the kingdom of darkness versus the Kingdom of light. Some of the answer lies in the church presenting the gospel as a religion of "dos and don'ts" rather than a loving relationship with the Creator of the universe.

Jesus didn't get into the "whys" of opposition. He merely stated to His disciples (and us) that there would be opposition and prepared them for it. He spoke in terms that could be easily understood in that culture. Farming was the main industry of that day, so Jesus identified His disciples as "sheep in the midst of wolves" (Matt. 10:16). Easy to understand—and scary. He then warned them, "Beware of men, for they will deliver you up to councils and scourge you in their synagogues. You will be brought before governors and kings for My sake..." (Matt. 10:17-18). He was speaking of arrest, accusation, and punishment.

Jesus then made it personal, stating that their own family members would turn on them—brother against brother, parents against children and vice versa—turning them in to authorities for prosecution and even execution (see Matt. 10:21). All for their faith in Christ and taking a stand for righteousness. Jesus summed it up by saying, "you will be hated by all for My name's sake..." (Matt. 10:22). Quite scary indeed.

Can this happen in America? A well-known Hollywood star recently said in an interview—in reference to "Tea Partyers," "conservatives," and "evangelical Christians"—that they should all be rounded up and herded into "re-education camps," and if they can't be re-educated, then "behead them." Speaking out against moral issues, such as homosexuality, has already been added to the Federal Government's list of hate speech. Hated by all, Jesus said.

It is after these and other dire warnings of what lay ahead for the disciples that Jesus made the stunning statement, "Therefore do not fear them" (Matt. 10:26). What? You're kidding, right? No, He was not. Prior to this statement, Jesus explained that the disciple is not above his teacher but rather is like his teacher (see Matt. 10:24-25). Jesus was saying this level of persecution was what He was facing, so they should expect to be tested in the same way (see Matt. 10:25).

Why all this rage? Jesus had just imparted His authority to the disciples to overrule the kingdom of darkness (see Matt. 10:1,5-8). It was a preview of what would become their reputation in the Book of Acts: "These who have turned the world upside down have come here too" (Acts 17:6). Then, through the coming of the Holy Spirit with power, we were given the same authority to wreak havoc on that same kingdom of darkness, doing even greater works than Jesus did (see Luke 24:49; Acts 1:8; Matt. 28:20; John 14:12). Should we expect any less opposition than He did?

Why, then, should we not fear? Because Jesus said He would reveal their heart: "...For there is nothing covered that will not be revealed, and hidden that will not be known" (Matt. 10:26). As I write this, a scandalous cover-up is being revealed regarding the terrorist attack on our Libyan embassy that resulted in the death of four Americans, including our ambassador, this past September 11, 2012. My wife and I have been praying that God would drop the scales from the eyes of the American voters, exposing both the lies and the truth. It is breathtaking to watch God respond!

God has always been and still is more interested in character and heart issues than in deeds and performance. He will reveal the hearts of our per-secutors while we pray for them to have an encounter with the God who loves them as much as He loves us (see Matt. 5:44). No matter how much they attempt to justify their bitter hatred by referring to separation of church and state or racism or any other cover-up motive, God will take the cover off and expose and disclose the true heart motivation. It is the New Testament fulfillment of David's frequent cries for vindication in Psalms.

One of the results of the Holy Spirit infilling in Acts 2 was boldness to preach. That boldness got them hauled before the authorities, threatened, and eventually beaten (see Acts 4:1-3,21; 5:40), after which they rejoiced, having been "...counted worthy to suffer shame for His name" (Acts 5:41). Being preserved and protected from physical harm didn't seem to be the apostles' top priority. Quite the opposite, according to Acts 5:41. A footnote to this verse in my New King James Bible says, "(This) response...would be unusual for some Christians today. Jesus does not guarantee perpetual happiness if we agree to serve Him, but He does promise us joy that is 'inex-pressible and full of glory' (1 Pet. 1:8)."

Unusual indeed. Our perspective must change. Jesus said He no longer calls us "servants" but "friends" (see John 15:15). That statement came right after He said, "Greater love has no one than this, than to lay down one's life for his friends" (see John 15:13).

He has called me *friend*. There is no greater honor. He paid the ultimate price to make that relationship possible. He has captured my heart. I will honor Him with my love, devotion, and, if necessary, my life. Life has no meaning without Him anyway. "…I will not fear. What can man do to me?" (Ps. 118:6). Is this last paragraph your testimony as well? I pray it is. It is His testimony of you!

FEAR IS FOR THE BIRDS

Do not fear therefore; you are of more value than many sparrows (Matthew 10:31).

Does God really care? Whether the question is in reference to world events or our own world, we've all asked the question. We know the answer—in our head. It's the 18 inches from there to our heart that proves difficult. In the midst of personal or global turmoil, are we really convinced He is still in control? How can we get the "do not fear" of this verse into our hearts? The answer is found in the next phrase—*value*. Webster's New World Dictionary lists one of the meanings of *value* as "that which is desirable or worthy of esteem for its own sake." How valuable are we to Him?

It has been made abundantly evident throughout this devotional. One that comes to mind is Day 62, which comments on Isaiah 43:1. There, Father says He named us and we belong to Him. We are His possession. To possess something, one must buy it, unless it was given as a gift. As His possession, both are true of us: "knowing that you were not redeemed [bought back] with corruptible things, like silver or gold...but with the precious blood of Christ..." (1 Pet. 1:18-19), and "For by grace you have been saved through faith, and that not of yourselves; *it is the gift of God*" (Eph. 2:8).

When God said in Isaiah 43:4, "you were *precious* in My sight," He was saying you are "rare and heavy with value" (Strong's, H3365). He also said that "...You have been honored, and I have loved you." The word God uses to describe us here as being *honored* is the same word that describes His glory (*kabad*)! *Wow!* He's saying we have His glory! It's time to flush the lies we've been told about our being worthless failures who will never amount to anything and embrace the truth of who Dad says we are.

The context here is the same as the previous chapter. Jesus is still referring to the persecutors, those who can "kill the body but cannot kill the soul" (Matt. 10:28). Yes, our confidence, trust, and most of all our love for Him can become so strong and intimate that even martyrdom will not produce fear, but with Paul we will say, "...to be absent from the body and to be present with the Lord" (2 Cor. 5:8). Paul, in the context of the resurrection, saw martyrdom as an event to be anticipated rather than feared.

Martyrdom, you say? Why speak of martyrdom in America? Well, what if? What if laws were passed such that, if evangelical Christians refused to obey them, they would be incarcerated in re-education camps and/or executed? What if we were labeled home-grown terrorists because we refused to deny Christ and righteousness? Paul was in prison when he wrote, "For me, to live is Christ, and to die is gain" (Phil. 1:21). He was actually torn between the two, knowing that to be with Christ was better for him, but to remain here was needful for the church (see Phil. 1:23-24). At this point of his life, Paul's love for Christ was so intense that this life on earth was beginning to dim by comparison.

Is the same true of us? He has expressed to us how valuable we are to Him. How valuable is He to us? The value of this life for Paul was viewed through the prism of those he could influence for Christ. We must do the same. Hold loosely the material aspect of this life and focus on the eternal. Paul concluded:

> *While we do not look at the things which are seen, but at the things which are not seen. For the things which are seen*

are temporary, but the things which are not seen are eternal
(2 Corinthians 4:18).

Our value to Him has shaped our eternal destiny! So do not fear the persecutors. Leave it for the birds!

THE STAKE IN THE HEART OF FEAR

But the angel answered and said to the women, "Do not be afraid, for I know that you seek Jesus who was crucified" (Matthew 28:5).

"I know who you're looking for, and He's not here." Isn't that a reason *to* fear? The women came to the tomb to anoint and dress the body of Jesus. They were heartbroken over His death and came to mourn their Savior, or who they *thought* was their Savior. But if He was, why was He dead? How could this have happened to the Messiah, whose mission was to establish His Kingdom and overthrow Rome? Confusion, fear. Now, to add to that fear, an angel appeared, telling them His body was not there. More confusion—until the next verse.

Have you ever felt so isolated from His presence that it seemed God *had* died? Though your head knows it's not true, your heart grieves as though it were. As with these women, you recall, in memory only, the day of joyous reveling in His presence, when you heard His voice, perhaps even audibly or through a prophetic word. You said with psalmist, "…I used to go with the multitude; I went with them to the house of God, with the voice of joy and praise…" (Ps. 42:4). But now, "My tears have been my food day and night, while they continually say to me, 'Where is your God?'" (Ps. 42:3). Yes, where is His presence?

But "He is not here" is not the end of the angel's message. In fact, that is not the message. The message is: "He is risen, as He said..." (Matt. 28:6)! New life at a supernatural level replaces the natural realm of knowing Him.

Bill Johnson says God never hides things *from* us; He hides things *for* us, so that, by seeking Him, we find a deeper level of intimacy that far supersedes what we had become satisfied with. The women at the tomb longed for the Jesus who had physically walked among them. But that level of relationship was gone. They were told to not be afraid because they were about to experience Him at a higher level—in resurrection power. Paul later cried out "that I may know Him and the power of His resurrection..." (Phil. 3:10). When God seems to withdraw from us, it is so He can draw us deeper into Him in order for us to experience Him more intimately. The word Paul uses for *know* speaks of marital intimacy, that embraces the ultimate experience in love of one person toward another.

Hopeless mourning exploded into joy: "So they went out quickly from the tomb with fear and great joy, and ran to bring His disciples word" (Matt. 28:8). Even though they still had some fear, probably the "Can this really be true?" type of fear, they ran out of the tomb with great joy.

It is time to put a stake in the heart of fear—the fear that He is no longer with us, no longer cares about us, is disappointed in us, or has died to our dreams and destiny. Enough! We need to take our rightful place, seated with Him in heavenly places (see Eph. 2:6), so that we might "reign in life" (Rom. 5:17), assured that we are "more than conquerors through Him who loved us" (Rom. 8:37). We believe a lie when we come to the garden to be with Him thinking our fellowship with Him is dead. There has been a resurrection! He is alive! And that same Spirit that raised Christ from the dead dwells in you because your body has become His dwelling place (see Rom. 8:11; 1 Cor. 6:19; Ps. 91:1).

The angel told the woman, "...you seek Jesus who was crucified" (Matt. 28:5). That's the problem. We rightly come to the cross to acknowledge His death (in communion), but then we stay there. We never move, as the women did, from the cross to the tomb. Many times we worship a dead, impotent Christ, who doesn't care to or is unable to impart power to us for victorious living. The women went to the tomb expecting Him to still be dead (a picture of religion—lifeless worship, powerless living). So that's okay. Come to the tomb with an asking heart. You will encounter Him, not in the tomb, but in the garden in resurrection life and power. Then do what the women did— run quickly from the tomb with great joy and bring the word of resurrection power to a world desperate for an encounter with Him.

We owe the world that much!

FEAR OF NOT BEING HEARD

But the angel said to him, "Do not be afraid, Zacharias, for your prayer is heard; and your wife Elizabeth will bear you a son, and you shall call his name John" (Luke 1:13).

This year marks 50 years since I accepted the Lord as my Savior (I was just a child!) and 40 years that I have served Him in ministry. In all that time, I cannot say that I have seen an angel as a result of my prayers or ministry, although I expect that to change as "on earth as it is in Heaven" becomes more of a reality in my life (see Matt. 6:10). I can understand Zacharias' response to his experience: "...when Zacharias saw him [the angel], he was troubled, and fear fell upon him" (Luke 1:12). That probably would have been my initial response, too.

A couple of things caught my attention as I read this story. The first was that Zacharias and Elizabeth were, "righteous before God" (Luke 1:6). That means they were in right standing with God. Having nothing blocking our fellowship with Daddy keeps open the channel of our love language between us, whereby He can respond to the desires of our heart with His.

The next thing was they were, "...walking in all the commandments and ordinances of the Lord blameless" (Luke 1:6). *Blameless* here means "irreproachable" (Strong's, G273). It doesn't speak of perfection, but of the heart condition. With 600-plus laws to keep, they had to have a heart to obey, and they did. They kept an Old Testament culture of law with a New Testament heart of tender love toward God. Obedience must flow *from* relationship rather than create one.

From the confidence of relationship, they felt safe to approach God with their heart's desire—to have a child. Evidently, they had persisted in this request, because, "…Elizabeth was barren, and they were both well advanced in years" (Luke 1:7). Two aspects of prayer can bring discouragement—the physical impossibility for it to happen (barrenness) and time (well-advanced in years). They probably had been praying since they were young, in their prime, and able to produce children. If Elizabeth's barrenness prevented it, then their advanced years cemented the impossibility now. Yet they were still praying! There was no inkling that God had even heard their prayers, much less responded.

There is evidence of Zacharias' discouragement over the years of unanswered prayer from his response in verse 18: "And Zacharias said to the angel, 'How shall I know this? For I am an old man, and my wife is well advanced in years.'" Disappointment may have led to a root of bitterness to a degree, even though he remained faithful in his ministry (see Luke 1:8). I don't know about you, but I identify with Zach here more times than I care to admit. Have you been praying for the salvation of a spouse, child, or parent for X years? With no evidence of change, you begin to wonder if God has even heard you. Then you begin looking for a reason: Is there sin in my life (see Ps. 66:18)? Do I not have enough faith (see Heb. 11:6)? Is it really His will (see 1 John 5:14)? If the answers to these questions line up with His word and God is not speaking any personal word to you as to the reason for delay, discouragement can set in. Sickness—and no healing. Financial lack—and no supply. What's wrong? Is He not even hearing me? What kind of Father would not even respond to His child's cry?

I believe our answer may lie in this verse: "So it was, that *while he was serving* as priest before God…" (Luke 1:8). Faithfulness. Their breakthrough came while Zacharias was doing the mundane, daily responsibilities—serving as priest. It was just another day. Doing what he did every day, ministering to the Lord, carrying out his assignment before the Lord. In the middle of his normal day—*bang!* The angel appeared. No wonder he was afraid!

Bill Johnson says he has determined he will not question or focus on what God has *not* done, but rather focus on what He has done. Maybe none of the above questions apply to you. Everything is in order. Then just continue to be faithful in "serving as priest," as Zacharias did. Love on Him, be faithful in the little things, and let Him love on you. You are preparing the atmosphere for your breakthrough. It was while Zacharias was doing what he was called to do that the angel appeared with his answer.

To me, the greatest part of the answer is the first part: "Do not be afraid, Zacharias, for your prayer is heard..." (Luke 1:13). I'm no angel (except in my wife's eyes, which may be an aging problem with her), but insert your name in place of Zach's. You do not need to be afraid; your prayer has been heard. Perhaps this same angel gave this same message to Daniel: "Do not fear, Daniel, for from the first day that you set your heart to understand... your words were heard" (Dan. 10:12). Your words and prayer have been heard, too.

Faithfulness leads to expectancy. You are expecting! I can't understand why the term expecting is used to describe a pregnant woman. She's not expecting; she's sure! But I digress. As you continue to be faithful in ministering to Him in worship, you will feel an expectancy welling up inside you, knowing that Father has heard your prayer: "I love the Lord, because He has heard my voice and my supplications" (Ps. 116:1). As long as there is no hearing problem in Heaven, there should be no fear problem on earth—on earth as it is in Heaven.

GOOD NEWS OR BAD NEWS?

Then the angel said to her, "Do not be afraid, Mary, for you have found favor with God" (Luke 1:30).

Some biblical historians theorize Mary may have been as young as 14, but if not, she was definitely a teenager when this event happened. Why would God choose someone so young for something so important? And why Mary? The only clue we have is in verse 28: "highly favored one." Gabriel's use of the word *favored* is interesting. It is the Greek word *charis*, from which we derive the English word *charismatic*. However, it is not used in the context of how we use it today to describe someone "filled with the Holy Spirit with the evidence of speaking in other tongues." It is used in its original meaning: "graciousness...of manner or act...especially the divine influence upon the heart, and its reflection in the life; including gratitude" (Strong's, G5485). Mary was a gracious young lady with a tender heart toward God reflected in her lifestyle, which drew the Divine influence. In other words, her tender heart and love relationship with God got God's attention—and response.

Mary's response was understandably troubled, disturbed, and agitated out of fear. Who wouldn't be? It goes on to say that Mary "...considered what manner of greeting this was" (Luke 1:29). *Considered* is the Greek translation of what we get our word *dialogue* from. Mary was so "shook up," she talked to herself! And eventually to Gabriel (see Luke 1:34). Yeah, I guess if you're just going through your normal day and suddenly Gabriel appears in your living room while you're sweeping the floor, it might shake you up a bit? Notice, Mary wasn't asking for an angelic manifestation. She wasn't even praying and fasting for the Messiah to come. She was just living her normal life in relationship with God, when *suddenly…*! I don't know about you, but that gives me hope. As we live our daily lives in tender fellowship with Him, we never know when He might choose to speak to us "suddenly."

Mary's reaction (described above) may imply her initial response of fear was because she didn't know if this was good news or bad news. It's like when I was in school and was called to the principal's office over the loudspeaker. My heart pounded as I walked that endless hallway from my classroom to the office. Good news or bad? Such a call seldom engendered joy and anticipation; it was more like foreboding. But on this occasion it was different. I was called to the office so that the principal could inform me that I had been chosen as one of the finalists in the Kiwanis Club's annual "Most Outstanding Teenage Young Man" contest (which I eventually won). That certainly was good news.

I grew up in a strict, religious family that taught that God was usually disappointed if not angry with us. If we participated in any activity besides church, Bible reading, and prayer, we were sinning. We were to "come out from among them and be separate" (2 Cor. 6:17). *Total* separation, as in having *nothing* to do with "worldly people" (their phrase). Unfortunately, that also included witnessing to them. Let them "find Jesus" by going to church, or to a Billy Graham crusade or something. If they didn't, oh well.

In that environment we feared God—literally. If we had an encounter with Him, angelic or otherwise, we would probably die. When I encountered Bill Johnson's teaching that "God is in a good mood," that He "rejoices over me with singing" (see Zeph. 3:17), and there was nothing I had to do or could do to earn what was already mine—His love—the bondage of performance was shattered in me and suddenly I realized God encounters were something to be desired and anticipated rather than feared.

Gospel means "good news." If you study angelic encounters in Scripture, they always bring good news to the righteous. Destruction is reserved for the unrepentant.

When Mary understood the nature of Gabriel's visit, she said, "Behold the maidservant of the Lord! Let it be to me according to your word" (Luke 1:38). "Okay, Lord. That's *good* news! I am so honored that You have chosen me. I will joyfully do Your will."

It is Father's heart to reveal Himself to you in intimate fellowship. In that fellowship, He may reveal His plan for your destiny, as He did with Mary. Special, singled out, chosen, desired, loved—all reasons for Father's sudden breakthrough from His world into ours. Maybe that's why my favorite Bible verse has become, "For I know the thoughts that I think toward you, says the Lord, thoughts of peace and not of evil, to give you a future and a hope" (Jer. 29:11). That sounds like pretty good news to me.

Fear of the Lord is a healthy, awesome respect for His power and holiness, not a cowering fear of Someone who wants to destroy us. Peter writes that "…[God is] not willing that any should perish but that all should come to repentance" (2 Pet. 3:9). Once we do repent, we are adopted as sons and daughters into His family (see Rom. 8:15) and given the privilege of free access into His presence: "Let us therefore, come boldly [with confidence] to the throne of grace, that we may obtain mercy and find grace to help in time of need" (Heb. 4:16).

I feared my earthly father because the only time I had encounters with him was when he scolded or spanked me. Hey, good news! Daddy wants to talk to you. He wants to announce that you have been chosen as one of the finalists for "Most Outstanding Child," and I heard a rumor—*you won!*

"BLUE-COLLAR" FEAR

Then the angel said to them [the shepherds], *"Do not be afraid, for behold, I bring you good tidings of great joy which will be to all people"* (Luke 2:10).

As I've mentioned before, I was raised on a dairy farm. We never saw ourselves as the elite of society. My dad always referred to us as "us poor people." I now realize what a negative confession that was, but to him it was a fact of life. What it did to us was minimize our significance in our eyes (see Num. 13:33), in the eyes of others, and (we thought) in the eyes of God. Men of God like Oral Roberts, Billy Graham, pastors, and evangelists were the important ones to God. We were just the peons, the common folk who worked hard, lived for God the best we knew how, and hoped it would be good enough to get us to Heaven.

I can't help but wonder if the shepherds felt the same way. They were the "blue-collar" workers of their day, caring for dirty, smelly sheep and emitting that wonderful fragrance wherever they went. They were looked down upon by businessmen and spiritual leaders alike—an unimportant yet necessary segment of their society, right down there with those stinky, uneducated fisherman. *Hmmmm*…and who were the first people to whom the Messiah was revealed?

This may help to explain why these shepherds "were greatly afraid" (Luke 2:9). "What's going on? Why are angels appearing to us? Is everyone seeing this or just us? And what *are* we seeing? Is this real, or should we not have smoked those funny-looking weeds yesterday?" (Well, it's possible!)

Think of it—the revelation of the greatest event in human history was given, not to the Pharisees or kings, but to shepherds! Revelation of God's plan and purpose is not reserved for the clergy. God, out of intimacy of relationship and fellowship, desires to share His heart with any of us who desire that intimacy.

> *The secret things belong to the Lord our God, but those things which are revealed belong to us and to our children forever, that we may do all the words of this law* (Deuteronomy 29:29).

Did you see that? The secret things of God's heart that He reveals belong to us! You, me—the blue-collar workers of the Kingdom! Like the shepherds, the thought of angelic revelations can scare us because of our taught sense of unworthiness. Who are we to think we can handle the precious things of God? *Lie!* The truth is, His blood has made us worthy! We have been adopted into His family and, as sons and daughters, own all rights to family secrets (see Rom. 8:15). The intimacy of our relationship with Him is expressed by Jesus when He uses the term *friends* in place of *servants*:

> *No longer do I call you servants, for a servant does not know what his master is doing; but I have called you friends, for all things that I heard from My Father I have made known to you* (John 15:15).

Friends and family discuss private matters, personal dreams, and heart issues.

Consider the significance of the revelation that was given to the shepherds: "We are announcing good news that will bring great cheerfulness, delight, and gladness that will apply to everyone in the world" (see Luke 2:10). Then that message was given in Luke 2:11-12: The Messiah had come! The One who was prophesied for thousands of years had arrived! What a message—and God entrusted the greatest announcement of all time to...shepherds? Israel's blue-collar workers?

The disciples—common fisherman, tax collectors, and the snubbed by society—were the ones Jesus entrusted to "turn the world upside down" with the proclamation and demonstration of this life-changing Gospel (see Acts 17:6). When they were hauled before the Sanhedrin in Acts 4, the disciples were described as "uneducated and untrained" by the Sanhedrin (see Acts 4:13). These words, when translated from the original Greek, literally mean, "illiterate and idiots." Did you get that? The Sanhedrin's opinion of the disciples was that they were illiterate idiots! But they also made one other observation: "And they realized that they had been with Jesus" (Acts 4:13). That's the key. That's why it also says in that verse that they *marveled*. Of course! How could illiterate idiots move in such power? Answer—they had been with Jesus.

Are there any more blue-collar disciples out there besides me? The message to us is this: Papa God has entrusted us with the greatest, most powerful life-transforming message the world has ever heard. And we are today's blue-collar disciples He has chosen to declare and demonstrate this powerful message. Paul said it like this:

> But God has chosen the foolish things of the world to put to shame
> the wise, and God has chosen the weak things of the world to put
> to shame the things which are mighty (1 Corinthians 1:27).

That's us gang! We're described in First Corinthians 1:26: "For you see your calling, brethren, that not many wise according to the flesh, not many mighty, not many noble, are called." What an honor to be chosen by Him to take this glorious message and "leak" it wherever we go on those who desperately need to hear it. So do not fear to be His blue-collar disciple. Wear that collar honorably and with confidence. Let's join with the shepherds who, after receiving the angelic announcement, went to see Jesus and then "...

made widely known the saying which was told them concerning this Child" (Luke 2:17).

FEARING HIS OMNIPOTENCE

For he [Simon Peter] *and all who were with him were astonished at the catch of fish which they had taken; and so also were James and John, the sons of Zebedee, who were partners with Simon. And Jesus said to Simon, "Do not be afraid. From now on you will catch men"* (Luke 5:9-10).

These were seasoned fisherman. This was what they did; it was their livelihood. They knew the best times and places to fish. Despite all their efforts, they came up empty after working all night (see Luke 5:5). They probably hadn't slept all night; now, tired and frustrated, they were cleaning their nets. What an inopportune time for this new itinerant preacher to show up. (Isn't that just like Jesus?) Not only did He show up, He asked Simon for the use of his boat as a platform for preaching. Such a request might elicit some not-so-friendly language from these rough fishermen. But Simon wearily complied.

Jesus really pushed the envelope when, after His sermon, he told Simon to "launch out" and throw out his nets (see Luke 5:4). That was the last straw! Having a carpenter for a father, Jesus might have the ability to build Simon's boat, but to tell him how to do his business? That takes a lot of nerve! Maybe Simon was too exhausted to argue, so he obeyed (see Luke 5:5). *Wow!* It's a good thing he did! Enough fish to break the nets and sink two ships!

Suddenly Simon knew he was in the presence of Majesty. He was flooded with remorse and a sense of unworthiness (see Luke 5:8). Jesus now had the undivided attention of these rough-edged professionals. His statement gave prophetic meaning to what had just happened. "What you just gathered in fish, you will gather in men." They probably had no idea what He meant, but they would.

When God intercepts our mundane day with a supernatural encounter, He has a reason for it. We often focus on the miraculous event and miss the message of His heart He is trying to communicate to us. Jesus' purpose was to call these men to a supernatural ministry—the harvest of souls into the Kingdom. If we don't understand His heart, we may be frightened at His unexpected and sudden invasion into our lives.

His power displayed can be frightening if we don't remember that He is for us and not against us, that His thoughts for us are precious and more in number than the sand of the sea, and they are for good and not for evil (see Rom. 8:31; Ps. 139:17-18; Jer. 29:11). He actually wants us to partner with Him in the supernatural because it is that demonstration that proves His love and compassion for people (see John 10:38).

Healing of cancer carries a message: He is greater and wants to establish a cancer-free zone wherever you carry His presence. Deliverance from addiction carries the message that He wants to destroy the works of the devil (see 1 John 3:8). Joy expressed in laughter is the crown of His presence (see Ps. 16:11). Financial abundance is a supernatural breakthrough of our love-giving to Him.

But the overall purpose of His sudden display of omnipotence is to harvest those for whom He paid the ultimate price—humankind (see Rom. 5:8). His love is so intense for us He will go to any extent to express it, even through supernatural manifestation. We are said to be the temple in which His Spirit resides (see 1 Cor. 6:19).

He does not want us to fear His presence. That's what Jesus told Simon and that's what He tells us—*do not fear*. He invites us into His supernatural realm to live in intimate fellowship with Him and to lower the net of His love that will attract a net-breaking, boat-sinking load of objects of Papa God's love.

FEAR OF TRAGIC LOSS

But when Jesus heard it, He answered him saying, "Do not be afraid; only believe, and she will be made well" (Luke 8:50).

No parent should have to bury a child. Yet it happens. The obvious question is always: why does it happen? There are many theories and suggestions, but only one answer that makes sense to me. And that is that we live in a fallen world. Death, tragedy, and pain came into it as a result of that fall. That still begs the argument that if God is all-powerful, why doesn't He intervene to protect and prevent tragedy?

I know I am stepping through a minefield here and there are no satisfactory answers for everyone. I could advance many theories and possibilities, none of which would offer comfort to you if you have walked through the tragedy of losing a child.

Bethel Church in Redding, California is experiencing a powerful move of God, especially in the area of miraculous healings. When Bill Johnson was senior pastor (his son, Eric, now is), he declared Bethel a cancer-free zone. Many have had cancer and tumors disappear during worship services. Yet Bill's own father, himself a former pastor of Bethel, died of cancer, even after months of faith-filled prayer and declarations.

Bill addressed disappointment in detail in his and Randy Clark's book, *The Essential Guide to Healing*. When the results of our prayers do not turn out as we hoped, we must deal with disappointment. Bill addresses the issue in Chapter 7, "Creating a Faith Culture." A few of his statements are worth noting. "Disappointment is inevitable for everyone pursuing this miracle lifestyle." He says many pastors try to explain it away in an attempt to comfort the family by saying things like, "...[God] needed another angel in heaven."[1] Bill's response to this statement is clear:

- This statement may give temporary comfort to a grieving family, but it is a lie on several fronts. God does not turn the dead into angels, and He did not cause the death of that child.

He also points out:

- There is a potential power in loss that gets lost itself in a cloud of disappointment. The lie also keeps them from pursuing a breakthrough anointing so that other parents do not have to feel the same grief and loss.[2]

He warns: "One of the most spiritually vulnerable moments in a Christian's life is when loss or disappointment comes."[3]

Although it is normal for questions to arise during loss, Bill cautions that "the danger comes when these questions lead us away from God..." to question God's goodness. We must remember that God's goodness is "...the cornerstone of our theology" and "...[to] question the goodness of God is one of the most dangerous spiritual diseases."[4] Bill concludes: "Dwelling on what God is not doing opens us up for the spirit of offense, which always leads to the ultimate sin of unbelief."[5]

In our text, Jesus told Jairus to "only believe." The word *believe* there means "to have faith in a person" (Strong's, G4100). Jesus was telling Jairus to have faith in Him and trust His word that "...she will be made well" (Luke 8:50). I believe Jesus wanted Jairus to focus his faith in Him, Jesus, not the miracle. I also believe that is still His message to us today. It takes the unexplainable for us to experience the peace that passes all understanding (see

Phil. 4:7). We must settle the issue that God is good—all the time. Please turn to Habakkuk 3:17-19. The prophet/farmer said when the bottom falls out of life, he will still "rejoice in the Lord" and "joy in the God of my salvation" (Hab. 3:18). How could Habakkuk do verse 18 in the light of the total tragedy of verse 17? Because of verse 19: "The Lord God is my strength."

That's the only foundation of life that cannot be shaken. It is our unshakable confidence in a Person, the same Person to whom Jairus looked in his hour of desperation. Jesus gave Jairus his daughter back. There are a growing number of documented stories of people being raised from the dead. Jesus said we would do greater works than He did (see John 14:12), and these will become more commonplace as the church arises and moves into her walk of authority as the return of her Bridegroom approaches.

We can literally call forth life into those whose life is prematurely cut off. If resurrection happens, it is to His glory. If it does not, we will commit to His hands our loved one and forsake any entertainment of questioning His goodness as we declare with the psalmist: "Oh, give thanks to the Lord, for He is good! For His mercy endures forever" (Ps. 118:1).

NOTES

1. Bill Johnson and Randy Clark, *The EssentialGuide to Healing* (Grand Rapids, MI: Chosen Books, 2011), 153-154.

2. Ibid., 154.

3. Ibid., 155.

4. Ibid., 156.

5. Ibid., 159.

FEAR HINDERS
INHERITING THE KINGDOM

Do not fear, little flock, for it is your Father's good pleasure to give you the kingdom (Luke 12:32).

This passage is Luke's account of what has become known as the "Sermon on the Mount" in Matthew 5–7. This text is in reference to His teaching against being anxious over our daily provisions (see Luke 12:22-34).

Many have the ability to multi-task. (I'm not one of them.) But in that multi-tasking, we must necessarily prioritize, formulating a mental "to do" list. Why? Because our focus must center on one thing—that which we determine is most important. Jesus identified that "one thing"—the Kingdom (see Luke 12:31).

Jesus realized that human nature tends to focus on daily material needs—food, drink, and clothing. To have those needs met, we must have money. To have money, we must be employed. It is a row of dominoes, and when one falls, like employment, all the rest fall with it. So our life can be one filled with anxiety over the threat of the reality of that happening. Jesus did not minimize the importance of these needs; He addressed the Source of their supply so that our focus can center on the one eternally more important issue—the Kingdom.

First, Jesus pointed out the futility of living in anxiety over these things: "And which of you by worrying can add one cubit to his stature?" (Luke 12:25). Worry doesn't supply the need; it only robs us of joy and leaves us emotionally and physically ill. It has been said that 80 to 85 percent of illnesses can be directly or indirectly traced to stress and/or anxiety. One much wiser than I has said, "A merry heart makes a cheerful countenance, but by sorrow of the heart the spirit is broken" (Prov. 15:13). I was always one of the shortest boys in my class when I was in school. I worried about it. But doing so never added one inch to my height. Worry about an unpaid bill never produced the money to pay it. So why do we worry, especially when we have a Father who "...knows that you need these things" (Luke 12:30)?

Second, Jesus put our material needs in perspective compared to seeking the Kingdom (Luke 12:31). Matthew words it, "Seek first the Kingdom..." (Matt. 6:33). He set the priority at *first*, or "firstly in time, place, order, or importance" (Strong's, G4412). Jesus' promise is if we represent, or "re-present" His Kingdom as the number-one priority of our lifestyle, He will make sure everything else (our needs) is taken care of. Jesus is also saying that advancing the Kingdom should be our only priority. That's our assignment. We are called "ambassadors for Christ," reconciling the world to Him (see 2 Cor. 5:18-20).

To be an ambassador means to act as a representative for a government. As such, we carry all the authority of that government while in the country to which we are assigned. While fulfilling the role of ambassador, the government he or she represents totally funds everything they need—housing, transportation, food, clothing, etc. So it is with *His* Kingdom. While acting as His representative, He funds everything we need. Our focus is representing Him; His focus is taking care of us. Ambassadors don't worry about their finances, health care, retirement, or anything else. Their concern is properly representing their government; their government's concern is providing everything they need so they can properly represent their country. For us? Greater Kingdom, greater Provider!

Finally, Jesus said, "…it is your Father's good pleasure to give you the Kingdom" (Luke 12:32). We are not to fear even our *seeking* the Kingdom. How many of us worry, "I really *want* to represent Him well as His ambassador, but I fear I won't"? So Jesus encouraged us not to fear this, because as we seek first His Kingdom (making it our lifestyle priority), the Father will gladly implant that supernatural Kingdom lifestyle within us so that it flows out from us and becomes evident to each person He leads us to impact. We don't need to anxiously strive to seek the Kingdom—just live the supernatural lifestyle we allow Him to implant in us daily until it becomes a naturally supernatural lifestyle. It's the Father's heart to give us the Kingdom. Is it your heart to seek Him to do it?

FEAR THAT HE WON'T SHOW UP

Then Jesus, when He had found a young donkey, sat on it; as it is written: "Fear not, daughter of Zion; behold, your King is coming, sitting on a donkey's colt" (John 12:14-15).

I n the old Western movies (if you're under 50, you're asking, "What's a Western movie?"), the cavalry always seems to come charging over the hill at the very last moment to the rescue of desperate settlers under attack.

The picture of Jesus arriving on the scene to rescue Israel from their oppressors was prophesied for hundreds of years. In fact, this text is a quote of Zechariah's prophecy, which was made some 480 to 500 years before Christ. (see Zech. 9:9). To get that in perspective, the U.S. celebrated her 236th birthday this year. Going back to the first Pilgrim settlement is 400 years. Now another 100 years and you're back to Magellan's cruise around the world. Now that's a long time to wait for a prophecy to be fulfilled!

Have you ever been or are you now in a place where you have God's promise of intervention in a situation and you're still waiting for the "cavalry" to show up? You may even be wondering at this point if He ever will.

Good news! He already has. Jesus made the promise to His disciples when He commissioned them to carry the Gospel message to the world (see Matt. 28:18-20). The promise was repeated in Hebrews: "I will never leave you nor forsake you" (Heb. 13:5). I guess it's all a matter of focus. We all know the story of Jesus calling to Peter to walk to Him in the storm-tossed water (see Matt. 14:28-31). As long as Peter focused on Jesus, he walked atop the churning waves, but when the threat of the waves captured his attention, fear gripped him and he began to sink. You see, Jesus was there the whole time. The only thing that changed was his focus. What about ours?

Remember, Jesus was there, present, while Peter looked at Him *and* when he looked away. We spend unnecessary prayer time calling on God to come and intervene in our situation. He is already present. He has taken up residence in us as His temple (see 1 Cor. 6:19; 2 Cor. 6:16). We are no longer waiting for Him to come to us sitting on a donkey. He is the victorious risen King of kings seated at the right hand of the Father! And what's more, we are seated *with* Him in the heavenly places (see Eph. 1:20; 2:6). So the fear of His not showing up on our behalf is a lie. It must be identified as such, rejected, and we must embrace the truth of His abiding presence.

Of course, the purpose of His coming was salvation. Jesus stated this in Luke 4:18-19, a quote from Isaiah 61:1-2. Even His name, *Jesus*, identifies His purpose. It is the Greek version of the Hebrew *Joshua*, which means "Jehovah is salvation." Gabriel, in assuring Joseph that Mary's pregnancy was Holy Spirit-originated, added, "…and you shall call His name Jesus, for He will save His people from their sins" (Matt. 1:21). He was further called "Immanuel," which means, "God with us" (Matt. 1:23).

Bill Johnson makes the statement: "Anything that concerns you concerns Him." He is not neutral in our affairs. He cares, as a father has tender love toward his child (see Ps. 103:13). The word used in that Psalm is *pities*, which doesn't convey the intensity of how Father feels toward us. The word more closely pictures feeling compassion or tenderly loving as a parent with an infant. That parent will provide and protect that child to the laying down of their life if necessary, providing for their needs and saving them from danger.

Our focus is to be on Him because His focus is on us. Waiting for Him is not necessary because He sent His Spirit to reside in us and upon us (see

John 14:16-18; Acts 1:8). The next time He comes, He will not be riding a donkey; it will be on a white horse to bring all kingdoms into subjection to Him, and we will rule and reign with Him. "Casting all your care upon Him, for He cares for you" (1 Pet. 5:7).

Have you? Will you? He is present in your life now. Commune, soak, enjoy His presence. And in that presence, speak, "Peace, be still," to your storm and He will back you up.

FEAR OF
APPEARING BEFORE CAESAR

Saying, "Do not be afraid, Paul; you must be brought before Caesar; and indeed God has granted you all those who sail with you" (Acts 27:24).

Today is November 6, 2012. My wife and I have just returned from voting in the 2012 presidential election. We arrived five minutes after the polls opened and the line was already out the door. We are all aware of the incredible, defining day today is. It is still in the morning as I write this, so we won't know what the results will be for at least another 12 hours. By the time you read this, we will be into our national future. The path will be determined today. It is being said that this is the most historic election since 1860, when the "Civil War President," Abraham Lincoln, was elected.

I believe this election will also determine whether we as believers will face a government that will defend our First Amendment right: "Congress shall make no law respecting an establishment of religion, or prohibiting the free exercise thereof; or abridging the freedom of speech, or of the press; or the right of the people peaceably to assemble, and to petition the Government for a redress of grievances…" or whether we will live under a government that will "bring us before Caesar" for our faith. Today, I am praying for the former, but am prepared for either. By the time you read this, we will be living in one or the other. My last entry will be written tomorrow, after the results are in and our national path has been determined.

Paul's future had already been determined and defined by God: "you must be brought before Caesar." That was not a warning to fear; it was an assignment to carry the glory of the Kingdom to a king. It was a king who had absolute authority to order execution of anyone or any group that appeared a threat to him.

So regardless of the outcome of this election, Father's message to us is to *fear not* and stand before Caesar (an antagonistic government), if necessary, to continue to advance the Kingdom. How are we able to do it? Here are a few thoughts that come to my mind:

1. At His ascension, Jesus assigned the disciples to advance the Kingdom, making disciples of all nations, which might tend to upset some heathen governments. That's why His final statement was, "…I am with you always, to the very end of the age" (Matt. 28:20 NIV).

    His presence makes all the difference. If we must defend our faith to an antagonistic government, we must remember Jesus' promise:

    When you are brought before synagogues, rulers and author-ities, do not worry about how you will defend yourselves or what you will say, for the Holy Spirit will teach you at that time what you should say (Luke 12:11-12 NIV).

That promise was re-emphasized in Acts 1:8. The book of Acts is *the* story of the apostles preaching with signs following, being intimidated, threatened, beaten, imprisoned, and in some cases martyred by the religious and political authorities. Yet the Kingdom of God exploded across the then-known world. His Presence will *always* be with us, regardless of government.

2. In that Presence resides power (see Acts 1:8). The Greek word for *power* is *dunamis,* from which we derive our word *dynamite.* The Gospel must be a Gospel of power—God's supernatural power. Paul said, "My speech and my preaching was not with enticing words of man's wisdom, but in demonstration of the Spirit and of power" (1 Cor. 2:4 KJV).

   Rather than living in fear, the apostles, after being threatened and beaten for preaching Jesus, returned to the church and prayed for even more boldness to preach with even greater power (see Acts 4:29-30). Presence, boldness, and power characterize the revivalist, not fear.

3. Protection in the storm. God's words to Paul in this text were given to him while aboard ship in the middle of a hurricane-like "Nor-easter" (see Acts 27:14). His words to Paul were a promise that he would survive the storm and fulfill his destiny before Caesar.

   So will we. Whether we walk through an economic collapse, political persecution and loss of freedom—whatever. We have a divine destiny to fulfill, an assignment to complete. So God's prophetic word to Paul becomes ours—we will be protected in whatever storm we must walk through—individually or as a nation—because His Kingdom *will* come and His will *will* be done on earth as it is in Heaven. Declare Psalm 91 over yourself, family, and loved ones. Stand strong as Joshua was commanded to do and put on the full armor of God (see Eph. 6:10-18).

4. That protection and provision extends to those who are with you: "God...has granted safety to everyone sailing with you" (Acts 27:24 NLT).

   Your family, friends, all who are "sailing" with you on this revivalist journey will experience the same Psalm 91 protection promised to you. Association grounded in agreement increases and extends the anointing on the assignment.

When Elisha's servant panicked as he saw them surrounded by the enemy, Elisha's response was, "Fear not: for they that be with us are more than they that be with them" (2 Kings 6:16 KJV). Elisha prayed that God would open his servant's eyes, and when He did the servant saw "...the mountain was full of horses and chariots of fire round about Elisha" (2 Kings 6:17 KJV). If our mountain is now loss of freedom or economic collapse, know that not only are we, too, surrounded by His protective angelic hosts, but we have a better covenant—the Holy Spirit dwelling *in* and upon us.

The coming years will be the greatest years of opportunity for the harvest and advancing the Kingdom regardless of who resides in the White House. That has always been historically true. The church has always experienced its greatest revival and growth under the worst forms of governmental oppression—from her inception in Acts to Communist and Nazi oppression in Russia, China, and Germany to current intimidation from Muslim nations. Supernatural appearances of Christ, creative miracles (severed limbs growing out, metal rods and screws disappearing, the dead raised, etc.) are becoming common in the nations of the world. As a result, millions are coming to Christ. This is the most exciting time in history to live. The greater works that Jesus prophesied are happening because the Greater One who lives in us is indeed proving Himself to be stronger than he who is in the world (see John 14:12; 1 John 4:4).

Yes, it is election day, 2012. And before I know the results, I rejoice as I anticipate participating with you and the army of believers who Paul describes as, "...more than conquerors through Him that loved us" (Rom. 8:37 KJV). Time to march into our destiny in Him. Ready? Let's go conquer, setting the captives free! You are blessed, mighty, and victorious because of who you are—a prince or princess of the King of kings and Lord of lords! Hallelujah!

THE FIRST AND LAST
REASON TO FEAR NOT

And when I saw Him, I fell at His feet as dead. But He laid His right hand on me, saying to me, "Do not be afraid; I am the First and the Last" (Revelation 1:17).

It is Wednesday, November 7, 2012, the day after our presidential election. As you know, our president was re-elected. I will not become political here, only encouraging us to pray for our leaders and submit to their rule unless and until it comes into conflict with God's principles.

A couple thoughts as we close this book:

First, if you are in anger, anxiety, or fear over the results of the election, I encourage you to once again re-focus on who is still in charge. Today's text contains a reminder from Jesus that *He* is the "First and the Last." He is never surprised in the affairs of man. He was in charge before there was time and will be in charge through eternity future. Remember "The king's [or president's] heart is in the hand of the Lord, like the rivers of water; He turns it wherever *He* wishes" (Prov. 21:1). He is still in charge! That's why He tells John (and us), "Do not be afraid."

Second, God has ruled over righteous and unrighteous leaders throughout history. We are reminded, "Exaltation comes neither from the east nor from the west nor from the south. But God is the Judge: He puts down one, and exalts another" (Ps. 75:6-7). Men rule with the permission of God. But men do have a hand in that permission. Joshua told Israel:

> *And if it seems evil to you to serve the Lord, choose for your-selves this day whom you will serve, whether the gods which your fathers served that were on the other side of the River, or the gods of the Amorites, in whose land you dwell. But as for me and my house, we will serve the Lord* (Joshua 24:15).

This morning I asked the Lord why He didn't answer the church's prayer of Second Chronicles 7:14 and overrule evil and establish righteous rulers who will bring our nation back to God. His answer was Joshua 24:15—choice. God was faithful in exposing the corruption and evil in our nation, but from the Garden of Eden to today, after showing the contrast, He stands back and allows us to choose—even if it turns out to be the wrong choice, as in the Garden.

There are consequences for choices. America has chosen to legalize drugs and same-sex marriage and to fund abortion while abandoning our support of Israel. Continue to intercede for our nation, because the consequences of choices, historically and scripturally, do not end well for the nation that embraces them (see Ps. 9:17).

Third, the Lord chastened me for putting my trust in political solutions rather than spiritual ones. Only another Great Awakening will save our nation. We have had two in our history and each time it changed a generation—but only *that* generation. Old Testament Israel's history was one of a cycle of sin, repentance, restoration, complacency, and back to sin. The reason—they did not teach what they experienced in God to their children. And throughout Church history, revivals have died for the same reason. God commanded Israel to teach His word to their children (see Deut. 6:6-7).

They didn't; neither have we. And into that vacuum a "new normal" has rushed in that is now being voted into law, along with an entitlement mentality that violates the scriptural work ethic of Proverbs and Second Thessalonians 3:10: "If anyone will not work, neither shall he eat."

Finally, I want to encourage you that God's Kingdom was birthed and grew explosively under the iron fist of the Roman Empire (see the Book of Acts). Today, the greatest moves of God are going on in the most oppressed nations of the world. Hunger for intimate relationship with God has never been greater. Supernatural manifestations of His presence through extraordinary miracles are sweeping those same nations. We are carriers of His glory. Our assignment is to be the salt of the earth. That assignment has not changed. Rather than react to the influence of evil, we are to be an influence for good (see Rom. 12:21). Every person is a treasure to God, and we are called to be treasure hunters—to find the gold in them. The Great Awakening happens as lives are changed by the grace and glory of God changing their core values. When values are changed to embrace His values, national change will happen in life, economics, and at the polls.

Matthew 11:12 says, "...the kingdom of heaven suffers violence, and the violent take it by force." I have committed to advance His supernatural Kingdom by training and raising up an army of revivalists who will experience and move in the raw power of God. Will you join me? It is not time to retreat into survival mode, but to pray with the apostles in Acts 4 for more boldness to proclaim Jesus with mighty signs following. Let's put on His armor, and in *spiritual* violence use the weapons of our warfare to co-labor in this last-day harvest ingathering (see Eph. 6:10-18; 2 Cor. 10:4-6).

These may be the days that try men's souls, but they are also the days when the gates of hell shall not prevail against His church (see Matt. 16:18). Courage, determination, vision, and passion for Him and His people are the qualifications for this assignment.

I bless you in the name of the Lord and speak His passion of love over you. I speak His abundant provision, divine health, clarity of purpose, and revelation of His calling and purpose over your life. Our journey into a new realm of His plan has begun. It is not a journey we walk alone; the promise of His presence still stands (see Matt. 28:20; Ps. 23:4). Will you walk it with me?

I feel impressed to close this book with His encouraging words rather than mine:

> *...Rejoice in hope of the glory of God. And not only that, but we also glory in tribulations, knowing that tribulation produces perseverance; and perseverance, character; and character, hope. Now hope does not disappoint, because the love of God has been poured out in our hearts by the Holy Spirit who was given to us* (Romans 5:2-5).

DECLARATIONS

Death and life are in the power of the tongue, and those who love it will eat its fruit (Proverbs 18:21).

There's something about verbalizing Papa God's promises to me that confirms and personalizes them. As a result, I am encouraged and my faith is built up. It also transfers my fear—to the devil. So enjoy eating the fruit of these declarations[1] about being fearless, and be strengthened and encouraged. And satan—be afraid. Be *very* afraid!

I will not fear:

- My prayers going unheard or unanswered because my prayers are powerful and effective (Mark 11:24; James 5:16).

- Financial lack because Papa God richly supplies *all* my financial needs (Phil. 4:19).

- Living under God's judgment for my sin because I am dead to sin and alive to His supernatural life (Rom. 6:11).

- Sickness or disease because I walk in divine health (Ps. 103:1-3; Isa. 53:3-5).

- Danger, harm, or terror because I live under Papa God's supernatural protection. Therefore, any sudden enemy attack or tragedy that is headed my or my family's way is canceled right now in Jesus' name (Ps. 91).

- Isolation, loneliness, or broken relationships because I grow daily in favor with God and man and all my relationships prosper (Luke 2:52).

- Spiritual insignificance because I am God's channel through which God encounters flow out to everyone I meet (Mark 16:17-18).

- Being rejected by God because through Jesus I am totally accepted in the Beloved, loved and worthy to receive all of God's blessings (Eph. 1:3-6; Col. 1:12; 2 Pet. 1:3-4).

Furthermore, I declare that:

- Each of my family members comes to know Jesus and is therefore awesomely blessed and radically saved (Acts 16:30-31).

- With Him who sits in the heavens, I laugh hilariously at every threat of the enemy (Ps. 2:2-4).

- My words set the course of my life so I only speak words that bless, build up, and encourage (Num. 14:28; Prov. 12:19; 18:21; Matt. 12:36-37).

- God is on my side; therefore I have no reason to take ownership of the four Ds: defeat, discouragement, depression, or disappointment (Rom. 8:37; Ps. 46; Phil. 4:13).

- As I speak God's promises and call those things which are not as though they are, they come to pass (Rom. 4:17; 2 Pet. 1:2-4; 2 Cor. 1:20).

- No enemy opposition can derail or hinder God's plan for my life (Isa. 54:17; Mark 11:23-24; 2 Cor.10:4-5).

- Because I have asked Him, Papa God has given me His wisdom today for every situation I will face (James 1:5).

- Because I have the mind of Christ, I will think the right thoughts, say the right words, and make the right decisions today (1 Cor. 2:16; Col. 3:1; Phil. 4:8; John 16:13; Luke 12:11-12; Ps. 32:8; Prov. 3:5-6).

- I expect to have powerful divine appointments today to do the works and greater works Jesus commanded me to do (John 14:12; Matt. 10:1,7-8; Luke 9:1-2; Mark 16:17-18).

- My angels are carrying out God's Word on my behalf and ministering my inheritance to me (Ps. 103:20; Heb. 1:14).

- I will not live under a spirit of fear because God has given me His Spirit of love, power, and a sound mind (2 Tim. 1:7).

- I will not be afraid of evil tidings (news) because my heart is steadfast, trusting in the Lord (Ps. 112:7).

- I will not receive the spirit of bondage again to fear because I have been adopted into His family and therefore have the right to call Him "Daddy, God" (Rom. 8:15).

And, finally:

- I speak to the raging waters in my life—peace, be still. I say to my mind—peace, be still. I say to my emotions—peace, be still. I say to my body—peace, be still. I say to my home—peace, be still. I say to my family—peace, be still (Mark 4:39; John 14:27; Phil. 4:6-7).

- I speak to every mountain of fear, every mountain of discouragement, every mountain of stress, every mountain of depression, every mountain of lack and insufficiency, and I say, "Be removed and cast into the sea in Jesus' name!" (Mark 11:22-24).

- And I speak to this day and I call you blessed. And I declare that I serve a mighty God who today will do exceedingly and abundantly beyond all that I can ask or think (Eph. 3:20). I say You are a good God and I eagerly anticipate Your goodness today.

NOTE

1. Taken from Steve Backlund's book *Igniting Faith in 40 Days.* Used by permission. For more information about Steve's ministry, go to www.ignitinghope.com.

BIBLIOGRAPHY

Komolafe, David. *365 Days of Fear Not*. Enumclaw, WA: Pleasant Word, 2008.

Strong, James. *New Strong's Exhaustive Concordance of the Bible*. Nashville, TN: Thomas Nelson Publishers, 1990.

Webster's New World Dictionary: 2nd College Edition. New York, NY: Simon & Schuster, 1970.